D1052924

In Search of the

BLUES

In Search of the

BLUES

Marybeth Hamilton

BASIC
BOOKS

A Member of the Perseus Books Group
New York

Copyright © 2008 by Marybeth Hamilton

Published by Basic Books
A Member of the Perseus Books Group

Books published by Basic Books are available at special discounts for bulk purchases in the United States by corporations, institutions, and other organizations. For more information, please contact the Special Markets Department at the Perseus Books Group, 2300 Chestnut Street, Suite 200, Philadelphia, PA 19103, or call (800) 255–1514, or e-mail special.markets@perseusbooks.com.

DESIGNED BY JEFF WILLIAMS

Library of Congress Cataloging-in-Publication Data
Hamilton, Marybeth.
    In search of the blues / Marybeth Hamilton.
        p. cm.
    Includes bibliographical references and index.
    ISBN-13: 978-0-465-02858-0 (alk. paper)
    ISBN-10: 0-465-02858-6 (alk. paper)
    1. Blues (Music)—History and criticism. 2. Field recordings—United States—History. I. Title.

ML3521.H34 2008
781.64309762'4—dc22

                                                                                2007034444

10 9 8 7 6 5 4 3 2

For Jackson and Lukas

⌐ CONTENTS ⌐

one

The Delta Revisited

O N OLD HIGHWAY 61 IN MISSISSIPPI, BETWEEN LULA and Robinsonville in the heart of the Delta, stand the remains of a wooden railroad bridge partially submerged in a murky swamp. The air enveloping the bridge is sticky and fetid, thick with the smell of decayed vegetation, and the dark, stagnant water stretches far into the distance, flooding the banks, engulfing the trees. To look at the scene is to peer at an eerie, apparently timeless landscape, primordial and untouched by history, the world Noah might have glimpsed after the flood.

I photographed this bridge in May 1999 while driving south through the Mississippi Delta, aware all the while of following a well-worn trail. The trek through the Delta in search of the roots of the blues has been a trope of music writing since the early 1960s, the opening years of the blues revival, when white Americans and Europeans rediscovered a music that African Americans had long left behind. My aim in coming to the Delta was, I thought, more sophisticated: to get a handle on the pilgrim experience, to reconstruct the breathless hunt for the authentic origins of the blues. And yet here I was, slamming to a halt on a desolate highway, bewitched by the sight of that decaying bridge, transported into what felt like a mystical landscape, a world frozen outside the passage of time.

This mythology of the Delta arose with the land itself. The region's first boosters, in the early twentieth century, portrayed it as a place outside history. Though it had only just been opened for agriculture—as late as 1860, 90 percent of the Delta was covered in swamps—by 1910 railroad developers had enveloped it in the romantic imagery of the Old South. "Nowhere in Mississippi have antebellum conditions of landholding been so nearly preserved as in the Delta," rhapsodized the owners of the Illinois Central Railroad. "The Negro is naturally gregarious in instinct, and is never so happy as when massed together in large numbers, as on the Delta plantations."

This idea of the Delta as "the Old South reincarnate," with its nostalgic evocation of mint juleps and magnolia blossoms, took on a more sinister cast in the mid-1930s, as northern anthropologists flocked to the region. Those observers—John Dollard, Hortense Powdermaker, Allison Davis—painted a stark, vivid portrait of a land of unparalleled brutality, marked by naked extremes of wealth and destitution and by caste domination in its most blatant forms.

But it was the blues revival of the 1960s that created the most luminous, enduring mythology of the Delta. The decade saw a flood of record collectors and folk music enthusiasts head south from Memphis and north from Vicksburg, armed

The ruins of a bridge, Mississippi Delta.

with tape recorders, cameras, and notepads, determined to cut through the dross churned out by the commercial record companies and capture the sound of the real thing. The real thing was the Delta blues, the name they devised for the intense voices they found on scratchy 78s and newly issued LP compilations: singers like Son House, Skip James, Charley Patton, and Robert Johnson. What distinguished the music, above all, was the arresting character of the singing. As the pilgrims described it, it was "rough, spontaneous, crude and unfinished," dominated by "stark, unrelieved emotion," an intense distillation of the music of slavery, "only a step from the wordless field cries and hollers of an older generation." In those recordings these new listeners heard the birth of the blues: impassioned voices echoing with pain and privation, emanating from a flat, waterlogged, primitive landscape seemingly untouched by the modern world.

As I made my way south—past the bridge to Clarksdale, Tutwiler, Itta Bena, Parchman, all the places whose names resonate in accounts of blues history—I found myself wholly caught up in the pilgrimage whose mythology I had set out to debunk. Everything seemed to demand to be photographed, as my trek was punctuated by enchanted moments when the Delta looked as it was supposed to look: trees submerged in water, crumbling sharecroppers' cabins, arid fields under a moonlit sky.

It took several months for the spell to be broken. Over time, once I'd returned to a frenetically urban, postindustrial London, my photograph of the railway bridge on Old Highway 61 began to tell a new tale. Looking at the swamp's stagnant water, I came to recognize that the primeval scene was in fact the product of a very modern process, which had absorbed the efforts of thousands of black workers in the late nineteenth century, of draining and clearing the wetlands to open the Delta for cotton crops. And in the submerged bridge I saw also remnants of the rail network that had reached the Delta in the early twentieth century, bringing musicians from New Orleans, businessmen from Memphis, and labor agents from factories in Chicago.

Every landscape is a work of the mind, shaped by the memories and obsessions of its observers. What I glimpsed was a Delta that memory had forgotten, full of bustle and noise and machines.

——•——

I FIRST HEARD OF THE DELTA BLUES SOMETIME AROUND 1977, when I was going to high school in San Diego, about as far southwest as you can get in America without crossing the Mexican border. As a child I had thrown myself into fleeting, solitary, bookish obsessions, and in my early teens I discovered music. My initial passion was for the New York Dolls, a scruffy band of dropouts from Queens and Staten Island whose music contained early stirrings of punk. I loved the way that their songs sounded rough and unfinished—partly because they could just barely manage their instruments—and I pored over the cover of their first album, on which the musicians slumped across a sofa in drag, their faces slathered in pancake makeup, the band's name scrawled across the top in lipstick.

At first this obsession was solitary too, but eventually I found friends who shared it, some my age and some a bit older, who had dropped out of college or never bothered to go. On Saturday nights five or six of us would cram into a Volkswagen Beetle and drive to Los Angeles to the Whiskey a Go Go on Sunset Boulevard to see and hear whoever was playing: Patti Smith, Talking Heads, the Ramones, Blondie, the Germs, the Screamers, the Dickies, X. Our cohort considered itself to be a musical avant-garde, and our manifesto was *Creem,* an iconoclastic compendium of salacious party gossip and flamboyantly articulate record reviews published monthly out of a commune in Detroit. Like most of the *Creem* writers, we took pride in the fact that the stuff we listened to was too edgy and raw for the radio to handle (though once, en route to L.A., we heard a local AM radio station play "Pretty Vacant" by the Sex Pistols, and in the shock and exhilaration that followed we almost careened off the road).

One day at the library I saw that a writer whose name I knew from *Creem,* Greil Marcus, had published a book called *Mystery Train: Images of America in Rock 'n' Roll Music.* Though his subjects were, by and large, musicians I didn't particularly care about, the book made surprising connections— between Randy Newman and Herman Melville, or Elvis Presley and the Puritan Jonathan Edwards, who left his mark on American history with a fire-and-brimstone sermon called "Sinners in the Hands of an Angry God." Marcus explored the ways in which the greatest rock artists, like the greatest writers, reworked enduring American stories. At their best and most risky, they contested "the very idea of America," teasing out its dark undercurrents and exposing something "complicated, dangerous, and alive."

Most dangerous of all was a musician Marcus profiled early on, a Mississippi blues singer named Robert Johnson. I had never heard his name before, and even Marcus knew only the barest facts of his life: that he was born in 1911 and died violently and mysteriously in 1938. But it was his music that mattered: the twenty-nine songs he recorded in 1936 and 1937, songs that loomed over every blues singer and every rock and roller that followed, because they went further than any artist had dared into the underside of the American dream. Johnson sang of "a world without salvation, redemption, or rest," of anguished, incessant wandering, of being pursued by baying hellhounds, of Satan knocking at his door. While blues in general "made the terrors of the world . . . more real," Johnson's made them more real than anyone else's. His greatest recording, "Stones in My Passway," was "a two minute image of doom that has the power to make doom a fact."

This was serious, heavy stuff. Whatever unvarnished truth I thought I was hearing in punk, Robert Johnson had gotten to it first, and in his shadow everything else became playacting: flimsy, trifling, inconsequential, and fake. Reading about him left me feeling challenged and, in some obscure way, affronted. Marcus's rhapsodic praise of the tormented drifter seemed somehow to exclude me—as a woman if nothing else. Perhaps that was why it took me fifteen years to get around to listening to Johnson's recordings, and why, when I did, I heard very little, just a guitar, a keening vocal, and a lot of surface noise. I certainly did not hear the tale of existential anguish that Marcus and others discerned within them. I wondered if my reaction revealed some defect in me, or if there might be another blues story to tell.

———

THE RAW MATERIAL FOR EVERY BLUES STORY, THE ONLY real evidence for how the music sounded, is of course the recordings. The earliest that survives dates from August 1920, when OKeh Records released "Crazy Blues" by Mamie Smith and her Jazz Hounds. It was, by any measure, a landmark: the first commercial blues recording issued by an African American singer. Though sold in black areas almost exclusively and steeply priced at one dollar (by contrast, admission to the movies cost ten cents), "Crazy Blues" stunned virtually everyone by selling hundreds of thousands of copies, seventy-five thousand in its first month of release. Its success revealed the scale of a musical market that the recording industry had long refused to believe existed. That African Americans would buy phonograph records in disproportionate numbers became

OKeh's advertisement for Mamie Smith.

startlingly audible in those last weeks of summer: people said that you could hear Mamie Smith's recording playing in every black neighborhood in the United States.

Recordings by Ma Rainey, Ida Cox, Victoria Spivey, Alberta Hunter, and a host of performers with the surname Smith all followed. The record industry called them "race records" because their audience was assumed to be exclusively black. Ten inches in diameter, made of a shellac derivative, they spun on an electric or hand-wound turntable at 78 revolutions per minute. Until 1943 (when a wartime ban on recording intervened), race records sold in the millions in black neighborhoods across the United States, conveying the voices of hundreds of performers on a range of labels: Paramount, OKeh, Victor, Columbia, Black Swan, Electrobeam Gennett. Pharmacists kept stocks of them behind the counter; so did department store owners, barbers, and funeral directors. African American newspapers like the *Chicago Defender* ran advertisements for new releases, with slips at the bottom so readers could order by mail. Traveling out of New York and Chicago, Pullman porters carried boxes of disks on their journeys and would sell them wherever they found demand, in small towns across the Midwest and the South.

That much of that output has now been forgotten owes to a single development. Beginning in the late 1920s, some of the race labels set out to cater to more specialized rural markets, and they sent mobile recording units across the South in search of musicians with local reputations whose recordings could conceivably sell. The talent scouts had dubious credentials: technicians and salesmen, nearly all of them white, with scant familiarity with African American music. So it was largely by chance that they captured the voices of Charley Patton, Son House, Skip James, and Robert Johnson, itinerant guitarists from the Mississippi Delta. They recorded them in a few fleeting sessions in record-pressing plants, hotel rooms, and warehouses, paid the performers in small change and whiskey, and sent them back out on the road.

Over half a century later, those voices dominate virtually every blues story. Patton, Johnson, House, and James became the model for a new kind of American icon: the mournful drifter roaming the Delta, pouring his desolation into his music. In their recordings, blues chroniclers heard African American song making stripped down to its essence, exuding the elemental despair bred by Jim Crow and slavery, the alienation from which, they believed, the blues sprang. That interpretation of the music's development has proven especially bewitching to scholars of black American history. In the lyrics of those Delta drifters they found resonant historical documents that were compelling, even mystical in their power to evoke the experience of the faceless black masses, whose lives mainstream historians had too long ignored. To listen to Robert Johnson, argues the Pulitzer Prize–winning historian Leon Litwack, "is to feel—more vividly and more intensely than any mere poet, novelist, or historian could convey—the despair, the thoughts, the passions, the aspirations, the anxieties, the deferred dreams, the frightening honesty of a new generation of black southerners and their efforts to grapple with day-to-day life, to make it somehow more bearable, perhaps even to transcend it." The searing voices of Delta blues singers seemed to provide direct access to a submerged history of African American suffering, forming a kind of audio snapshot of the innermost truths of the past. As blues chronicler Robert Palmer puts it: "How much history can be transmitted by pressure on a guitar string? The thought of generations, the history of every human being who's ever felt the blues come down like showers of rain."

It is enormously seductive, this idea of the Delta blues as history transmitted by a guitar string. In a virtual reality world of replicas, pastiches, and hybrids, one cannot but crave that direct connection, the opportunity to hear the sounds and feel the rhythms that touched the lives of the folk themselves. Yet there is something unsettling about it too. Historians ordinarily pride themselves on their methodological rigor, the unsparing eye with which they scrutinize evidence. Why is it, then, that when they turn to the blues that pose of critical distance evaporates and their writing takes on the hues of romance? The argument for the elemental and immediate power of the blues recalls nothing so much as the claims made, decades ago, for oral history: that it allows us to bypass the dangers of historical interpretation by removing the need for an historian, that it enables us to communicate with the past directly by presenting past experience in its purest form.

Enraptured by the immediacy they heard in the music, historians have neglected some basic questions. For the recordings of Johnson and Patton to be used as evidence for the ideas and emotions of the black masses, it needs to be clear that black Americans bought them, that they absorbed and identified with what they heard. Yet the awkward fact is that, as newly minted 78s, Charley Patton's recordings sold only moderately in the 1920s and 1930s; those of Son House, Skip James, and Robert Johnson sold barely at all. Even in the heart of the Mississippi Delta, the so-called Delta bluesman had limited appeal. A Fisk University sociologist who surveyed the black bars of Clarksdale in 1941 found not a single local performer upon the jukeboxes. Instead, the top sellers were the same as they were in black areas across the United States: Louis Jordan, Lil Green, Count Basie, Fats Waller, all patently urban and unabashedly sexual, their songs laden with double (and sometimes single) entendres, backed by a sophisticated, jazz-inflected sound.

In fact, the Delta blues was not born in the bars and dance halls of Mississippi. That Robert Johnson and Charley Patton came to dominate blues history owes to more elusive mediators and shapers of taste. The idea of something called the Delta blues dates from the late twentieth century. It was discovered—or, if you like, invented—by white men and women, as the culmination of a long-standing fascination with uncorrupted black singers, untainted by the city, by commerce, by the sights and sounds of modernity.

A key emblem of that corruption, beginning in 1920, was the race record. It was a mechanical object that offered mass-produced music, and it was embraced by a people long celebrated for free, unscripted, spontaneous singing. To many whites, its jangling sound evoked a new and disheartening world. Between 1914 and 1930, nearly two million African Americans left the South; the black population of New York more than trebled, and that of Chicago rose by 500 percent. In the city black migrants joined the ranks of factory labor; they went to the movies; they bought automobiles, radios, and phonographs. Many whites—and not only southerners—liked to envision African Americans as an unspoiled peasantry. By the 1920s, it became clear that such an image, if it was ever accurate, belonged to a rapidly fading past.

In that context, a small group of white men and women set out on a quest to salvage endangered black voices—rich, stirring, singular voices that the cacophony of race records threatened to drown out. Some of these pilgrims are well-known in the annals of blues history, such as the father-and-son folklorists John and Alan Lomax, who combed the Depression-era South in search of black song and found authenticity in a Louisiana convict named Leadbelly. But other, more obscure characters emerge as well—individuals who may seem unlikely characters in a blues context: the southern sociologist Howard Odum; the Texas novelist Dorothy Scarborough; the jazz historians Frederic Ramsey, Charles Edward Smith, and

William Russell; and a reclusive record collector named James McKune.

These seekers made extraordinary discoveries, but perhaps more interesting are the fears and obsessions that propelled their quest. All were captivated by the idea of (in John Lomax's term) "uncontaminated" black singing, all embarked on quests to unearth it, and all, in different ways, addressed the same question: How did you capture and preserve the real black voice when black people themselves were embracing reproductions? Answering that question meant engaging with the very technology whose impact they feared, ferreting out singers with portable phonographs and, eventually, riffling through bins in used record stores, searching for voices that sounded archaic, willing themselves to hear past the machine.

———

FOR THE FIRST GENERATION OF AMERICAN INTELLECTUALS to encounter race records, hearing past the machine rarely came easily. In a business that cut every corner, manufacturers of recordings intended for the African American market were notorious for their shoddy materials. The biggest race label, Paramount, was determined to drive its production costs below the $1.50 per hundred that the industry considered the bottom line. Skimping on shellac, the most expensive ingredient, Paramount packed out the "dough" with low-quality filler. The result was a "tin-pan tone," as one retailer put it, a disk that sounded worn and scratchy before it was ever put on a turntable. "You couldn't get anything on Paramount," talent scout Harry Charles lamented years later. "I put some good songs on there; you'd never know it."

All the more startling, then, was the sheer zeal with which America's black population embraced those recordings. Their response made a sharp contrast to the reaction of the white middle class. Though by 1900 the phonograph had become a familiar object in the middle-class parlor, to most such consumers it was little more than a diverting novelty. Playing mass-produced recordings on a machine seemed a poor substitute for hearing music live in concert halls or for displaying one's virtuosity at home on the piano. As late as 1917, when the Edison Corporation set out to market its state-of-the-art Diamond Disk phonograph, it had to hide the machinery inside decorative cabinets and unveil demonstration models in concert halls to dispel a persistent skepticism of recorded music, a widespread unwillingness to accept it as "real." None of those techniques of persuasion were needed when it came to African Americans. All they required was for someone to put their music on phonograph records, and even men like songwriter Perry Bradford, who had spent years promoting black singers, were unprepared for the sheer volume of disks they purchased.

Ten years later, black America was awash in recorded music. That transformation was viewed by some black intellectuals with outright dismay. The African American folklorist and novelist Zora Neale Hurston was astonished at the end of the decade by the extent to which "the mechanical, nickel phonograph" had come to dominate the turpentine, logging, and phosphate camps of rural Florida, where homemade songs had once reigned supreme. "No, ma'am, they don't make up many songs," one foreman told her. "The boys used to be pretty bad about making up songs but they don't do that now." Instead, such made-up songs with their roots in the region gave way to "Pine-top's Boogie-Woogie" and other songs learned from recordings. Seemingly overnight, commercial records from the city had inundated what had been an oral culture, and a long-standing love of song making seemed simply to have died off.

Hurston found this development deeply alarming. On the road in the South in the late 1920s, she searched for a black voice that she was convinced was disappearing, a vocal majesty and creativity that were in the process of being drowned out. "Enclosed find all of the material that I have transcribed into ink," she wrote to the anthropologist Franz Boas in 1927. "It is fortunate that it is being collected now, for a great many people say, 'I used to know some of that old stuff, but I done forgot it all.' You see, the Negro is not living his lore to the extent of the Indian. He is not on a reservation, being kept pure. His negroness is being rubbed off by close contact with white culture." Her report concluded: "The bulk of the population spends its leisure in motion picture theatres, or with the phonograph and its blues."

Preserving pure "Negroness" was Hurston's concern, and the race record endangered that purity. That fear was echoed by other African American intellectuals who, like Hurston, were entranced with the power of black folk song and speech. The writer Jean Toomer, a native of Washington, D.C., moved to a "crude . . . but strangely rich and beautiful" part of rural Georgia in 1921 and was distressed by what he encountered, only one year after "Crazy Blues" had burst in upon the African American soundscape.

> There was a valley . . . with smoke-wreaths during the day
> and mist at night. A family of back-country Negroes had only

recently moved into a shack not too far away. They sang.
And this was the first time I'd ever heard the folk-songs and
spirituals. They were very rich and sad and joyous and
beautiful. But I learned that the Negroes of the town
objected to them. They called them "shouting." They had
victrolas and player-pianos. So, I realized with deep regret,
that the spirituals, meeting ridicule, would be certain to die
out. With Negroes also the trend was towards the small town
and then towards the city—and industry and commerce and
machines.

Machines were the problem: like the city, like industry, like
commerce, they corrupted whatever fell in their path. "The
supreme fact of mechanical civilization is that you become
part of it, or get sloughed off," Toomer wrote to his friend
Waldo Frank in 1922. "Negroes have no culture to resist it
with (and if they had, their position would be identical to the
Indians), hence industrialism the more readily transforms
them." Even Hurston, more sanguine than Toomer about the
persistence of folk song in some black rural areas, felt that this
survival could only be temporary, that the "lush glades of primitive imagination" would inevitably be "drained by mechanical
invention."

Central to that process of depletion were the standardized
products of commercial amusement. Even before the recording industry developed, many feared that authentic folk songs
were being drowned out by assembly-line replicas. That no
piece of sheet music could be an authentic folk song was accepted virtually without debate. Folk music was composed
anonymously, transmitted orally, and suffused with the spirit of
the peasantry, and since that unspoiled people was fast disap-

pearing, genuine folk song was fading fast. Its gentle tones could not compete with the strident strains of commercial popular music. "There is an enemy at the doors of folk-music which is driving it out, namely the common popular songs of the day, and this enemy is one of the most repulsive and most insidious," noted the British composer Hubert Parry in 1899. "In true folk songs there is no sham, no got-up glitter, and no vulgarity. . . . [T]hese treasures of humanity are getting rare, for they are written in characters the most evanescent you can imagine, upon the sensitive brain fibres of those who learn them, and have but little idea of their value."

Yet if Hurston and Toomer's distaste for commercial recordings was part of a broader elegy about the disappearance of folk music, it also had meanings that were specifically racial. Since the mid-nineteenth century, African American intellectuals had stressed the importance of song as communication, a critical source of expression for a people otherwise forced into silence. The slave-turned-abolitionist Frederick Douglass wrote in 1845 of the significance to be found in music that genteel whites dismissed as childlike gaiety or primitive noise. "Rude and apparently incoherent" though the slave songs might be, beneath the surface they contained unfathomable depths of suffering: "They were tones loud, long, and deep, they breathed the prayer and complaint of souls boiling over with the bitterest anguish. Every tone was testimony against slavery, and a prayer to God for deliverance from chains."

In the wake of emancipation, African American writers and activists built on Douglass's reflections. The black sociologist W. E. B. Du Bois, writing in *The Souls of Black Folk* in 1903, stressed the spirituals' importance as testimony, a powerful refutation of historians' claims "that life was joyous to the black slave, careless and happy." However guarded their language, the sorrow songs confronted the listener with "death and suffering and unvoiced longing toward a truer world," a yearning for deliverance to a place and time where "men will judge men by their souls and not by their skins." And in an era of rampaging commerce and industry, they offered a simplicity and purity of spirit unparalleled in a nation effectively born in modernity, a nation that lacked a peasant past. "There is no true American music but the wild sweet melodies of the Negro slave," he concluded. "All in all, we black men seem the sole oasis of simple faith and reverence in a dusty desert of dollars and smartness."

But what would happen if black men abandoned that role? That was the danger Hurston and Toomer feared in the pell-mell embrace of race records. Northern labor shortages in World War I had intensified urbanization, black people's movement from field to factory, and the explosive growth of urban enclaves like Harlem. Such dramatic modernization promised African Americans increased opportunity, but Hurston and Toomer saw dangers too. With its crowds, electric lights, and machines, the city offered new forms of stimulation, and it could eat away at the bonds of tradition. Race records embodied that threat. By standardizing the song-making process, they could kill off the patterns of call-and-response, as well as the processes of invention and improvisation on which black music had long relied. Even the likes of Langston Hughes and Sterling Brown, who saw the blues as a modern folk music, shared something of Hurston's apprehension. Though devoted consumers of race records, they confined that enthusiasm to their private letters; their published writings celebrating the blues as an expression of black memory and community (like Hughes's 1930 novel *Not Without Laughter* and Brown's 1930 poem "Ma Rainey") effaced the recorded disk and depicted the music in live performance.

It would not be until 1952, when the nameless protagonist of Ralph Ellison's *Invisible Man* burrows into his hidden basement in Harlem, lights up a joint, drops Louis Armstrong's 1929 recording "What Did I Do to Be So Black and Blue" on the turntable, and finds "a new analytical way of listening to music," that an African American novelist reflected on the possibilities opened up by the phonograph record. In those three decades of silence, it would seem, lay unspoken tensions about the impact of mechanical reproduction and of this strange process of hearing music by putting a platter on a recording machine.

IF EVEN BLACK INTELLECTUALS FOUND THE EMERGENCE OF race records unsettling, it was all the more jarring for white men and women enchanted by African American singing, whose numbers were greater than one might suppose. That enchantment stretched back at least to the mid-nineteenth century and the development of minstrel shows (whose racism disguised a fascination with the vitality of black music), yet it reached a new peak during and after the Civil War, when the South was flooded with white northerners, veterans of anti-slavery efforts, who traveled among the emancipated slaves and were riveted by the music they heard. The spirituals, the work songs, the "long, lonely sing-song of the fields," were beautiful, haunting, somehow unearthly. They strained the white listener's capacity to describe them, to fix them on paper in musical notes. "It is difficult to express the entire character of these negro ballads by mere musical notes and signs," wrote the abolitionist campaigner Lucy McKim in 1862. "The odd turns made in the throat; and that curious rhythmic effect produced by single voices chiming in at different irregular intervals seem almost as impossible to place on score as the singing of birds, or the tones of an Aeolian Harp." The antislavery activist William Allen felt the same sense of awe at the strangeness and singularity of the black voice. "The best we can do . . . with paper and types, or even with voices, will convey but a faint shadow of the original. The voices of the colored people have a peculiar quality that nothing can imitate; and the intonations and delicate variations of even one singer cannot be reproduced on paper."

In the years that followed, the elusiveness of the black voice, its resistance to reproduction, became an indispensable axiom, the eye of the needle through which any discussion of African American song had to pass. As the cult of the spirituals grew in the 1870s and 1880s with the international success of the Fisk Jubilee Singers, white intellectuals in America and Europe lauded what they saw as a wholly untutored artistry that owed its power to the "remarkable musical capacity" of a "half-barbarous" race that remained tied to the natural world. In that indescribable, irreproducible voice, enthusiasts heard a purity of spirit and a wild, untamed longing, a mournfulness that spoke not just of slavery but of something universal in the human soul. As onetime Union commander Thomas Wentworth Higginson put it, "Never, it seems to me, since man first lived and suffered, was his infinite longing and suffering uttered more plaintively." Deepened by suffering, honed by anguish, the black voice could reach peaks of emotion that white voices could not; through rapt attention, white listeners could absorb it and experience something of the sublime.

All the more unsettling, then, to hear that sublime, untutored, primitive voice corrupted by this most modern of modern technologies and to see America's black population shelling out millions to buy those disks up. To connoisseurs of the spirituals, the new music sounded cheap and tawdry, and the titles verged on the pornographic: hit releases like "Black Snake Moan," "Meat Cutter Blues," "I Got the Best Jelly Roll in Town." Few observers were as blunt as the song collector Robert Gordon, who stated that in preserving black folk song he aimed to help "the whites of the South to keep *one* bunch of negroes from becoming utterly worthless and *modern* in the city coon sense." Yet many shared the feeling underlying Gordon's pronouncement: that the cultural value of African Americans lay in their remaining rural and primitive and that as they abandoned that role, something essential was being lost. "When black [*sic*] takes on the prowlings and pratings of the white race and becomes a strutting chrysalis in silk shirts and Ford cars, the mystery is gone forever," wrote one journalist. That lament went hand in hand with a yearning for "real" black music, emanating from African American singers who successfully resisted the pull of the modern, urban world.

What follows are the stories of a few white men and women who went in search of those spellbinding voices, who set out to stem the tide of mass-produced replicas by uncovering the sound of the real thing. In writing this history of exploration and connoisseurship, inevitably, I have been selective. For many enthusiasts of African American singing, the recording machine posed grave dangers even as it opened up new possibilities: at once the prime destroyer of authenticity and an unparalleled tool of authentication. I have looked for people whose experience seemed to shed light on that contradiction, whose passions and vulnerabilities I felt for, and whose struggles I thought I could bring alive.

Out of those struggles, over time, emerged the idea of the Delta blues. By now it should be obvious that mine is not a conventional Delta blues history. I make no attempt to cover the ground mapped in Robert Palmer's canonical *Deep Blues*, with its focus on the development of a musical style and lines of artistic transmission (Charley Patton begets Son House begets Robert Johnson begets Muddy Waters). In such a history, quite rightly, the protagonists are black. My central characters are white. All of them set out to find an undiluted and primal black music. Behind that obsession lay an emotional attachment to racial difference that extends back at least to the mid-nineteenth century, to abolitionists' enchantment with the peculiar power of black singers, their uncanny ability to allow their white listeners to experience an unimagined transcendence, a level of emotional intensity otherwise out of their reach.

The folklorists, critics, and collectors I've written about were all searching for that vicarious ecstasy. All were born in the era of segregation; in different ways, all felt imaginatively tied to the South. Throughout their lives, they made racial assumptions that were hackneyed, condescending, and often offensive. Yet as I read their words, tracked their obsessions, and revisited their journeys, I came to appreciate what they have left us, the reservoir of recovered music, the chain of knowledge and expertise. In time, I learned to admire the sheer fortitude it took to engage with an art form that few whites of their generation respected. Even as they feared black modernity, they struggled to cope with it and sometimes to transcend their racist beginnings.

In the end, theirs is not a straightforward history, with a discernible chronology, a specifiable time line. To excavate the idea of the Delta blues is to describe something more amorphous and intangible: a history of voices and responses to voices, of the memories and emotions they generate, of how those associations change over time. What emerges from their stories is a genealogy of feeling and sensibility. Out of that journey of the imagination was created what we know as the Delta blues, a music of archaic, uncompromised voices, captured on commercial recordings and yet—magically, paradoxically— pristinely untouched by the modern world.

≈ *t w o* ≈

Impartial Testimony

I N THE MIDST OF THE VAST, FLAT EXPANSE OF SWAMP AND field that is the Mississippi Delta, there is a small, deteriorating hamlet called Tutwiler. On the side of the road, fifteen miles south of Clarksdale on Highway 49, stand two wooden signs built in the shape of a railway depot. From one hangs a large replica of a harmonica, from the other an outsized guitar. "Tutwiler," they announce, "Where 'Blues' was born."

There were few signs of blues, or indeed of much else, on the day I drove into Tutwiler. A few wooden buildings, some boarded up, lined the main street, along with a larger building bearing the words "U.S. Post Office, Tutwiler, Mississipp." It took only minutes to reach what must have been, in earlier days, the town center: a dirt square abutting a small patch of grass. When I got out of the car the air was humid and stagnant, the only sound the occasional rush of a truck on the distant highway, and I crossed a grass verge alongside a railroad track and looked at what I had come there to see.

On the near side of the track was a brass plaque mounted upon a stone pillar that had been placed there in 1976. It read:

A LANDMARK OF AMERICAN MUSIC

In his autobiography *Father of the Blues*, W. C. Handy stated that he first heard the blues, a native Negro ballad form, in the railroad station of Tutwiler in 1895.

Presented by the National Music Council,
Mississippi Music Educators Association and Exxon.

On the far side of the track, painted on the back wall of a long brick building, was a mural in the form of a triptych, the left panel showing a steam locomotive and the right showing bluesman and native son Sonny Boy Williamson, who is buried nearby. The middle panel depicted two black men sitting on a wooden bench, one stiff and rigid in a dark suit, the other in ragged jeans and work shirt and holding a guitar. Between the first and second murals was a painted sign.

In 1903, while touring the Delta and playing musical engagements, W. C. Handy was waiting for a train in Tutwiler.
At the train depot an unknown musician was singing while
sliding a knife blade down the strings of his guitar.
The sound and effect were unforgettable to Handy and
became the music known worldwide as "The Blues."

It was hard to know what to make of these monuments. As memorials of the blues they were remarkably feeble, not least in the fact that the memorializers could not agree about the year in which this encounter took place. Yet that very uncertainty points to a truth. So little is known about the early blues that it is not at all clear when or even where the form originated. Though in the wake of the blues revival historians have routinely rooted the blues in the Mississippi Delta, in point of fact they have had little hard evidence to back up that claim.

As a music of a denigrated, impoverished class, the early blues left the barest traces behind it. While scholars agree that its signature AAB verse form first appeared in the early twentieth century, even that is less fact than inference: nothing resembling that form appears in the reports of nineteenth-century ballad hunters. It all comes down to guesswork. No one knows who sang the first blues, or where they sang it, or when.

Lacking documentation, historians have relied upon stories like the ones emblazoned on these monuments, told retrospectively by well-placed observers about encountering the blues for the first time. By far the most frequently told of those tales is W. C. Handy's description (in his 1941 autobiography *Father of the Blues*) of his late-night encounter sometime in the Mississippi Delta, when "one night in Tutwiler, as I nodded in the railroad station while waiting for a train that had been delayed nine hours, life suddenly took me by the shoulder and wakened me with a start."

A lean, loose-jointed Negro had commenced plunking a guitar beside me as I slept. His clothes were rags; his feet peeped out of his shoes. His face had on it some of the sadness of the ages. As he played, he pressed a knife on the strings of the guitar in a manner popularized by Hawaiian guitarists who used steel bars. The effect was unforgettable. His song, too, struck me instantly.

Goin' where the Southern cross the Dog.

The singer repeated the line three times, accompanying himself on the guitar with the weirdest music I had ever heard. The tune stayed in my mind.

In recent years Handy's story of the ragged man at the Delta train station has become a blues legend, repeated by chroniclers from Robert Palmer to Greil Marcus, all eager to assert the primacy of the Delta in blues history despite the lack of demonstrable proof. In their recountings of the history of the Delta blues, Handy's vagrant is transformed into the archetypal bluesman: drifting aimlessly, owning nothing, singing, but not to any purpose, singing simply to while away the time. In the process of singing, he gives voice to melancholy, the emotion that Handy says powered the blues. "Suffering and hard luck were the midwives that birthed these songs," wrote Handy. "The blues were conceived in aching hearts."

Handy's drifter is understandably appealing to chroniclers of the blues because he so closely resembles the musicians whose recordings they venerate, Delta drifters like Charley Patton, Son House, and, above all, Robert Johnson, self-accompanied acoustic bluesmen who are championed by blues historians as the real thing. But there is a deeper reason for the vagrant's appeal. Handy's story captures the blues in a state of nature, as it must have existed before recording companies got hold of it. It is a foundation myth, a story that conveys something essential and incontrovertible about the origins of the blues tradition. To its enthusiasts, the blues evokes the raw, anguished voice of African American suffering. Handy's tale makes sense in this context because it is a story of discovery rather than invention. The blues, the story implies, is something eternal, primeval, entering into history through the accident of Handy's first encounter. A sorrowful wanderer drifts in the timeless landscape of the Mississippi Delta, appearing before him as if from a dream.

There is another story to be told about the discovery of the blues. It lacks the magic and mystery of Handy's account, that luminous moment when the bluesman stands before us in exactly the form in which we want him to appear. In this tale there is no such wondrous revelation. Here our view of the singer is obscured by the presence of the narrator, a young white southerner with no ear for music and scant knowledge of African American culture who was deeply unsettled by what he heard.

A decade and a half before the advent of race records, one unknowable day in 1907, a bespectacled twenty-three-year-old, Howard Odum, saddled his horse and set out from Oxford, forty miles east of the Mississippi Delta in Lafayette County. His aim was to collect research materials for a study of (as he would eventually title it) "the social and mental traits of the Negro." Strapped to his saddle was a graphophone, a cylinder recorder for capturing sound. With that equipment he would make what seem to have been the first field recordings of African American song.

Odum embarked on his trek with all the zeal of a new convert. He had just turned his back on the study of classics that had earned him a master's degree at the University of Mississippi and had thrown himself into social science, a revolutionary new field that applied to the study of human beings and society

Howard Odum outside the log cabin he built on his farm, ca. 1928.
From Howard Washington Odum Papers, courtesy of Southern Historical
Collection, Wilson Library, the University of North Carolina at Chapel Hill.

the rigorous empiricism of a laboratory experiment. Social scientists disdained texts and libraries in favor of the real world,
people and places observed at close range. That zeal for fact
gave it limitless potential to shape public policy, to arbitrate conflict—ultimately, Odum thought, to remake the South. Odum
knew the region's backwardness and degradation firsthand, and

he liked to envision it cleansed of its troubles and brought into the modern world. Social science, he believed, could do just that, and it offered its practitioner a chance to be a leader, even while dedicating himself to higher things, to the service of man, truth, and God.

The South needed leaders. Of that Odum was certain. Looking beyond the university at the bare hills and rolling fields of Lafayette County, he saw white families edging steadily into poverty, as more and more of them lost control of their farms and fell into tenancy and sharecropping. Schooling was minimal, even for whites, outside the university town of Oxford, and lives were shaped by superstition, tales of the shrieking ghosts haunting Cassidy's Bayou and of the spectral panthers to be glimpsed in the swamps, their fur gleaming black, their eyes burning yellow, their jaws dripping with blood.

There was a more palpable ghost as well: the lingering presence of the Old South. Its physical and psychological echoes gave the place an eerie, dreamlike feel that its native son William Faulkner would capture when he named the region "Yoknapatawpha," a Chickasaw term that translated roughly as "water runs slow through flat land." As a young graduate student trekking through the county on horseback, Odum would have seen the skeletal remains of country manors like Abbeville, once the pride of the county but burned in two Civil War battles and then lingering in slow decay, overgrown by weeds, engulfed by jungle, as the westernmost fringes of the Appalachian forest encroached ever further, seemingly ready to claim the land back. There were flesh-and-blood ruins too, sons and daughters of the deteriorating gentry who were tormented by the past. Once, when one of those young men, whom he knew slightly, lost his precarious hold upon sanity, Odum set out to bring him home, chasing him on an unbroken colt for forty miles from Toccapola to New Albany, "in and out across swollen streams and backwoods and pinehills," as he recalled it in a memoir, "often reflecting a physical reality stranger than fiction." In Odum's native northern Georgia, only a fraction of the antebellum population had owned any slaves, and the plantocracy was a distant presence. Here, memories of plantation grandeur hung over the landscape like a malignant spirit. "I myself have known Yoknapatawpha and it is no purely imaginary fantasy," he remembered thirty years later. "I have been close enough to Faulkner's quicksands to sense something of its terrors and have often imagined, behind the cedars and columned houses, that anything could happen there."

In among the cedars and columned houses were the cabins of African Americans. Comprising 45 percent of the county's population, they had powerful ghosts of their own—slavery and, still within living memory, the betrayal of Reconstruction. Here as in the rest of the South, hopes of forty acres and a mule gave way to the reality of the sharecropping system, in which families leased land from a planter, grew what he ordered (invariably cotton), and promised him one-half of the yield. Inevitably, they mortgaged away even more. During the growing season, from March through August, families kept themselves alive with loans from planters and merchants, who provided them with food and farming supplies. Only if the value of their crop exceeded that of their "furnish" did they end the year with a profit. In years when cotton prices were low, families were often poorer after the harvest than they had been before the season began.

Concurrently with sharecropping came systematic racial oppression and ostracism. Black Mississippians were kept from the polls by force, fraud, and, after 1890, provisions in the state constitution that withheld the vote from those judged to be vicious or ignorant. The state's first "Jim Crow" statute, mandating separation of the races on railway coaches, was passed in 1888, formalizing a practice of racial exclusion that had been customary for at least fifteen years. In schools, hospitals, restaurants, hotels, railway stations, streetcars, and prisons, African Americans were kept separate from whites. Those who broke the rules, who appeared sullen or uppity, or who allowed their eyes to meet a white woman's could be harassed, beaten, jailed, or lynched. Over two hundred black men and women were lynched in Mississippi in the decade around the turn of the century, more than any other state in the South. "If necessary every Negro in the state will be lynched," stated Governor James K. Vardaman in 1907. "It will be done to maintain white supremacy."

Before he arrived at the University of Mississippi, Odum gave no more thought than most other white southerners to life on the other side of the color line. In the Civil War stories that haunted him as a boy, the principal victims were white. His mother's family had been successful slaveholders wiped out by the advance of Union troops, and both his grandfathers had served in the Confederate Army and returned broken in body and spirit. He grew particularly close to his paternal grandfather, John Wesley Odum, a small farmer who had owned no slaves. The elder Odum spent much of the war sick and despondent, suffering near-fatal injuries and a nervous breakdown in battle. When his company marched a few miles from his farm, he "slipped off and went home," depressed and confused. The young Howard Odum, at his grandfather's knee, heard the tale of his desertion over and over. At commemorations to mark the Confederate dead, he watched him burn with shame and discomfort, "his broad forehead moist with perspiration . . . his big blue eyes peering straight ahead with the hurt look of the innocent wounded."

In time Odum would fuse his grandfather's story with the tragedy that was southern history. As a boy, however, he felt only humiliation, to which he added a despair all his own. He was born in 1884 near the tiny village of Bethlehem, Georgia, the second son of a struggling truck-and-dairy farmer, William Pleasants Odum, and his wife Mary Ann Thomas. Odum's mother nursed painful memories of her comfortable girlhood on a plantation. Fueled by a bitter hatred of Yankees, she pushed her children to learn, to achieve, to regain something of the family's lost standing. She shaped their home as a rarefied world of books and music and spiritual devotion, and Howard, an early reader, soon became the focus of her ambitions. He wanted to please her, but it was difficult. The scrappy, arid plains around Bethlehem; the threadbare school that he attended erratically; the harsh, pious Methodism that terrorized him: it all made his every effort seem futile. He had a big nose, he lisped, he was cripplingly shy, and his early memories were shadowed by death. As a young boy, too sickly for farm chores, he had been left to look after his three younger siblings, all of whom died—one from burns suffered in a brush fire, one from a spinal injury after falling from a tree, and the last from diphtheria. Though none of the deaths were the result of his negligence, he felt profoundly responsible, and a sense of guilt and self-loathing would haunt him for the rest of his life.

In 1904, Odum graduated from Emory College in Georgia, having earned a bachelor's degree in classics without making an impression on anyone. His ambitions to move ahead in the world were undercut by his awareness of his own marginality.

"I [had a strong sense of being] what I designated as A. I. U. P.,"
he remembered, "awkward, ignorant, ugly, and poor." He took
the only job that he could find, as a schoolteacher in Toccapola
in northern Mississippi; six months into the post, he enrolled
at the University of Mississippi as a graduate student in classics. His aim, now, was to become a college lecturer, teaching
classics to keen undergraduates—not exactly his mother's
dream that he serve God and redeem the South, but still a step
up in the world. He traveled the twenty miles to Oxford on
horseback, shuddering at the dense forests and swamps that
he passed through, and settled into life immersed in the
tragedies of Oedipus and Antigone, tales of fatalism, defeat,
and disaster that he sometimes merged into his own.

Then one day in 1906, Odum stumbled into a graduate
seminar on the "Psychology of the Negro Problem," led by a
charismatic professor of social psychology, Thomas P. Bailey. By
Mississippi standards, Bailey was cosmopolitan. Though born,
raised, and schooled in South Carolina, he found his first teaching posts at the University of Chicago and the University of
California at Berkeley and built a national reputation for psychological investigations that probed the making of human
character, the means by which men and women mastered their
instincts to become rational, disciplined, self-motivated adults.
Those studies imbued him with a messianic sense of the importance of the social scientist's task. Labor unrest, urban crime: as
Bailey conceived them, they were deviant forms of human behavior, the consequence of unmastered instinct, and they
needed impartial, rigorous, expert attention if they were to be
kept under control. Arriving at the University of Mississippi in
1903, he conveyed to his students that same sense of urgency.
"Science, and science alone, star-eyed science, truth-loving

science, spiritually intellectual science," with its empirical methods, its verifiable facts, could help the South find its way out of its most vexing dilemmas—above all, out of the problem of race.

"Does the Negro show potentialities as a race?" The question drove Bailey's research in Mississippi and guided his seminar on Negro psychology. What could black men and women make of themselves, if genuinely given the chance? It was indisputable, Bailey acknowledged, that at this moment African Americans were inferior to whites; indisputable too that segregation was wise, necessary, and natural, if only to avoid racial amalgamation and keep up what he described as "the physical stock of the higher racial types." Yet who was to say for how long that would remain imperative? Blacks were currently "less developed" than whites, but that did not mean that they were inherently "lower"—no one knew what their capacities were. A full and reasoned judgment of Negro capacity awaited the verdict of science—ideally, a team of scientists, sponsored by leaders from across the country. Until then, it was up to individual researchers to ask the questions that needed answers. Was the Negro capable of reaching a mature standard of white Christian conduct, of exercising rational self-control? "Is the Negro really adaptable, or is he parasitic? Is his slowness of development due to deep-lying anatomical and physiological causes or to environmental causes? Is the Negro deteriorating? If so, why?"

Odum was accustomed to the sight of African Americans, but not to asking questions about them. With his eyes opened by Bailey, he found it impossible to stop. Those dark faces that turned away when they saw him watching: What did the men and women behind them feel? What did they think? Surveying the bent figures in the cotton fields outside Oxford, he saw a compelling enigma, a mystery that needed unraveling. "The Negro has a life and an environment of his own which the whites do not see, which after all may be at the bottom of his actions," he wrote in 1910. Some way had to be found to penetrate that life, that environment, if the South were to move forward—some way of seeing beyond surface appearances deep into the heart of African American character, of reaching past the mask for a glimpse of the genuine Negro face.

And it was eventually toward folk song that he turned to find the answer. In the songs he sang at home, work, and leisure, the Negro revealed his true self, as Odum put it: "what he *is* rather than what he appears to be." Odum took his interpretation of folk materials from sociologist William Graham Sumner's 1907 book *Folkways,* which explored the power of tradition and custom at primitive stages of social organization. Prize apart a traditional song or tale, and you could identify the distinctive mindset of a culture: primitive traditions and rituals grew out of basic desires and mental traits, and they resisted all pressure to evolve or change. With Bailey's help, Odum devised a plan for a doctoral study in social psychology. He would travel through Lafayette County collecting black song with a graphophone, transcribing the lyrics, and analyzing the social and mental traits that the lyrics revealed. The result would be "impartial testimony," objective data revealing the truth of a bewildering race.

That impartial evidence was all the more crucial in light of the misguided notions that had long surrounded black music. Odum had read the rapturous accounts of the spirituals written just after the Civil War, and he had read W. E. B. Du Bois's *The Souls of Black Folk,* and in Du Bois's erudition Odum found ominous indications of where the cult of the spirituals was bound to lead. In the spirituals Du Bois had heard a political music, full of eloquent protest against racial oppression and "faith in the ultimate justice of things." No matter that in 1903 Du Bois was very much a lone voice; no matter that with popularization the spirituals were being steadily stripped of political overtones, their grammar cleaned up, their imagery conventionalized, so the songs were fit to sing (as one song anthology of the period put it) "at all manner of occasions, from funerals to yachting parties." To champion the sorrow songs, Odum believed, was effectively to pose them as "the truest representation of the negro's real self," songs whose transcendent power gave cheering hopes for cultivation and refinement in African American life.

To Odum, that was sentimental nonsense. The spirituals were beautiful, but they were hardly representative: artificially preserved by choirs and sheet music publishers, they did not reflect what black southerners were singing now. Though "the religious songs of the Negro have commonly been accepted as the characteristic music of the race," he maintained, "observation for the most part has been made by those who have heard the Negro songs but have not studied them." By working with a graphophone, he would change that, replacing facile understandings with irrefutable, objective facts, uncovering at last the stark, brutal truths of Negro psychology.

———

THOUGH NEW TECHNOLOGIES ARE COMMONLY CELEBRATED as either miracles or inevitabilities, every mechanical innovation is the material expression of an idea. In the case of the

The earliest known photograph of a Graphophone in use. Frances Densmore records Blackfoot leader Mountain Chief.

Courtesy of the Archive of Folk Culture, the Library of Congress.

phonograph, the idea was to do for the ear what the daguerreotype had done for the eye: to freeze sensory impressions that would otherwise be evanescent, to protect them from the destruction of time. "We will be able to preserve and hear again . . . a memorable speech . . . the last words of a dying man . . . of a distant parent, a lover, a mistress," explained Thomas Edison in 1878, one year after inventing the talking tinfoil. The phonograph could be an aid to business, making dictation possible without a stenographer. It could uplift the blind through "phonographic books," mechanical recordings of classic texts. And human knowledge and learning would be enriched through the machine's ability to reproduce foreign languages, to teach elocution, or to record a teacher's lessons to be heard at home.

Number four on Edison's inventory of possibilities was the reproduction of music. That it did not rank higher owed partly to his priorities ("I don't want the phonograph sold for amusement purposes, it is not a toy," he told an associate in 1894), but also to the limitations of the technology. The original tinfoil phonograph produced an indistinct sound, just about clear enough to convey human speech but nowhere near nuanced enough for musical subtleties. It would take another two decades of technical innovations to produce machines that could convey resonant musical sounds. In 1886 Alexander Graham Bell and his cousin Charles Tainter devised a wax cylinder recording machine called the graphophone with far better sound quality than Edison's model; it was also more practical, since the wax cylinders could be removed, stored, and replayed, while the tinfoil-wrapped cylinders, once removed, were destroyed. The wax cylinder recorder would be eclipsed in turn by the disk-playing gramophone introduced by Emile Berliner in 1887. The gramophone pared down the cost of the Bell graphophone by offering only half its functions: it could play music but could not record it. Consumers liked the savings; phonograph vendors liked the guaranteed market for pre-recorded disks. Over the next ten years sales of disks and disk players grew steadily, with the manufacture of wax cylinder phonographs ceasing altogether by 1913.

Yet in one area the cylinder was not supplanted: in the new scholarly discipline of social science, where it had been embraced as an indispensable tool nearly from the moment of its invention. In his visionary excitement about the technology, Odum tapped into a sense of the machine's possibilities first expressed in 1890, when the ethnographer Jesse Walter Fewkes pioneered the use of a phonograph to record the language patterns of Maine's Passamaquody Indians. "The apparatus proves to be a means by which the actual sound itself of which a music consists may, even in many of its more delicate characteristics, be stored up by the traveler, in a form permanently accessible to observation," noted the psychologist Benjamin Gilman on hearing Fewkes's recordings. "[The recording] can be interrupted at any point, repeated indefinitely, and even within certain limits magnified, as it were, for more accurate appreciation of changes in pitch, by increasing the duration of notes." The Hungarian composer Béla Bartók, who made field recordings of eastern European folk music around 1900, found that the cylinders made audible "notes between the notes" that "cultured" westerners ordinarily could not discern. The phonograph, in other words, expanded and intensified sensory perception, just as the microscope had for the eye. By extracting the voice from its human context and reproducing it in mechanical form, the machine allowed the investigator to strip bare its workings, to probe and manipulate, to parse and dismember.

That capacity for verisimilitude has shaped how the phonograph has been written into the history of African American music. In sharp contrast to the story of recording for profit is the story of recording for knowledge: the story of what since the 1950s has been labeled "field recording," in which men and women who felt passionately that endangered music *mattered* set off down the back roads lugging unwieldy equipment to capture what commerce and industry threatened to drown out. Employed in this fashion, as a tool for preserving marginal cultures, the recording machine seemed a progressive instrument, part of the intellectual revolution that anthropologist Franz Boas produced in early-twentieth-century social science. At the heart of that revolution was an attack on the evolutionary precepts that propelled Victorian anthropology, which focused on elaborating grand theories of social development, the human progression from savagery to civilization. Boas insisted that humankind should not be measured by one uniform standard of cultivation. Instead, he spoke of "cultures": the customs, traditions, and forms of expression created by particular societies at particular times. In the process he inveighed against scholarly racism, disputed the idea that some peoples were "primitive," and urged his students to value all the peoples they studied by making accurate records of their words and their sounds.

Yet though they used phonographs routinely, Boasian ethnographers in 1907 did not study African American music. The purpose of fieldwork, as Boas conceived it, was to map particular societies' "culture patterns," and for that reason his students focused on Native Americans, who had elaborate, picturesque, and obviously doomed expressive systems that needed to be documented, analyzed, and explained before they disappeared. But even though African Americans had songs and animal tales that ethnographers noted with a fair bit of interest, no one at that stage, not even the liberal Boas, believed that those practices cohered into a distinctive and integrated whole. Bluntly put, black Americans did not have cultural patterns of any depth or richness—they had lost their African traditions in crossing the Atlantic: so believed Boas, so believed (with a few conspicuous exceptions, such as Zora Neale Hurston) virtually every early-twentieth-century ethnographer. The fact that African Americans were renowned internationally for their resonant singing did not in itself arouse the interest of ethnographers. Though between 1890 and 1930 ethnographers studying Native American song made some fourteen thousand cylinder recordings, of African American voices they appear to have made only a handful.

Howard Odum, it seems, was the first, and he was not a Boasian. He had little interest in mapping cultures holistically or uncovering cultural patterns in their entirety; nor could he endorse Boas's cultural relativism. Eventually, as the South's premier sociologist, his views on race would become more liberal, and he would come to oppose segregation privately and on principle while seeking its incremental abolition in practice. But in 1907 he took up his cylinder recorder in the same spirit that physical anthropologists of the day took up calipers—to provide hard and objective proof of black inferiority.

———

THOUGH HOWARD ODUM EMBARKED ON HIS SEARCH OUT OF devotion to science, in the process he stumbled upon History. As he traveled across Lafayette County, he found something curious: songs made up of a single line, repeated two or three times. He heard them from itinerant players—"music physicianers," "musicianers," and "songsters," they called themselves—who carried their songs and guitars along the back roads and sang into his graphophone in return for small change. They adapted their songs to suit their mood, and they could stretch them out for what seemed like hours, fusing lines from different tunes to take them straight from one song to another and sliding a knife or a bone along the guitar strings to make the instrument "talk" in response. The effect was hypnotic, and the words they sang were elliptical and haunting. "I'm po' boy long way from home," one bedraggled man intoned. "I got the blues, but I'm too damn mean to cry."

What Odum found, he later realized, was the blues in formation. Whether the form had yet acquired the name "blues" is debatable, since none of Odum's informants labeled it as such. They spoke of "coon songs," "rag times," "knife songs," "devil songs," "breakdowns," and any one song could have a variety of labels, depending on the context in which it was played. His findings were largely a collection of musical fragments combined and reused in song after song, barely distinguishable from the minstrel show tunes, ballads, and Tin Pan Alley standards that made up the itinerant player's repertoire.

As a label for a particular musical form, the term "blues" seems to have been coined around 1912, with the first publication of such song titles on sheet music; ten years later, in the wake of "Crazy Blues," that label was everywhere. To most white observers the music seemed to have materialized instantaneously. Odum, however, eventually matched up what he was hearing on records with what he had captured in the field two decades earlier. In 1925, poring over his findings, he drew up the following list:

LINES AND TITLES OF SONGS COLLECTED TWENTY YEARS AGO	LINES AND TITLES OF RECENT POPULAR BLUES
Laid in jail, back to the wall.	Laid in jail, back to the wall.
Jailer, won't you put 'nother man in my stall?	Look here, mister jailer, put another gal in my stall.
Baby, won't you please come home?	Baby, won't you please come home?
Wonder where my baby stay las' night?	Where did you stay last night?
I got my all-night trick, baby, and you can't git in.	I'm busy and you can't come in.
I'll see her when her trouble's like mine.	I'm gonna see you when your troubles are just like mine.
Satisfied.	I'm satisfied.
You may go, but this will bring you back.	I got what it takes to bring you back.
Joe Turner.	Joe Turner blues.
Love, Kelly's love.	Love, careless love.
I'm on my las' go-round.	Last go-round blues.

Reading Odum's list today is tantalizing and frustrating in equal measure, for it is the sole indication of the importance of what he found. Equipped with his cylinder recorder, Odum captured the Holy Grail: the voice of the blues before record companies got to it, the sound of the music in its natural state. Yet we have no way of hearing the voices he heard, no means of recovering the sounds that he documented. Odum seems to have lost or discarded his cylinders at some point in the 1920s, after his research assistant Guy Johnson made use of them. They form no part of the voluminous collection of his papers and artifacts held at the University of North Carolina; that we know of them at all comes down largely to the recollections of family, like his daughter Mary Frances, who can locate neither cylinders nor field notebooks but (she has written me) can picture them in her "mind's eye." Odum himself never described the process of recording and never itemized the cylinders' contents. That the recordings themselves might become objects of interest does not seem to have crossed his mind.

What mattered to Odum was scientific truth, not the music he uncovered, yet in stumbling upon (and then losing) the blues, he discovered things that he had not foreseen. He went into the field styling himself a hard-nosed scientific explorer, but he had not anticipated the difficulties he faced. Most unsettling was the enforced intimacy required by his work. Odum's search for the facts of black song demanded that he act as spy and voyeur, exploring black neighborhoods, eavesdropping on singers, and coaxing them to sing into the horn. He had grown up believing in cleanliness of body and spirit; in the purity of hearth and home; in the values of self-restraint, hard work, and service. "We should all try to discharge our duty," read the maxim on the calendar Odum kept at his bedside; in the margins he scribbled a fervent "Yes." Face-to-face with black southerners, he encountered a world in which, to his eyes, such ideals were entirely absent.

Nothing in Odum's devout, driven, duty-bound upbringing prepared him for the itinerant players from whom he collected the bulk of his songs, men who struck him as dissolute, self-indulgent drifters guided by "an independent ethics of vagrancy." "The Negro has little home conscience or love of home, no local attachment of the better sort," he maintained in 1910. Love among them was fleeting and casual, its expression carnal and animalistic, a state of moral pollution reflected in the general dirt and disorder. "Filth and uncleanness is everywhere predominant. One must refrain from a description of the worst phase of the Negro's personal habits." The songs the musicians performed for him grew out of those noxious surroundings: they were "openly descriptive of the grossest immorality," "vicious and obscene," "rotten with filth." The more he heard, the more the whole enterprise of song gathering repelled him. "The student finds difficulty in holding himself to the persistent, sustained, and laborious effort that a searching investigation requires," he admitted. "Many incidents growing out of the efforts to secure his information are repulsive, not to say nauseous and gruesome. Only the hardiest scientific interest in discoverable facts can sustain the investigator."

Given the violence of his response, it is perhaps not surprising that Odum soon abandoned the study of black music. The songs he gathered in Mississippi provided the raw material for two Ph.D. dissertations: a 1909 study of African American religious songs that brought him a doctorate in psychology from Clark University, and a 1910 thesis on "the social and mental traits of the Negro," for which he earned a doctorate in sociology from Columbia. Thereafter he turned to the study of white rural underdevelopment, the subject on which he would build his career. Nor should it be surprising that Odum's journey did not compel other investigators to follow up. It would not be until the mid-1920s that scholars again recorded itinerant black singers, and not until the mid-1930s that they took much care to preserve the results. Field recording, Odum discovered, brought a physical proximity that could be unsettling, so much so that for the next two decades most folklorists employing phonographic technology preferred to avoid black informants outright.

Intriguingly, however, Odum did eventually return to the subject. In 1924, prompted by the race record phenomenon and by a new wave of white interest in African American culture and in what would soon be described as "the New Negro," he got his research assistant Guy Johnson to read through his field notes from Mississippi and shape them into a book. Published in 1925 as *The Negro and His Songs*, it won praise from many reviewers, including the African American poet Countee Cullen, who deemed it "a serious attempt to delve into a mine of rich and varied ore . . . done with a scholarly acumen for detail and a dispassionate notation on the specimens." That favorable reception prompted Odum and Johnson to undertake a follow-up volume, haunting construction sites and logging camps for itinerant singers to interview and record.

One day in the summer of 1925 Odum passed a construction site in Chapel Hill and heard one of the laborers singing, and something about the voice prompted him to stop. The man was a rambler and a guitarist with a prodigious repertoire—to Odum's ears he seemed to remember every song he had ever heard—and Odum was transfixed by the sight of him, "his face with blood vessels standing out and perspiration bursting out and his physical earnestness." Over a few days Odum plied him with whiskey and got him talking. A few weeks later he wrote to his friend H. L. Mencken:

> John Wesley Gordon, alias "Left Wing," has lived, worked, loafed, fought, bled, and died in no less than 36 of the States, in support of which he gives concrete and vivid evidence, fearfully and wonderfully made. I propose, as a matter of recreation, and as a substitute for other forms of entertainment, such as the less highbrow might find pleasing, to present the annals of Left Wing, perhaps under the title of "The Left Wing Blues."

The result, in 1928, was a life history of Left Wing Gordon entitled *Rainbow Round My Shoulder*, billed by Odum's publisher as "the Negro's own story, the autobiography of the Negro supertramp." Just who Gordon was, if indeed he existed, would never be entirely clear. The book appeared to be based on verbatim testimony from a single, larger-than-life black adventurer, and that, indeed, was how Odum had sold it to his editor, Gordon's words reproduced "exactly as given," "all pictures, all concreteness," an "untouched phototype." Yet no transcriptions of Gordon's words or those of any other black laborer appear in his private papers. To judge by the reminiscences of his colleagues, the book seems to have taken shape less through transcription or compilation than through minstrelsy or, perhaps, self-conducted psychoanalysis, as Odum cast his imagination back from Gordon to the drifters he had met in Lafayette County in 1907. Dictating in his office for hours at a stretch, eyes closed, stock-still, he sang and spoke in the voices he remembered, as his secretary struggled to get down every word.

What lay at the heart of the book were the songs Gordon sang, the same songs Odum had heard two decades earlier, which he now thought of as the "folk blues." Odum devised that term to distinguish the songs he had heard in Mississippi from the "formal blues" now being sold on race records. Looking back on the former now, he remembered their earthy natural charm, their freshness and innocence, which were being cheapened on record by thinly veiled double entendres and a spirit of calculation and artifice. Partly the distinctions he made came down to the singers—the phonograph records were dominated by women, while the songsters he had recorded had all been men—but the transformation ran deeper. The tone, the sensibility, had been transformed, and in the process, something precious was fading away.

Bringing that something precious to life was his purpose in writing about Left Wing Gordon. As Odum evoked him, Gordon gave his life story in speech and in song, but the text made little distinction between them. So fully did Gordon embody the blues in Odum's retelling that his speech and his song often elide into one:

Good Lawd, I can't be satisfied. If I been back here mo' 'n twenty times, maybe I'll come back twenty mo' an' maybe I won't. I don't stay noplace mo' 'n three weeks, leastwise never mo' 'n fo.' I'm gittin' out o' here now for Philadelphia see does my baby know right from wrong.

> O Lawd, if I feel tomorrow
> Like I feel today
> Good God, gonna pack my suitcase
> Lawd, an' walk away.

In those ceaseless wanderings that once had repulsed him, Odum now perceived something poignant and noble, a "Black Ulysses," as he called him, driven by a yearning, restless spirit untamed by the constraints of family or home. In the blues that Gordon could never stop singing, Odum heard songs "so strange and varied as to reveal a sort of superhuman evidence of the folk soul." Although he held out some hope that folk blues and formal blues could continue to exist side by side, that could only happen so long as black laborers remained uncorrupted, permeated by an essential simplicity. "There will be the folk blues," Odum concluded, "as long as there are Negro toilers and adventurers whose naivete has not been worn off by what the white man calls culture."

Protecting those toilers from corruption was thus imperative, but Odum knew from his own experience how hard that would be. Though by 1928 he had waxed rhapsodic about the simple, unworldly singers he had met in Mississippi, his cylinders, were we now able to hear them, might well have told a different story. Though he went into the field with a messianic vision of science, his cylinder recorder a bit player in that larger drama, in practice the machine proved an intrusive third party in his encounters with the guitarists whom he persuaded to sing into the horn. As traveling performers at dances and on roadsides, they were accustomed to playing to the crowd, and in their recording sessions they sought to demonstrate their up-to-date repertoires, which, Odum realized the more he encountered it, was decidedly not what he was after. "All manner of 'ragtimes,' 'coon-songs,' and the latest 'hits' replace the simpler negro melodies," he lamented. "Young negroes pride themselves on the number of such songs they can sing, at the same time that they resent a request to sing the older melodies." Far from being inhibited by Odum's cylinder recorder, they welcomed it as a means of broadcasting their music. Odum was particularly unsettled by "the young negro who wished to call out his name before each song which he was singing into the graphophone. 'Song composed by Will Smith of Chattanooga, Tennessee,' he would cry out, then begin his song; for, he maintained, these songs would be sung all over the world, and he deserved the credit for them."

In Will Smith, Odum heard a sophistication he had not expected, a welcoming of technology and a worldly ambition that the recording machine seemed not simply to capture but to provoke. Though he had seized upon the phonograph as a scientific tool, he discovered that it could propel his subjects into distinctly unfolkish behavior. That twenty years on he discarded those cylinders should perhaps not surprise us. Faced with the voices that race records generated, he wanted to remember voices that were purer, more magical, voices that sang the "simpler Negro melodies," the "soft, stirring melodies of a folklife."

three

On the Trail of
Negro Folk Songs

OFTEN IN THE YEARS THAT FOLLOWED, DOROTHY SCAR-
borough recalled the night when her search first promised fruition, when after months of letter writing and
interviews she heard the sound of the uncorrupted black
voice. It came to her in 1921 in the Manhattan townhouse
owned by John Allan Wyeth, a seventy-six-year-old Civil War
veteran and surgeon of national renown, onetime president of
the American Medical Association and founder of the Poly-
clinic Hospital, the first postgraduate school of medicine in the
United States. Seven years earlier, Wyeth had published his
memoirs, *With Sabre and Scalpel*, which included accounts of
slave songs and dances he had learned growing up on his family's Alabama plantation. Scarborough was desperate to meet
him, and a doctor friend offered to make introductions. Letters were sent, an appointment was made, and on a breezy

spring evening the friend brought Scarborough to Wyeth's door.

With his leonine head and stern, chiseled features, Wyeth was an imposing figure, reserved and formal and accustomed to deference. But Scarborough soon felt at ease. At forty-three, she had a calm, sweet, daughterly manner, and though she had spent the last few years in New York City teaching creative writing at Columbia University, she had an intimate knowledge of southern patriarchs. Her father, John Bledsoe Scarborough, had been a Confederate veteran from Louisiana. Like his wife, he was a child of slave owners, and like Wyeth, he had risen in the war's aftermath to a position of power and influence. Trained as a lawyer, he worked as a judge in a series of Texas towns before settling in Waco, home to Baylor University, whose board of trustees he soon joined.

Dorothy Scarborough grew up in the shadow of this pillar of the local community, which proved particularly burdensome after her mother's early death. As the lone unmarried daughter, she was expected to serve as her father's hostess. She had ideas and determination; in her quiet way, she rebelled. By her twenty-first birthday in 1899, she had earned a bachelor's degree and a master's degree in English at Baylor, and when her father died in 1905 she instantly put her training to work. Over the next twelve years, she taught intermittently at Baylor while pursuing a doctorate in English literature, traveling first to the University of Chicago and then to Oxford University, only to discover to her dismay that this bastion of higher learning refused to grant women degrees. In 1915 she enrolled at Columbia University and began a doctoral disserta-

Dorothy Scarborough.

tion on the supernatural in English fiction, and almost immediately Columbia's extension division offered her a teaching
post. She quit her job at Baylor, shipped the last of her belong-
ings, and settled in New York City for good.

Until then, Scarborough's writing had focused on the lore
and literature of distant lands, but abruptly, when she moved
to New York, she began writing about the South. In 1919 she
published a memoir of sorts entitled *From a Southern Porch,* a
celebration of languorous days spent on her sister's front porch
in Richmond, Virginia, where she fled every summer when
Manhattan's gasoline fumes became stifling and the streets
grew gummy with melted tar. There she would sit from early
morning until the last traces of light disappeared from the sky,

with a notebook in her lap, observing the procession of life. "I can see a black woman going by on the road, a basket of clothes balanced on her head—swaying but never in danger of falling," she wrote.

> Groups of laughing gay young Negroes pass by to their work or to errands in town. Little boys, as black as the berries they have in their buckets for sale, are on their way to market. An old mule ambles restfully down the road, drawing a cart that creaks with rheumatism and years, and that has one hind wheel at an alarming angle with the body of the cart. But the driver, an ebony antique, is unagitated, and the animal at ease of mind. Not for any inducement would that mule quicken his pace. Autos from the city whirl by with sophisticated snorts and honk-honks, raising dust in whorls.

What Scarborough reveled in from that front porch in Virginia was a South that felt and sounded unchanging. It could not have been more different from what she encountered on her roof garden on West 113th Street, where her attempts to lose herself in reverie were continually foiled by the screech of argumentative voices, the honking and roaring of cars and buses, and the jangle and crackle of Victrolas pumping canned music from all directions, meshing and merging with the noise of the city, "the hurdy-gurdy of the street beyond." By contrast, the black folk she saw from the porch could have stepped straight out of the mid-nineteenth century. "Not for any inducement would that mule quicken his pace"—nor, she might have added, would the "ebony antique" who drove him. On foot and in horse carts, calm and unhurried, they exuded a placid contentment that was altogether unshakeable, that could not be disturbed even by the passing automobiles, with their "sophisticated snorts and honk-honks."

So Scarborough had believed in 1919. But the next year brought Mamie Smith's "Crazy Blues," and with it a drastic and steep rise in the black audience for recorded music all across the United States, including the South. Suddenly her portrait of a people doggedly resisting technology seemed much harder to sustain. Suddenly those mellifluous voices that she heard from the front porch seemed in danger of falling silent, and although she could not have said what it was, exactly, she knew that something essential was under threat.

And so, in January 1921, five months after "Crazy Blues" began reverberating across her roof garden, Scarborough sent Wyeth a letter on Columbia University stationery asking for his help in collecting black songs. The spirituals, she argued, had been well documented, but Negro folk song was a far broader category. "I am trying to make as complete a collection of these as possible, since these interesting and valuable reflections of our southern life may soon be forgotten if they are not preserved in some permanent way," she noted. "It is the genuine negro songs that I wish, not those written by white people, but the ones made and sung by the colored race."

As she came into Wyeth's parlor, Scarborough would have seen evidence of his long and distinguished career all around her: the plaques commemorating his surgical innovations (ligation of the external carotid artery, bloodless amputation at shoulder and hip joints), the medals for his Civil War service. She would have observed the long lines in his face that spoke of his sixteen months of imprisonment in a Union prison, where he contracted pneumonia, malaria, and typhoid and watched thousands of Confederate prisoners die of starvation, an experience he later chronicled in an article for *Century* magazine that, with its accusations of Union cruelty, created a national furor. Not long before, he had broken his hip, and now he walked with a cane. He settled into his chair slowly and carefully and turned to her to begin the interview with the grave dignity of a venerable man who had outlived most of his critics and felt sure of his place in the world.

Yet as he began to speak, it was as though time slipped away. Scarborough asked Wyeth about his childhood in the valley of the Tennessee River, and he told her about his parents, who, like "so many of the best people in the South" had been, at heart, emancipationists. They bought slaves for house service only because white domestic servants were not an option, and they treated them with a kindness that soon turned to love, nursing them through sickness and age. The slaves, men and women "of fine character," responded with unflagging devotion. Wyeth himself had been particularly close to an elderly slave, Uncle Billy, who had taught him how to sing and dance and play the banjo. "When the boy became more proficient than the old man," Scarborough related, "Uncle Billy put away the banjo and never played again." Like all the family's servants, Billy remained loyal during the war, and after the Confederate surrender, a Republican Negro cut his throat.

They were nearly all dead now, those old-time Negroes. Faithful, patient, submissive, contented, they had, Wyeth mused, a "charm of manner" that today's "colored citizens" utterly lacked. The trust and affection between the races had disappeared too. No white child growing up today could know what it felt like to sit at Mammy Tildy's hearth late at night listening to her "skeery" stories, or to sit on the steps of Uncle Billy's cabin, where he had learned to play the banjo, the slave's large hands guiding his small ones as they pressed and plucked the strings.

Long ago, after Billy was murdered, Wyeth had put his old banjo away, but he brought it out for Scarborough's visit. He could still remember the songs. The scientist in him found them intriguing. The Negroes' idea of rhythm, Wyeth explained to Scarborough, showed their "low order of development"—when dancing, they patted the ground, while the more evolved Indians reached away from the earth.

Sometimes, if he was lucky, Wyeth could capture the grain of Billy's voice. He sang "Jimmy Rose," a song that he believed Billy had made up, and "Run, Nigger, Run," a song Scarborough remembered her mother singing, about the comic misadventures of escapees attempting to elude the slave patrols. Wyeth showed Scarborough the instrumental techniques that Uncle Billy had taught him, demonstrating that he had never lost the proficiency that made his slave companion set the banjo aside. "He evoked melodies of wistful gaiety by drawing a handkerchief across the banjo strings," Scarborough noted, "and lively tunes by playing it with a whisk-broom." They were "magical tricks," she concluded. "This is astounding to anybody who has seen him in the operating room," her doctor friend whispered. "The rest of us feel honored at handing him a sponge, and no one could have convinced us he would turn himself loose on a banjo like this."

And then, in the dwindling light, the old doctor rose to his feet and tossed aside his cane. He wanted to show Scarborough some of the old breakdowns, the way the slaves themselves had danced them, so slowly, gingerly, he began moving his body as Uncle Billy had taught him to move. He clapped his hands, bent his knees, clicked his heels, and patted his thighs; he hopped and shuffled and kicked his legs skyward and hopped and shuffled and kicked again. As Scarborough watched, the surroundings seemed to fade, the tasteful décor and the expensive furniture and the roar and screech of the traffic below. Dr. Wyeth jumped and twirled. "I felt transported," she wrote years later, "to an old plantation of days before the war."

———

TO AN EXTENT THAT EDISON COULD NOT HAVE FORESEEN, the mechanical reproduction of music transformed human experience by freeing sound from its roots in communities, from the constraints of time and place. There may have been only one Mamie Smith, but by 1920 there were one million of her records in circulation, making it possible to hear her simultaneously from New Orleans to Chicago, from Charleston to Seattle, from London to Johannesburg.

Recording and mass-producing music allowed it to transcend more than just regional moorings: to an extent never before possible, African American songs could break through the color line. Once only encountered at house parties and barn dances, on street corners and the black showbiz circuit, by the 1920s the blues could be heard pouring out of speakeasies, nightclubs, houses, apartments, drug stores and barbershops, hardware stores and funeral parlors, anywhere race records were played or sold.

White people in cities could not avoid hearing it, and many were frankly appalled. "Hundreds of 'race' singers have flooded the market with what is generally regarded as the worst contribution to the cause of good music ever inflicted on the public," one aggrieved listener, a correspondent for a music industry trade paper, noted. "The lyrics of a great many of these 'blues' are worse than the lowest sort of doggerel and the melodies are lacking in originality, lilting rhythm and any semblance to musical worth." For some, it was vulgarity pure and simple, and they gave it no more thought than that. But for others, no less dismayed but more reflective, it was something more unsettling: the emergence of a new black urban world.

From her apartment on the fringes of Harlem, Dorothy Scarborough saw that world everyday. Her 1921 appeal for "genuine Negro songs," the appeal that took her to Wyeth, culminated in her 1925 book *On the Trail of Negro Folk-Songs*. Part song anthology, part history, part folklore compendium, part memoir, the book is virtually unread today. Scarborough herself has slipped into the peculiar obscurity of southern apologists, those white men and women who lamented the passing of the gracious days of the plantation and who were, on the face of it, utterly untroubled by what W. E. B. Du Bois famously called "the problem of the color line." Without doubt, the book makes for difficult reading. Scarborough's prose, "delightful" according to her original reviewers, has a studied whimsy about it that now feels affected and cloying. More troubling still are the assumptions she makes: that the music passed down by black southerners reflects "the lighter, happier side of slavery"; that the songs' syncopated rhythms and singular wordplay speak of the irrational, illogical "colored mind."

Yet behind the book lies an obsession with black voices that rewards close attention. Scarborough's 1921 interview with Wyeth launched a four-year search for "genuine Negro melodies" that took her across the South, as she met up with white informants who re-created the voices of the kindly aunties and uncles who had fed them, played with them, and sung them

100   NEGRO FOLK-SONGS

It has a little swing that is individual and yet characteristically "darky."

The Negro's music goes from one harmony to another, with no discord, and is like the harmony of nature. Dr. Wyeth gave an old dance-song, *Jimmy Rose*, which he said a Negro on his plantation had made up. "You can just hear in it a darky jog along in a jog-trot on a mule."

JIMMY ROSE

Jim - my Rose, he went to town,—Jim - my Rose, he went to town,—

Jim - my Rose, he went to town,—To 'com - mo-date de la - dies.

> Jimmy Rose, he went to town,
> Jimmy Rose, he went to town,
> Jimmy Rose, he went to town,
> To 'commodate de ladies.
>
> Fare ye well, ye ladies all,
> Fare ye well, ye ladies all,
> Fare ye well, ye ladies all,
> God Ermighty bless you!

Dr. Wyeth performed magical tricks with a banjo, as he had been taught by old Uncle Billy in slavery times. He evoked melodies of wistful gaiety by drawing a handkerchief across the banjo strings, and lively tunes by playing it with a whisk-broom. And when he danced some of the old breakdowns for me, just to show how they went, I felt transported to an old plantation of days before the war. Another of the dance-songs he gave me was *Johnny Booker*.

> I went down to de back of de fiel';
> A black snake cotch me by de heel.
> I cut my dus', I run my bes',
> I run right into a horney's nes'.

Chorus

> Oh, do, Mr. Booker, do! Oh, do, Mr. Booker, do!
> Oh, do, Mr. Booker, Johnny Booker,
> Mr. Booker, Mr. Booker, Johnny Booker, do!

A page from On the Trail of Negro Folk-Songs.

to sleep. In none of that was she unusual. At a time when ethnographers documenting Native American ritual collected from Native Americans directly, enthusiasts of black song like Newman White, Robert Winslow Gordon, Emmet Kennedy, J. Frank Dobie, and Frank Brown preferred to rely on their own recollections or those of elderly white southerners whose reminiscences of a childhood soundscape were shot through with "the fairy tale of a happy slave civilization," as W. E. B. Du Bois called it.

What should we do with these re-creations? It is too simplistic, obviously, to take the stories at face value, as evidence of "slave culture." To give just one example: "Run, Nigger, Run," which Wyeth sang to Scarborough, did date back to the mid-nineteenth century, but it is unlikely that slaves themselves originated or even willingly sang it, at least not in the form of the comic ditty that Wyeth and Scarborough remembered. The slave patrols that it described were notorious for their brutality. Asked about the song in the 1930s, one ex-slave remarked, "Sometimes I wonder iffen de white folks didn't make dat song up so us niggers would keep in line."

The white informants who re-created black music for Scarborough were hardly disinterested observers. In Wyeth's case, the narrative of his idyllic childhood is permeated with a reactionary nostalgia that cannot help but tarnish whatever facts it might contain. The songs themselves seem almost incidental to the memories their performance evoked and (from Wyeth's side anyway) to the experience of projecting himself into an imagined blackness. Although he did not don blackface, it is impossible not to see his performance as minstrelsy. Inveighing against the Negro's "low order of development" while "turning himself loose on the banjo," Wyeth drew upon the minstrel show's legacy of ambivalent racial emotions: revulsion mixed with fascination, disgust with desire.

And yet, although these performances may be seen as merely the product of racist fantasy, they reveal a great deal about the complex emotions fueling white southerners' memories of black song. What passed between Wyeth and Scarborough was more than an interview—it was a ritual of belonging. Re-creating the voice of the plantation Negro had been an obsession for southern whites since the late nineteenth century, carried out in dialect fiction, stage performances, and state and local folklore societies. Scarborough drew on that obsession in her research. Her list of informants reads like a who's who of self-styled "darky dialecticians," from writers such as John Trotwood Moore to Louise Clarke Pyrnelle to Thomas Nelson Page, who built careers ventriloquizing the plantation Negro in memoirs, short stories, and novels that brought regional, sometimes national, renown.

Fearing that authentic black music was being drowned out by mass-produced replicas, Scarborough set out in search of the real thing. That the real thing turned out to be a white imitation invites us to consider the place of nostalgia, imagination, and fantasy in the shaping of the African American folk canon, and, indeed, the protean nature of "authenticity" itself. Claims of authenticity—in effect, assertions that some expressive forms are more "real" than others—are, unavoidably, political and social critiques. In proclaiming her capacity to distinguish the real from the spurious, Scarborough set herself up as a cultural arbiter, endowed with superior taste and discernment, a role that gave her the authority to contest the shape of popular art.

IN THE YEARS iT TOOK HER TO COMPLETE HER BOOK, Dorothy Scarborough made several trips to the South, relatively brief ones in 1921 and 1922 and then a year's sabbatical, beginning in the autumn of 1923. It is virtually impossible to track her movements, to pin down where she journeyed and when: she drew up no itinerary (or at least did not preserve one); nor did she keep a diary or field notes. The account that she published in *On the Trail* depicted less a purposeful trek than a set of meanderings: a lazy few days in South Carolina, a languorous week in Mississippi. In her remembrance they blended into each other, one long amble through an enchanted landscape. Like her friend Emmet Kennedy, a white native of Louisiana whose 1925 book *Mellows* was an ecstatic reminiscence of the black songs of his childhood, she was searching for a place that was not on the map, "a region of uncontaminated beauty and pastoral dreams," the magical land she had sensed as she watched Wyeth, the "old plantation of days before the war."

The idea of the "old plantation" as a source of transcendent black singing had rarely, if ever, been voiced by antebellum planters themselves. Although some encouraged their field hands to sing in order to speed up the pace of work, most seem to have heard in slave song only savage wails—barbaric, uncivilized noise. White southerners' rhapsodic accounts of black singing were an entirely retrospective affair, arising only in the late nineteenth century. Their emergence owed to new instabilities in politics and in matters of race. The end of Reconstruction saw the rise of a new southern elite, an uneasy mix of planters and industrialists united by their determination to reverse the fragile gains African Americans had won since the war. By the end of the century, the introduction of the sharecropping system was supplemented by a campaign of disenfranchisement, segregation, and lynching—a full-blown racial caste system backed up, when necessary, by violence. Yet the new racial order was never as stable as most southern whites would have liked. Despite all their efforts to keep African Americans tied to the soil, black men and women proved stubbornly mobile, leaving the farm, sometimes leaving the South, and in ways large and small, real and imagined, abandoning old habits of deference.

Against that backdrop, southern whites turned to visions of (in the phrase of the period) "the old-time Negro." By the late nineteenth century, that figure had the impress of social science upon it. In 1888 the newly founded American Folklore Society declared its intention to collect and study "the fast-vanishing remains of folklore in America," by which it meant "relics of old English ballads," myths and tales of Native Americans, and the "lore of Negroes in the Southern States." From the outset, the work of collecting the latter was dominated by white southerners, who set up state and local folklore societies at the turn of the twentieth century that defined how the study of Negro folklore would be pursued for the next thirty years.

Driving those folklore societies was an all-pervasive sense of nostalgia. Few of their members drew upon fieldwork. Instead, they excavated their memories, conjuring up the old-time Negro as a ghostly rebuke to the new, mourning the loss of a golden age of racial harmony, "the happy days of the plantation" when blacks and whites had lived in friendship and peace. Women played a key role in this process as cultural caretakers, conduits of plantation lore, transforming their domestic seclusion into privileged access to a remembered world of tender emotion. As late as 1930, the folklorist Robert Winslow Gordon, who prided himself on his scientific rigor, spoke of their value as informants. "Many a dear little Southern lady whose hair is now white [has told me] that she used as a girl to beg the Negro women to shout for her, and, if no men were present, had joined in with them—thus herself learning the art."

From the moment she published *From a Southern Porch,* Scarborough built a career as a southern lady, a genteel chronicler of what she fondly presented as the region's vanishing domestic life. In that persona she found that her memories were transformed into knowledge, that her writings won praise from reviewers as exemplary folklore, and that she herself was accorded respect. She had grown up, she once remarked, as "a queer combination of bookworm and tomboy," a studious girl who loved to climb trees and constantly butted up against social constraints. Once, when she was eight or nine, she had attended a religious revival, watching in awe as men and boys stumbled forward to confess their sins and profess their faith, yet when she rose and attempted to do the same, she heard the room erupt in laughter and found herself shunted back to her seat. If to grow up female in the South was, by and large, to confront that kind of belittlement, as a southern folklorist she could voice her ideas and emotions, and no one would question her right to speak.

Her interest in Negro folk song developed early, well before she started writing *On the Trail.* Her first foray into the topic came in 1915, when as head of the Texas Folklore Society she gave a talk on "plantation melodies" for her presidential address. Later, when she began writing fiction (*In the Land of Cotton,* a novel about white farmers in Texas, was published in 1921), she threaded black folk lyrics through the story and discovered that "readers found them more interesting than anything I had written myself."

Even in those early writings, she staked out her own, distinctively southern, approach to folk music. A voracious reader, she had ploughed through the books that defined the scholarly orthodoxy, the works of northerners like Francis

Child and George Lyman Kittredge. Although much of their argument struck her as insightful, their style and methods left her cold. She accepted the basics: a genuine folk song was of rural, communal origins; it had no single, definitive form; it was common property in the hands of amateur singers, who altered it freely according to their mood. Yet Child and Kittredge approached song collecting as an act of taxonomy, endlessly classifying and cataloguing multiple variants. For Scarborough, its lure was far more emotional and intuitive, an invitation to travel through time. "How many memories of my childhood and youth are associated with loved black faces!" she rhapsodized.

> How I enjoyed the songs the Negroes sang, even though I was ignorant of their value! . . . I see a procession of black and yellow and cream-colored faces that have passed through our kitchen and house and garden—some very impermanent and some remaining for years, but all singing. Now, when I sit on a porch at night, I am in fancy back at our old home, listening to the mellow, plaintive singing of a Negro congregation at a church a half-mile away—a congregation which "ne-er broke up" at least before I went to sleep, and which gathered every night in a summer-long revival. I can project myself into the past and hear the wailful songs at Negro funerals, the shouting songs at baptizings and the creek or river, old breakdowns at parties, lullabies crooned as mammies rocked black and white babies to sleep, work-songs in cotton field or on the railroad or street-grading jobs. All sounds of human activity among the Negroes in the South used to be accompanied with song. It is so now to a certain extent, but less than before.

In the modern world, she believed, genuine black melodies were fast disappearing, as those "loved black faces" gave way to anonymous new ones who were no longer disposed to break into song, who had fully succumbed to the lure of what she could only regard as "canned music." The more she read as she researched the topic in the early 1920s, the more convinced she became. African Americans' too-enthusiastic embrace of modernity, in the form of education, factory labor, and migration to cities, were eradicating what one commentator described as the Negro's "highest gift, his spontaneity. Songs start from nothing, from the loading of a truck, the possession of a banjo, the half-remembered line of a hymn, and grow in an hour, never to be exactly repeated. . . . The songs may live, but the best thing of all, the free impulse, the pattern of careless voices happily inventing as they go, if it dies it cannot be resurrected." That "free impulse," that "golden source," still existed in the souls of some black southerners, but its days were clearly numbered. "The plantation Master and the plantation Negro stand today definitely at the parting of the ways," lamented Scarborough's friend, South Carolina novelist DuBose Heyward. "The call of the city has already been heeded. The migration has commenced. They will be taken from our fields, fired with ambition, and fed to the machines of our glittering new civilization."

In the face of that disheartening prospect, capturing authentic black songs became an imperative for Scarborough. For sources she looked for elderly white southerners (often found through friends and relatives) who had absorbed the melodies they had heard from black caretakers with the wholehearted devotion only children could show. Though she had her own vivid memories of such figures, by and large she let her informants speak for her. They told of stealing away to the servants' quarters, treasured illicit moments in childhoods otherwise ruled by decorum. "I sat in the kitchen and learned songs, stories and the buck and wing dances, from when I was first able to carry a tune until I went away to school at thirteen," recalled Udly Jones Wheeler. "I didn't know what I was singing, I just sang as he sang." And they mourned the steady deterioration in the years that had followed. "Once the trusted servant and almost constant companion of the white man, the Negro, since he became free, has become shiftless, uncertain in his responsibility, and morally outcast," argued her informant J. E. Morrow. "The happy days of the plantation have passed; with them have gone 'Swanee Ribber,' 'My Ole Kentucky Home,' 'Uncle Ned,' 'Nellie Gray' and 'Old Black Joe'. . . No longer does the Negro sit about his little cabin and sing his rich old melodies to the plinky-plinky-plank-plank-plank of his banjo. No more the pathos of a heart longing to hunt for the possum an' de coon on de ole Kaintucky shore; no more the pining for the home far away; no longer the passion of a bereaved heart in a plaintive 'I shall nebber see my darlin' eny mo'.' The art of banjo playing has almost been lost and where it survives, the instrument has been prostituted to thumming out vulgar dances for dives or cheap ragtime songs for carnivals or medicine shows."

Scarborough would not have phrased it so bluntly, but at heart she would have agreed. What she heard and saw in her informants' singing and dancing was an evocative contrast to the ceaseless sound of race records drifting in through her windows in Manhattan. She had no doubts about the accuracy of her informants' performances or their value as historical artifacts. Black people themselves were no longer singing, at least not the kinds of songs she was after. Wyeth, in contrast, could evoke Uncle Billy's dancing and singing with scientific precision, and not only because he had memories to draw on. As Scarborough repeatedly maintained, "The Negro is by nature a mimetic creature, dramatizing all he knows, his experiences and the life about him, expressing everything in form and motion." Like most other white southerners of her generation, she assumed that slave songs and dances had originated, not from an African inheritance, but from imitation of the slaveholding class. That inborn disposition to mimicry explained both the high class of melodies developed under slavery, when blacks were in constant contact with aristocratic whites, and the danger of urban migration, since black men and women would inevitably take on the character of their surroundings. What Wyeth had enacted for her was not just a dance but an intimacy, a tender care and reciprocity that once existed between the races. Seen in that light, his performance became not a mere copy, but an imitation of an original that was itself an imitation, a hall of mirrors whose multiple refractions devolved from a source that once had been white.

Hence Scarborough's sense that obtaining black song need not involve speaking to black people, apart from those born into slavery or, in some indefinable but palpable way, touched with the spirit of the Old South. Occasionally in her travels she stumbled upon those gentle, submissive souls, and then it was as if time had stopped. Their backs stooped, their faces lined, in voices beautiful with old age's "quavering sweetness" they sang songs that no one else remembered, and when she pleaded for more they smiled indulgently, as though at the vagaries of a demanding child.

And sometimes she got more than songs: memories of loved ones who had been lost to her. Once in Natchitoches,

Louisiana, when she was wandering through the ruins of her family's plantation, an elderly black man approached her deferentially and introduced himself as Sebron Mallard, one of her late grandfather's slaves. Though he could not sing and could not help her directly, he was able to verify the antiquity of some of the songs she was investigating, and he had vivid memories of her father, a high-spirited boy who had run away to join the Confederates at age seventeen. "I was ploughing when I got the word that Mister Johnny's daughter was nigh here, and I drapped the plough and made tracks toward you," he explained. "Mister Johnny war de youngest of all de boys, but he knowed how to work harder and laugh more than any of 'em." He looked at her fondly. "He said, 'Li'l mistis, is you well? Is you happy?'"

"Yes, Uncle Sebron, I'm always well, and I'm very happy," I told him.

He looked at me with dimming eyes.

"My ole pappy tol' me befo' he died that good luck would be bound to go with ol' Marster's fambly becase they was allus so good to their pore slaves. They brought us up mannerble, and I brought my chillun up thataway, too. And ain't none of us never been arrested nor had no trouble. But some of the young folks these days isn't that way and it makes trouble. Us old folks sees when dey do wrong, and it hurts us, but we can't do nothing, cause we's feble and we's few.

"White folks and black folks look like they ain't live lovely together like they used to."

Voices like Mallard's, speaking words she could (and indeed might) have scripted, were for Scarborough the black

voices that mattered; to others she was largely indifferent. After leaving Natchitoches, she traveled to Texas and spent a few
days with a friend, the state's governor, Pat Neff, who urged
her to follow up an encounter he had on a recent visit to Central State Prison Farm. "A Negro man came up to him after
supper," Scarborough related, "and said, 'Will you listen while
I sing you a song?' He rendered a ditty whose refrain ran as
follows:

> "If I had the gov'ner
> Where the gov'ner has me,
> Before daylight
> I'd set the gov'ner free.
> I begs you, gov'ner,
> Upon my soul:
> If you won't gimme a pardon,
> Won't you gimme a parole?"

Ten years later, chasing his own dream of authentic black
voices, John Lomax would record another pardon song by that
same convict in Angola State Penitentiary in Louisiana, but the
prospect of hearing him did not entice Scarborough. She enjoyed Neff's anecdote and wrote down the lyrics, but for her,
the governor's rendition was real enough.

————

OPPOSITE THE MAIN ARCHIVIST'S DESK IN THE SPECIAL
Collections Library at Baylor University hangs a portrait of
Dorothy Scarborough. Painted, most likely, sometime around
1920, it shows a small-boned woman with light brown hair
and hazel eyes behind wire-rimmed glasses, her expression

composed and thoughtful, her glance bright and alert as a bird's. The heart-shaped face has a wistful smile and an understated, not wholly realized beauty—like a bookish spinster in a Hollywood movie, just before the hero removes her glasses and lets down her hair.

If anyone ever let Scarborough's hair down, she kept it quiet. To read the collection of her papers at Baylor, thick with manuscripts and letters from correspondents, is to be struck by her remoteness: carefully culled by her sister to remove anything unduly personal, the archive contains virtually no letters *from* her, barely a trace of her private voice. Nor can that private voice be made out in the pages she wrote for publication, where she dwells most on the memories of others and says relatively little about her own. What we are left with is that face in the portrait, the voice that Scarborough carefully cultivated: that of the archetypal southern lady—"our demure, delicate, poised, other-minded Dot," as one of her friends put it. That voice is persuasive even in *On the Trail*, where she moves with a freedom that few southern white women could have imagined. "I have wandered through the colored quarters of many towns and cities, hailing many an old mammy and uncle to beg for songs," she wrote.

> I have made friends with countless children, loitering to watch their play and hear their singing, stopping them from their errands, rousing them from their naps in public places. I have loitered in market places to watch the women buying their supplies, and overhear their conversation and their chance humming, and have strolled along levees and quays in many a town to hear the Negro men sing at their work.

That she seems no less refined and genteel for so doing simply heightens our sense of the magical landscape to which song collecting transports her: a world where racial boundaries do not impinge upon her, where danger never looms.

There is only one point in the book when her safety is threatened. While gathering songs near Natchez, Mississippi, Scarborough encounters a baptism being held in a pond on the grounds of a mansion that had burned down in the war. She had seen the ritual once or twice in her childhood, but framed by the ruins of an old plantation, this one unfolded with the power of a dream. The candidates for baptism filed to the edge of the water, ghostly figures enveloped in white, their voices raised in a weird, eerie dirge. As the preacher cried out in exhortation, each candidate plunged into the water and resurfaced, thrashing and wailing in ecstasy, while the hundreds of black worshippers gathered at the waterside responded with shouts and groans. For a time Scarborough watched the services from the top of the mansion's old marble stairway, but the drama grew too intriguing, and as "with each immersion the excitement grew, the shouting became more wild and unrestrained, the struggles of the candidate grew more violent," she moved into the crowd and pulled out her camera to capture the proceedings on film.

> The shouter would fall on the ground, writhing about as if in anguish, tearing her hair, beating off those who sought to calm her. Sometimes one, reeling too near in the throes of thanksgiving, would fall into the water and have to be fished out, somewhat subdued but still shrieking, and led off to dry in the sun.

I tried repeatedly to get a picture of the scene, but each time I adjusted the Kodak, some shouter would start up beside me and all but push me into the pond. That little black box seemed to have an unfortunate effect on the crowd. One time I thought I would persist, but in the melee I was all but crushed. I was between the pond on one side and a barbed-wire fence on the other, with no chance for escape but a tree which I might have climbed had it not been a *bois-d'arc,* full of hard thorns. The crowd surged against me, and I had to put up my Kodak hastily and become as inconspicuous as possible. I do not think they meant to harm me, but it was merely a matter of emotional excitement. Even my pencil taking down songs upset them.

Reading Scarborough's account of the baptism, it is tempting to interpret it as a kind of fable, a distillation of the corrupting power she saw at work in the Machine Age. In the crowd she discovers the unfortunate effect that a machine—"that little black box"—had upon the people whose rituals she was trying to capture. No wonder Scarborough so feared the impact of the phonograph: mechanical instruments like Victrolas and cameras created a dangerous kind of self-consciousness, and a primitive folk that had been simple and nurturing suddenly became a mob.

So powerfully does Scarborough evoke this moment that it comes as a shock to discover that throughout her research for *On the Trail* she collected songs with mechanical devices: a bulky disk recorder that she used near her home in Manhattan and a portable recording phonograph that she took into the field. Scarborough began hunting for the machines early on in her research, writing to Thomas A. Edison, Inc., requesting a

cylinder phonograph for home recording in April 1921. Just
what she recorded and when is uncertain—the cylinders wore
out after a few uses, and she apparently discarded them after a
musician friend transcribed their contents—but in her sessions with her white informants she appears to have used the
machine routinely. It seems almost certain that she had it with
her when she turned up at Wyeth's apartment, that he "turned
himself loose" on the banjo while facing a mechanical recording horn.

From the moment Scarborough embarked on her quest,
she had to grapple with a dilemma that had vexed song collectors for over three decades: how best to capture authentic
voices in the age of mechanical reproduction. That the arduous work of transcribing songs could be immeasurably eased
by the phonograph had been apparent to song collectors virtually from the moment of the machine's invention, yet the very
precision that first entranced Howard Odum made the cylinder recorder anathema to others, particularly those who had
experienced precisely how useful its assistance could be. "I
lack entire faith in the [making] of wax records," noted the
folklorist Natalie Curtis Burlin, shortly after recording black
students at the Hampton Institute in 1919. Mechanical accuracy, as she saw it, got in the way of folkloric truth, which celebrated "the instinctive song of un-self-conscious people—a
type of music which is by its very nature furthermost removed
from all idea of mechanism." Far more important was the folklorist's intuitive grasp of the songs she was hearing, gained
from living among the singers until their rhythms become part
of her own being. Scarborough had those words with her as
she embarked on her project, and her own practice endorsed
them. As a granddaughter of slave owners, she believed she

had inherited a body of knowledge that enabled her to distinguish the fake from the genuine, and like Burlin, she saw folk-song gathering as an intuitive and, by implication, quintessentially feminine practice. In her account of her meeting with Wyeth, she posed herself as a dutiful southern daughter, coaxing him back to a childhood soundscape of tenderness and emotion. To have shown the machine in her account would have shattered the illusion, revealing the modern researcher behind the plantation-bred lady, the writer and teacher who through her connections at Columbia had access to a technological aid.

That technological aid was crucial to her project. Scarborough used her cylinder recorder to capture music and lyrics, then threaded bits of musical transcription through her account of her subjects' reminiscences. When her subjects remembered the music but forgot the words, her transcriptions indicated that too. What she was after was not a songbook, a set of playable musical arrangements—rather, an impressionistic record of her own journey, in which memories slid into half-remembered musical fragments, shards of melodies that the reader could just about hum but not in any real sense recreate. To describe Scarborough's technique as documentation does not really capture it—it was more of a summoning of musical ghosts. Using a cylinder recorder allowed Scarborough to immerse herself in the illusion. With her hands freed from the work of transcription, she could slip into reverie, reliving, through her informants' mimicry, the transracial intimacy she felt she had known as a child.

Compelling her informants to sit at a machine and sing their songs into a horn made for a different sort of collecting encounter, far more formal, controlled, and artificial than she would ever admit to. Yet in many ways Scarborough's hidden machine is of a piece with other tensions at work in her story. For what is most intriguing about *On the Trail* is its erratic but unmistakable note of detachment, its intermittent reluctance to commit to the plantation myths that the book otherwise seems to purvey. Take, for instance, her discussion of that central southern archetype, the mammy. Though for much of the book Scarborough relies upon formula, a conventional elegy to the "crooning sweetness" of her remembered singing, to the wonder of "a racial mother-heart which can take in not only its own babies, but those of another, dominant, race as well," at moments she abruptly steps back. "What other nation of mothers has ever patiently and with a beautiful sacrifice put alien children ahead of its own?" she asks, adding, "in outward devotion if not in actual fact?" That the "actual fact" might have been different, that the mammy might have been playing a role, that she might have felt hostility toward her "alien" charges, was a possibility that few white southerners ever broached.

"We wear the mask," wrote the African American poet Paul Laurence Dunbar in a verse of which Scarborough was likely aware. Once Scarborough had completed her travels, she began writing the book in her New York apartment, and the longer she worked on it, the more her persona as a plantation-bred lady took on elements of a masquerade. The life she developed in the 1920s bristles with contradictions. On the face of it a professional southerner, she claimed to find the North cold, arid, and soulless, yet she never attempted to move away. Scarborough lived in New York until the end of her life, and her roots there became stronger as time went on.

Far more than the southern arcadia she sometimes evoked in her writing, New York City had been Scarborough's salvation.

In Texas and even in Oxford, her femininity constantly con-
strained her; in New York she could support herself as a writer,
teacher, and journalist, and she seems to have prized the crisp
professionalism of that identity. She never married; she lived
alone. And much as at times she aimed to hide it, she relished
the mobility and anonymity the city allowed, the possibilities for
loitering, wandering, eavesdropping, the same pleasures, indeed, of collecting black song. "She told him how on Saturday
afternoons she would explore the town as if it were a jungle no
one had seen before, would loaf for hours watching the life slip
by on the East River, would visit the piers to see the ocean lin-
ers, would mingle with the foreigners in the tenement section,"
she wrote in her final novel. "On subways at rush hours, on ele-
vated trains past the exposed domesticity of second-story windows, on buses up Fifth Avenue, up Riverside where grey
battleships lay in the river, on ferry boats to Governor's Island
with its army headquarters, to Staten Island and back to watch
the miracle of the New York skyline at sunset, or as dusk
brought out its million lights."

Scarborough's explorations of the urban "jungle" almost
certainly included Harlem. She lived on the fringes of what
she described as the "greatest Negro city in the world," and in
time she got to know people there. At Columbia she taught
and befriended the West Indian journalist Eric Walrond,
whose collection of short stories *Tropic of Death* she helped
nurse into print, and through him she met Charles S. Johnson,
Walrond's editor at *Opportunity* magazine, the journal of black
arts and politics produced by the Urban League. Though he
may not have known of her interest in black folklore, Johnson
admired her fiction, its attention to regional particularity, a
skill he believed black writers should cultivate. In September

1924, he invited Scarborough to serve as a judge for *Opportunity's* upcoming literary contest, which would award five hundred dollars in prize money to the most promising African American writers. Over the next nine months, as she wrote the final drafts of *On the Trail,* Scarborough read hundreds of pages of African American fiction, debating their merits with her fellow judges on the short story panel, including the black critic Alain Locke. On the first of May 1925, she joined Locke, Paul Robeson, James Weldon Johnson, Jean Toomer, Carl Van Doren, Carl Van Vechten, and three hundred other writers, artists, and critics for a banquet ceremony at the Fifth Avenue Restaurant, awarding prizes to Langston Hughes and Countee Cullen for poetry, Sterling Brown and E. Franklin Frazier for essays, and Eric Walrond and Zora Neale Hurston for short stories. "White critics, whom 'everybody' knows, Negro writers, whom 'nobody' knows, meeting on common ground," marveled the *New York Herald Tribune.* "The movement behind it means something to the race problem in general; certainly it means something to American literature. We are on the edge, if not already in the midst, of what might not improperly be called a Negro renaissance."

Scarborough stumbled upon that renaissance in the final stages of drafting *On the Trail,* and she could not have failed to miss its challenge to white southerners enthralled with black singing, who claimed the authority to delineate authentic black voices, those that evoked "our southern life." "The day of 'aunties,' 'uncles' and 'mammy' is gone," retorted Alain Locke bluntly on the eve of the *Opportunity* dinner. Those words would recur in his much-heralded anthology *The New Negro,* published in December of that year. The old-time Negro, he continued, had always been "more of a myth than a man," "a stock figure perpetuated as an historical fiction partly in innocent sentimentalism, partly in deliberate reactionism." Putting an end to that historical fiction demanded a reinterpretation of black folk song and folk tales, and of paramount importance in that process was "the energy and awakening of the Negro scholar and folklorist," wrote Scarborough's student Eric Walrond. "For it is more or less common property in these United States today that if you really want to get to the heart and spirit of the black people you must do it through the medium of one of their own."

What Scarborough was hearing, all around her, was the sound of her own obsolescence, assertions that reminiscences of black song penned by southern whites were, at best, inconsequential, revealing little more than sentimental platitudes about African American music's "heart and spirit." ("I am now struggling with Kennedy's *Mellows*," wrote Locke to Scarborough, "so charming in some respects, but so annoying in others.") Just what she made of these claims is unclear, since Scarborough never addressed them directly, but the tone of her comments suggests unease. "I am considered something of an authority on Negro life and literature, and the Negroes of New York think of me as a friend who is willing to help in constructive ways," she wrote to a journalist in the final months of completing the book. "I am often asked by editors to review books on the subject and I frequently act as judge in contests. . . . I am glad to do anything I can to help the Negroes develop their talents and find their audience, and I am gratified at the progress I see them making in education and citizenship and art." If Scarborough's talk of her "gratification" sounds an unmistakable note of condescension, it was surely fed by trepidation: fear that a new generation of black intellectuals was stealing away her subject matter and that her status as an authority on "genuine black music" was being downgraded by a new group of scholars who were far more genuine than she could ever be.

In the end, that fear proved impossible to ignore. Before she could finish her book, she had to embark on one last journey, which for one brief, startling moment would open her tale to the modern world.

———

"FOR THE LAST SEVERAL YEARS," SCARBOROUGH OBSERVES in the final chapter of *On the Trail*, "the most popular type of Negro song has been that peculiar, barbaric sort of melody called 'blues.'" It was, to her ears, at once disagreeable and compelling in its sheer oddity. Blues compositions had a jerky rhythm, "like a cripple dancing because of some irresistible impulse," and the abrupt stanzas, three lines instead of the customary four, gave them the shock of the unexpected, "like the whip-crack surprise at the end of an O. Henry story." Broadly available on recordings and sheet music, blues seemed on the face of it "to have little relation to authentic folk-music of the Negroes." But the music's singularity made Scarborough curious, and she set out "to trace it back to its origin," through referrals and tips making her way to West 46th Street and the music publishing office of W. C. Handy.

Scarborough had never heard of Handy before one of her correspondents, the Mississippi planter William Percy, passed on his name. Born to former slaves in Alabama in 1873, Handy had worked as a bandleader in the Midwest and the Mississippi Delta before settling in Memphis and, in 1912, publishing "Memphis Blues," among the first pieces of sheet music with the word "blues" in the title. Its success led to others: "Beale Street Blues," "Joe Turner Blues," and "St. Louis Blues," which in the hands of the race record industry became perhaps the best-known blues of all time. By the time Scarborough tracked him down, Handy had moved his thriving business from Memphis to Times Square and established himself among the city's best-known songwriters, though his international renown as self-proclaimed "father of the blues" was still over a decade away.

Scarborough peppered the composer with questions. Did the blues meet the criteria to be considered a folk music, based in rural traditions, remote from the world of cities, commerce, and machines? Had the form emerged anonymously? Did blues compositions spring up spontaneously? Were the songs, to any extent, sung communally—"taken up by many singers, who change and adapt and add to [them] in accordance with their own mood"? Yes, Handy replied, all that was true enough, but it did not get to the heart of the matter. What gave the blues its real standing as folk music was that it was "essentially of our race," rooted in a collective black past. "Each one of my blues is based on some old Negro song of the south, some folk-song that I heard from my mammy when I was a child," he explained. "Something that sticks in my mind, that I hum to myself when I'm not thinking about it. Some old song that is a part of the memories of my childhood and of my race."

Scarborough presented Handy's words without comment, unable, it seems, to digest them, and her silence leaves questions hanging in the reader's mind and, perhaps, in her own. Had Handy really had a mammy, that archetypal badge of genteel southern whiteness? Did he compose his songs out of a kind of nostalgia, though necessarily of a different character from that infusing the plantation myth? Above all, by Handy's criteria, what did the term "folk music" mean? Though Scarborough treasured authentic black song as the voice of an idyllic community, Handy, in words echoed by New Negro critics, asserted that the music's folkness lay in the fact that it was "essentially of [his] race," born of a history from which she was excluded, a black experience that she could not share.

Perhaps in Scarborough's encounter with Handy, and in those unasked questions, lay the seeds of what would become a retreat. By the mid-1920s she was spending her summers not at her sister's house in Virginia, but at her own cottage in Connecticut, where she cultivated a garden, wrote several novels, and enjoyed the relative quiet. Her New York apartment became a salon for minor literati, like her fellow book reviewers on the *New York Tribune,* friends like Fannie Hurst and Zona Gale, writing students like Carson McCullers, and displaced song gatherers like Emmet Kennedy. In time, those friendships became the most southern thing about her. Her 1925 novel *The Wind* can only be described as an antipastoral: based on a tale Scarborough originally heard from her mother, it follows a young bride who moves to West Texas, only to be driven mad by the bleakness of the landscape—above all by the "wild shouting voice" of a howling wind that never lets her "know the peace of silence." Though for most of the decade Scarborough continued to write regional fiction (tales of white Texas farmers interspersed with scraps of black folk song, which "seemed to me necessary to make the life of the section adequately real"), the setting became increasingly unspecific, and her final novel, 1932's *The Stretch-Berry Smile,* takes place by and large in New York.

In the process, she abandoned the study of black music. Though she planned for *On the Trail* to be the first of a series of books about black folk song, in fact she never returned to the topic. As her novels of the late 1920s moved ever-further from a southern setting, those black voices that once seemed so necessary "to make the life of the section adequately real" gradually lapsed into silence. The mounds of material on African American music she claimed to have accumulated appear nowhere in her private papers. When she died abruptly of influenza in 1935, she was at work on a book about song collecting, but the manuscript described her experience in the Appalachians, in remote communities where she was a stranger, gathering traditional melodies from mountain whites.

In all kinds of ways this account of song hunting differed from anything she had written before. Rather than relying on secondhand reminiscence, she describes collecting from the music's primary carriers, a remote, aloof people with whom she makes no claims of a shared past. She depicts their "incredibly arid and difficult" lives with the dispassionate concern of a social worker, pointedly acknowledging their jarring discrepancy with the South of plantation myth. "One sees log cabins or shacks, fields black and poor, people whose faces show the lines wrought by struggle, care, and despondency," she observes. "No beauty of Greek columns here—no dreaming lawns, no happy ease—but instead a terrible, proud poverty that cheats body, mind, and soul." Collecting songs in this region meant doing battle with isolation, reserve, and suspicion. That she succeeded at all owes in part to the intervention of teachers and missionaries, but more importantly to her appeal to wonder: in a region still "remote from the centers of commerce, inaccessible for lack of good roads," she offers her

subjects the chance to hear their voices played back on a
recording machine.

Ten years after *On the Trail*, Scarborough again hunted for
songs with mechanical assistance, but this time her narrative
makes no attempt to hide the machine. Her introduction de-
votes three pages to her efforts to find the appropriate mechanism, in the process lifting the veil on her use of a phonograph
a decade before. "On my trips to collect material for *On the
Trail of Negro Folk-Songs* I had used an old-fashioned recording phonograph of a type not now manufactured, but that had
been broken and so was not available," she explains in her introduction. Though she still owned a Speak-O-Phone disk
recorder, it was too bulky to take into the field; in the end, she
consulted technicians at the Dictaphone Corporation, who
built a cylinder machine to her specifications. "The Dictaphone records, being of wax, are not permanent, and can be
run off only a dozen to twenty, and they are less agreeable to
listen to than the Speak-O-Phone records, which are practically as good reproductions of sound as the radio or the phonograph," she observes. "But the Dictaphone served my main
purpose, which was to capture the tunes so that they could
later be transcribed." In the pages that follow, her Dictaphone
becomes a central player in the drama, a bulky contraption ar-
duously transported from the world beyond the mountains,
which her subjects regard with astonishment.

When she drafted the manuscript in 1932, no one was describing recording machines in this fashion—not ethnographers, whose scientific ethos demanded that they spotlight
their findings and excise the tools by which they obtained
them, and not even, at that stage, John Lomax, whose accounts
of his field recording experiments would not see print for well

over a year. But perhaps it amounts to a hesitant new start, an attempt to find a new voice. In *On the Trail*, Scarborough had written as a fond southern daughter, her expertise in black song based on the fact that "I was a Southerner born and bred, and that I had been loving the Southern Negroes ever since I could remember anything." Yet in the wake of the New Negro movement, she could no longer voice the old plantation platitudes, nor could she assume that her readers would accept her judgments simply because she was born in the South. In chronicling song in the Appalachians, she sought a visible, palpable badge of authority. Her recording machine transformed her into a documentarian, a fact gatherer driven by disinterested compassion. The Appalachians, she discovered, housed a genuine folk culture, a people immune to mechanically reproduced music. "There isn't a radio in the district," one of her informants noted. "We have to make our own music and provide our own amusement." Hence the care she takes to assure her readers that she employs the machine purely as a tool of transcription. To do otherwise, to produce recordings that were "agreeable to listen to," would run the risk of corrupting the culture whose music she sought to preserve.

Scarborough's death cut short this tentative transformation, and we cannot be sure where it would have taken her. Perhaps it would have provided a new beginning, a new voice of authority, that would have allowed her to return to collecting black songs. Yet that seems unlikely. Even at the peak of her involvement, the songs had always mattered less to her than the affectionate exchanges she had in collecting them. Mostly, and of necessity, she had those exchanges with white informants, but every so often she had stumbled upon elderly black men and women born in the era of slavery, and then all the pleasures of the past rushed in upon her. Once, at a garden party near the Alabama-Mississippi border, she heard a haunting melody "floating on the breezes"; parting a curtain of ivy, she found an aged black laundress "engaged in the mysteries of the washboard," singing a song that Scarborough remembered from childhood, when she drifted to sleep in her mammy's arms. That was the way of Negro folk songs: their notes cracked open worlds otherwise inaccessible, "songs I knew but did not know that I knew," memories she did not recall that she had.

Just how irrevocably that world was now lost to her had become clear in Handy's office. Though she presented him in *On the Trail* as benign and affable, yet another in her gallery of kindly old aunties and uncles, the reality of her encounter was far more unsettling than she ever let on. Soon after her visit, she wrote a draft account and sent it to her friend Ola Lee Gulledge, a musician and fellow southerner who had transcribed her disk recordings and had accompanied her to Handy's office. Gulledge sent the manuscript back with puzzled comments scrawled across the margins. Why, she wondered, had Scarborough left out so much of what their visit had really been like?

Why not say that it was typical of all publication offices— filled with vaudeville stars (both genders—black and white) and cigarette smoke. Do you think it out of place to stress how business-like it was—when the man said, 'Mr. Handy is in his office, is very busy, and will not be able to see you'— and so forth.

Though Scarborough could present, if not assimilate, Handy's New Negro vision of folk song, what she could not abide, could not even acknowledge, was the brusque indifference she met with in his office. No greater contrast could be imagined with the world to which song hunting had once transported her. Here the tenderness of her remembered South had been crowded out by a hard-nosed commercialism, faceless and altogether lacking in deference, as Scarborough found herself rebuffed in a smoke-filled office where white women and men jostled with black ones for the attention of a black entrepreneur. In the end, Handy's office is the silence at the heart of her tale, the unspeakable emblem of an unwelcome new world in which African Americans looked less like a "folk" than ever before.

~ *four* ~

Sound Photographs
of Negro Songs

L OUISIANA HIGHWAY 66 IS ONE OF THOSE MEANDERING
southern roads that seem to offer the traveler a straight
shot into the past. In places little more than a dirt track, it
winds past antebellum mansions shadowed by magnolias and
crumbling churches overgrown by kudzu, and the humid air
echoes with the plash of river water from the tributaries of the
Mississippi that straddle the road. The great river itself surges
against a levee a few hundred yards to the west, and to the east
rise the Tunica hills, their bluffs and ravines thick with copper-
heads, bears, and bobcats.

At a hairpin bend of the Mississippi, about fifty miles outside Baton Rouge, Highway 66 terminates in front of a high
wall topped with barbed wire, the entrance to Angola State
Penitentiary. Founded in the wake of the Civil War by a former Confederate major, Samuel James, it was set up on the

grounds of Angola Plantation, once a thriving agricultural center whose owner had named it after the region that had been home to most of his slaves. James was an entrepreneur who designed his prison to turn a profit, and convicts figured into his scheme as cheap and eminently disposable labor. Housed in flimsy, ill-ventilated dormitories built over malarial swamps, convicts spent their days shackled at neck and ankle, tilling cotton and sugarcane and building levees, driven with a degree of brutality that eventually became a national scandal. In the early twentieth century, new prison administrators fired the worst of the guards, built new dormitories, and abolished the much-despised convict stripes. But in the economic chaos of the Great Depression, Louisiana's governor left Angola to fall into decay, its guards took it over as a private fiefdom, and convict stripes were brought back.

On a hot July day in 1933, a dusty black Ford drove up to Angola's gates bearing a portly white man in a Stetson hat, who addressed the guard with the blustery charm of a Texan accustomed to getting his own way. His name was John Lomax, he was writing a book about folk music, and he hoped to spend two or three days at Angola, hunting for songs among the black prisoners. He wanted to talk to the inmates in their free time—whatever time they had free from their prison labors—and then (with the help of his eighteen-year-old son Alan) listen to anyone who had songs to offer. The best of their findings they would record on disk, via a bulky mass of phonographic equipment that he had been loaned by the Library of Congress. It went without saying that he would do nothing to stir up trouble among the inmates; he was, after all, born and bred in the South. Lomax produced a sheaf of letters from powerful acquaintances, including an old friend of the prison governor. With visible reluctance, the guard opened the gates and waved his car through.

Lomax had arrived at Angola in a state of near-euphoria. At age sixty-five he was a vagabond, quite a feat after a lifetime that sometimes had seemed to consist only of missed opportunities and failed hopes. He was born in 1867 in Goodman, Mississippi, his father a farmer and tanyard operator, the family situated (as Lomax liked to put it) "on the upper crust of the po' white trash." Two years later, they boarded two covered wagons and moved to the Bosque Valley in Texas, looking for a place to homestead. Lomax grew up immersed in farm labor, scratching corn and cotton out of the arid soil, attending school for short bursts between crops. Though he loved to read, cowboy stories especially, not until he was nearly thirty did he enroll at the University of Texas. He had hoped to become a teacher, but instead he spent most of the years that followed trapped behind a desk as a college administrator and later as a bonds trader in a Dallas bank.

Then came 1931, which brought catastrophe: the loss of his job, when the bank he worked for failed, and the death of his much-loved wife of thirty years. Lomax found himself an unemployed single father with two of his four children still living at home, and he might have succumbed to despair had not his eldest son, John, Jr., persuaded him to return to his first love, song hunting. Back in 1907 he had enrolled for a term of graduate study at Harvard and had been inspired by a course on folk expression and regional literature. On his return to Texas he took a cylinder recorder into the Brazos River Bottoms near Dallas, capturing enough cowboy songs to publish an anthology of them in 1910. His song gathering had been hampered thereafter by the pressure of a growing family, but the book had remained in print, with a new edition published in 1929. In 1932 Lomax, Alan, and John, Jr., drove across the United States, promoting it in public lectures. But the book sold poorly, and the three men bickered frequently; they had several flat tires. The trio returned to Texas uncertain about what to try next.

But John Lomax was nothing if not an optimist and an incorrigible entrepreneur. Midway through the dispiriting book tour, he had managed to sell Macmillan on a new volume of folk songs, a much bigger book than his cowboy anthology, drawing on fieldwork to be undertaken during the next summer among men and women from all walks of life. If his first book had focused on one picturesque group, this one would offer a portrait of a nation—a nation, he believed, that had a tradition of indigenous song as rich, robust, and vital as anything to be found in Europe.

That conviction placed Lomax at odds with a generation of scholars, his teachers at Harvard among them, who believed that America had no indigenous music, no body of song developed on its own soil. Folk music was composed anonymously, transmitted orally, and suffused with the spirit of the peasantry, and since America was singularly lacking in peasants, no such tradition could have taken shape. Lomax rejected that argument flat out. No less than his teachers, he valued quaint, even primitive, voices unsullied by contact with the industrial city, but he denied that such voices were only to be found among the traditional peasantry. Any ballad scholars who claimed there were no American folk songs had clearly not looked in the right place. The United States proved to be rich in folk music once you ventured outside the confines of polite society, once you scouted among "the down-and-out classes—the outcast girl, the dope fiend, the convict, the jail-bird, and the tramp."

Chief among those "down-and-out classes" were African Americans. Lomax's fascination with black singing stretched back to his childhood, and he would have pursued it in his studies at Harvard had his supervisor George Kittredge been remotely receptive. The unfettered emotion he heard in the spirituals, the vigorous exertion that echoed in the work songs: all that spoke of a folk tradition as vital and spontaneous as the open air. In the 1910s Lomax began putting his thoughts about Negro music on paper, often attending services in black churches and taking down the words to the spirituals, occasionally employing a cylinder recorder to capture the elusive melodies. Those trips gave him material for a few published articles and a series of after-dinner speeches, but he knew that he had done little more than scratch the surface. The collections of black song published in the 1920s by people like his friend and fellow Texan Dorothy Scarborough only reminded him how much remained to be done.

Once Lomax had sold Macmillan on his proposal, he began researching in earnest, traveling to Washington, D.C., and the newly established Archive of Folk Song at the Library of Congress. Set up in 1928 as an adjunct to the Library's Music Division, the archive was the brainchild of Robert Winslow Gordon, a forty-four-year-old Harvard graduate and folk song aficionado. A man of obsessive enthusiasms, tall, thin, and permanently disheveled, Gordon had scraped together a living in the early 1920s as a folk song columnist for a pulp adventure magazine, soliciting contributions from readers and building up a vast collection of work songs, ballads, and chanteys. On the basis of that material and his encyclopedic knowledge of folk song history and style, Gordon persuaded the Library of Congress to set up a national folk song repository. He would serve as the collection's "Specialist and Consultant in the Field of Folk-Song and Literature," making and transcribing field recordings and classifying and studying the results.

Yet however pioneering Gordon's vision, the man himself proved supremely ill-suited to giving it form. No sooner had he established himself as the archive's "Specialist and Consultant" than he retreated to Darien, Georgia, where he hid himself away in a one-room cabin and immersed himself in the minutiae of his subject (at one point he drove 2,500 miles to interview an informant about the real-life crime behind the ballad "Cooney Shot Delia"). His priorities seemed to lie less with filling the archive than with "solving the basic problems of folk song" in a mammoth text on the subject, very little of which ever got written. Absorbed in the excitement of his quest, he was incommunicado for months at a time, leaving letters from the library unanswered but occasionally issuing grandiose manifestos for the future of the archive when pressures from Washington became too intense to ignore. Meanwhile, the four rooms in the Music Division set aside for the archive remained more or less empty, and Music Division staff were fast losing patience. They were already planning to cut Gordon's funding when John Lomax stepped onto the scene.

The archive, it seemed, needed John Lomax. For his part, Lomax needed the archive—needed its stamp of approval, for a start, letters of introduction on library stationary that could get him past southern prison officials. Above all, he needed recording equipment. Back in 1907 he had used a portable graphophone with a horn and a spring-driven motor that recorded on wax cylinders, the same kind of machine employed by Howard Odum and virtually every other folklorist in the field. It had advantages—it was lightweight enough to be easily carried, and the windup motor allowed it to run in remote areas—but the cylinders were fragile, and the sound quality of the recordings was poor. By the early 1920s, recording companies like OKeh and Victor had devised a portable machine capable of recording wax master disks in the field, but the disks required factory processing to be transformed into permanent, playable records. Lomax wanted a device that was simple to use and easy to carry and that made durable, high-quality disk recordings that could be played back on the spot. No such machine had yet been devised, but late in the spring of 1933 the library rustled up the necessary funds to pay a recording engineer to devise an experimental model. Two weeks into his journey, Lomax picked up the machine in Baton Rouge. Consisting of two large batteries, a rotary converter, amplifiers, a button carbon microphone, a speaker, cables, and piles of blank aluminum disks, it weighed over three hundred pounds. In the end Lomax managed to transport it only by tearing the back seat out of his Ford.

John Lomax's recording machine.

Equipped with their machine, Lomax and his son set out on the road, by day speeding down rutted highways, by night camping on beaches, washed over by birdsong and the cool Gulf breezes. Within days, they found rich material. In a logging camp near the Louisiana state line, they "heard for the first time the wail of the Negro woodsman," who echoed the shuddering crash of the pines in a cry full of "music. . . and mystery and wistful sadness." At the Central State Prison Farm near Sugarland, Texas, they met two "lifers," Iron Head and Clear Rock, who knew "the words of enough folk songs to fill a volume of five hundred pages." Just as rewarding was the sweltering evening they spent near Wingate, Texas, with Henry Trevillier, leader of a railroad track crew, who knew an endless stream of work songs and chants but insisted that they record him with his cabin door shut and his windows bolted, "for his wife objected to his singing other than 'sanctified' tunes."

They were three weeks into their trip when they arrived at Angola, and at first the inmates proved a disappointment. Apart from a group of female prisoners who sang a haunting ballad of Christ's crucifixion—"how Christ took his persecution, the crown of thorns, the cruel nails through his feet and hands, . . . 'and he never said a mumblin' word'"—the bulk of the convicts had nothing to give them. Undoubtedly, the prison itself was partly to blame, since at Angola, Negro inmates were not allowed to sing as they worked. The Lomaxes spent three grueling days attempting to coax songs from indifferent convicts before concluding that the effort was fruitless.

But just as they prepared to pack up their equipment, Captain Andrew Reaux of Camp A brought one last inmate forward. He was a "trusty"—a convict of noteworthy skill and reliability—who had been at Angola for over three years. In that time he had won the confidence of prison officials, who had moved him out of the sugarcane fields, allowed him to serve as Camp A's laundryman and, from time to time, awarded him the privilege of entertaining the inmates on their days off. The number on his convict stripes read LSP 19469. Reaux introduced him as Huddie Ledbetter, but everyone called him Leadbelly.

He was short and stocky, with coal-black skin and a chiseled, somber, unwrinkled face; only his hair, gray at the temples, indicated his forty-five years. Across his throat a long, deep, horizontal scar could be glimpsed under the collar of his striped convict's overalls. In his arms he carried a battered twelve-string guitar, painted green and held together with twine, and his eyes bore the wary, deliberately blank expression born of ten years' confinement in three southern penitentiaries for violent offenses about which he remained stubbornly vague.

He began to sing, and John Lomax was transfixed. This was a find like no other. Spirituals, lullabies, cowboy tunes, shouts from the fields and the levee camp: Leadbelly appeared to remember every song that he had ever heard. He had a deep, booming voice that echoed down the prison corridors, and the propulsive twang of his twelve-string guitar set his vocals off to rich effect. Even when Alan set the recording machine whirling, the flood of songs never slowed. Leadbelly moved effortlessly from a novelty song, "The Western Cowboy," to the old whorehouse ballad, "Frankie and Albert," to a prison lament called "Angola Blues," much of which he seemed to have composed himself. He sang a Dallas saloon number, "Ella Speed"; a song about cocaine, "Honey Take a Whiff on Me"; and "You Can't Lose Me, Cholly," a dance tune that had been around for years. In with those raucous numbers was a gentle waltz called "Irene" that he sang in a lilting tenor. In the end they obtained seven disks, each so different from the others that it was hard to believe they were sung by the same man.

These songs were nothing like the homogenized stuff that clogged up the radio airwaves. To Lomax's ears they sounded archaic, wholly unsullied by contact with whites. Even the more upbeat tunes, with their undercurrent of melancholy, spoke of a profound isolation. In Leadbelly, Lomax found what he was after: a living, breathing musical artifact, a black voice that was free from contamination by the modern world.

———

"EVERYBODY KNOWS THE STORY OF HOW LEADBELLY SANG his way to freedom," writes critic and historian Francis Davis, and it is true that the tale of the convict-turned-folksinger commands attention in virtually every blues chronicle. The story is usually told like this: Born in 1885 in Mooringsport, Louisiana, Huddie Ledbetter won a pardon from his ten-year sentence in July 1934 after John Lomax returned to Angola and recorded "Governor O. K. Allen," a plea for clemency that Leadbelly composed and Lomax delivered to the state governor. That collaboration launched a stormy partnership. Initially employed as Lomax's chauffeur and manservant, Leadbelly traveled with him across the South, performing for black inmates in penitentiaries from Arkansas to South Carolina to give them an idea of the songs Lomax was after. Late in 1934 the pair arrived in New York, where Lomax regaled journalists with the pardon story, reenacted it in a *March of Time* newsreel, and booked Leadbelly into high-profile singing engagements up and down the East Coast. Though their rela-

John Lomax (right) and Leadbelly (standing).

tionship disintegrated quickly thereafter, Leadbelly's fortunes eventually revived, earning him recording contracts, concert bookings from Los Angeles to Paris, and an enduring reputation as a folk musician par excellence.

What we know less well is the figure in the margins of that story, the man who took the recorded disk to the governor and thus, as legend has it, engineered Leadbelly's release. John Lomax spent little more than a decade documenting African American music, and his career has long been overshadowed by the achievements of his son Alan. Yet in those few years he transformed the search for authentic black song by spinning around it a new kind of romance. The black renegade, the outlaw, the convict in chains: they were carriers of the folk spirit, and they would give up their treasures to the brave and intrepid who dared to venture off the beaten path. Not for nothing did Lomax title his 1947 autobiography *Adventures of a Ballad Hunter:* for him song collecting was a kind of safari, rough-hewn, vigorous, and consummately masculine, full of the excitement of sleeping in the rough, eating around a campfire, and driving down rutted, dusty back roads at midnight.

Enmeshed in that sense of virile adventure was an evangelical enthusiasm for recording technology. Unlike virtually every collector who preceded him, in writing up his accounts of his findings, Lomax made no effort to hide his use of the machine. He felt none of his predecessors' fear that the phonograph could distort the reality that it was meant to be capturing, or that admitting to using it would compromise his authority. Rather, it was the phonograph that had made a truly objective study of black music possible for the first time:

> Through the Music Division in the Library of Congress, we were provided with the latest improved-model portable-machine for electrical sound-recording, with all the necessary accessories, including a fine microphone. Edison batteries, operating a direct current, enabled us to record singing wherever we found a good voice, in camp, cabin, or field. Likewise, a music-reproducing apparatus made it possible to play back at once any song recorded, to the very great astonishment and enjoyment of our black convict friends, nearly all of whom manifested an eager and enthusiastic interest in the project. . . . Before starting on the trip, I was impressed with a cautioning word from Mr. Engel, chief of the Music Division: "Don't take any musician along with you," said he; "what the Library wants is the machine's record of Negro singing and not some musician's interpretation of it; nor do we wish any musician about to tell the Negroes how they ought to sing." The hundred and fifty new tunes that we brought to the Library at the end of the summer are, therefore, in a very true sense, sound-photographs of Negro

songs, rendered in their own native element, unrestrained, uninfluenced, and undirected by anyone who had his own notions of how the songs should be rendered.

"Sound photographs" were what Lomax was after: the black voice reproduced with machinelike precision. Lomax was convinced that metropolitan audiences would be transfixed by these rough, primal voices and that it was those voices that needed preserving, not just the folklorist's transcription of them. The disks, in other words, were what mattered. "The songs would make a sensation in cultured centers," he noted after a visit to Parchman Prison Farm in Mississippi, "if it were only possible to present them in their native, primitive style." His specially built recording machine made that dream a reality. Caught on wax, those evanescent voices could be stored for posterity in a federal repository— as one of Lomax's informants would put it, in a building that would never burn down.

Yet if Lomax's enthusiasm for recording technology was, among song collectors, unprecedented, it was also fraught with contradictions. However much he waxed rhapsodic about his state-of-the-art recording devices, his aim in employing them was to find archaic Negroes who inhabited a world where time had supposedly stopped and the phonograph itself was alien and unheard of. "Folk songs flourish, grow—are created, propagated, transformed—in the eddies of human society, particularly where there is isolation and homogeneity of thought and experience," he explained. Hence his enthusiasm for recording in prisons, which supplied isolation and homogeneity in abundance. Faced with a recording machine, Lomax maintained, convicts revealed their essential simplicity, with hardened criminals transformed into giddy boys, "contented and carefree as a group of children":

> Their excitement over the strange machine merged into laughing delight as the singers listened to their voices coming back to them from the newly made records. One man, not knowing what was going on and brought in suddenly from the barn to sing before the microphone, crumpled and fell flat on his back in amazed terror on hearing his own voice from the machine.

Contrast that account to Howard Odum's encounter with the blasé, savvy Will Smith three decades earlier. What made the convict, for Lomax, an ideal subject was what he saw as the singular lack of (in his terms) "contamination" ensured by the conditions of prison life. "Negro songs in their primitive purity can be obtained probably as nowhere else from Negro prisoners in state or Federal penitentiaries," Lomax argued. "Here the Negroes are completely segregated and have no familiar contact with whites. Thrown on their own resources for entertainment, they still sing [the distinctive old-time Negro melodies], especially the long-term prisoners who have been confined for years and who have not yet been influenced by jazz and the radio." He never doubted that such isolation was possible, even by the mid-1930s, when race records had been circulating for fifteen years. In stressing the shock of his "convict friends" when they heard their own voices replayed on the phonograph, he echoed comic writers like Joel Chandler Harris, who back in 1880 had lampooned Uncle Remus's befuddlement at the workings of "dish 'ere w'at dey calls de fonygraf," his naive astonishment at the disembodied voice booming out of the horn.

Yet time and again, Lomax would be bewildered by the worldliness of the men whose "primitive purity" he was meant to be documenting. At no point did that bewilderment loom larger, or have more painful consequences, than in his encounter with Leadbelly, when he transported him from Angola to New York and put him onstage as an embodiment of the uncorrupted folk-voice.

ONE KEY SHAPER OF THE LEADBELLY LEGEND WAS THE *March of Time* newsreel, filmed in February 1935, a few weeks after Leadbelly and Lomax arrived in New York. By that time the spectacle of the singing ex-convict had already provoked a media frenzy, to such an extent that Lomax had removed Leadbelly from the city; brought his lover, Martha Promise, up from Shreveport; and secreted them in a friend's house in Wilton, Connecticut. There the filmmakers arrived with barbed wire and guard dogs in an attempt to transform the rolling New England hills into a passable facsimile of the Angola swamps. The film that resulted was transcribed decades later by a German fan, Herman Gebhard.

> *Title: "Angola, Louisiana." At night. LEADBELLY and other black convicts, dressed in stripes, are shown huddled round a fire. Leadbelly plays his guitar, the sound covered by orchestral music.*
>
> ANNOUNCER
> To the Louisiana State Penitentiary goes JOHN A. LOMAX, Library of Congress curator, collector of American folk songs.
>
> *End of background music. Leadbelly sings and plays "Goodnight, Irene" as Lomax records him. There is a shot*

of the recording equipment in action. After a verse, Lomax interrupts.

LOMAX

Just one more, Leadbelly!

Leadbelly starts again with "Goodnight, Irene." He sings another verse.

LOMAX

That's fine, Leadbelly. You're a fine songster. I've never heard so many good Negro songs.

LEADBELLY

Thank you, sir, boss. I sure hope you send Governor O. K. Allen a record of that song I made up about him, 'cause I believe he'll turn me loose.

LOMAX

Leadbelly, I don't know this governor. You mustn't expect too much of me.

LEADBELLY

But Governor Pat Neff of Texas, he turned me loose, when he heard this song that I made up about him.

LOMAX

So you were in the Texas penitentiary, too, Leadbelly?

LEADBELLY

Yeah, I was serving thirty-five years for murder, but it wasn't my fault. A man was tryin' to cut my head off.

LOMAX

Mighty bad, Leadbelly.

> LEADBELLY

I believe Governor O. K. Allen, if you'll just send him a record of that song, I believe he'll turn me loose.

> LOMAX

Leadbelly, I'll try it.

> LEADBELLY

Thank you, sir, boss, thank you, sir, thank you!

He begins to play again. Scene fades. Next scene begins with a hotel entrance. Leadbelly, in jeans and with his guitar in hand, talks to the hotel clerk.

> CLERK

Yes, Mr. John Lomax is staying here. He's in room 109.

A typewriter is heard in the background.

> LEADBELLY

Is that on the first floor?

> CLERK

Yep.

Leadbelly runs up the stairs.

> CLERK

Hey, hold on a minute!

Inside Lomax's room. Lomax is sitting at a table, typing. A knock at the door.

> LOMAX

Come in!

Leadbelly comes in.

LEADBELLY

Boss, here I is!

LOMAX

Leadbelly! What are you doing here?

LEADBELLY

No use to try and run me away, boss. I came here
to be your man. I got to work for you the rest of my
life. You got me out of that Louisiana pen.

LOMAX

I—you can't work for me. You're a mean boy. You
killed two men.

LEADBELLY

Please to don't talk thataway, boss.

LOMAX

Have you got a pistol?

LEADBELLY

No, sir, I got a knife.

LOMAX

Lemme see it.

*Leadbelly produces a short knife. Lomax examines it and
hands it back.*

LOMAX

What do you do with that thing?

LEADBELLY

I'll use it on somebody if they bother you, boss.
Please, boss, take me with you. You'll never have to
tie your stri—shoe strings any more, if you'll let
me, long as you keep me with you.

LOMAX

All right, Leadbelly, I'll try you.

LEADBELLY

Thank you, sir, boss, thank you.

Claps his hands.

LEADBELLY

I'll drive you all over the United States and I'll sing all songs for you. You be my big boss and I'll be your man. Thank you, sir, thank you, sir.

End of scene. In the next scene, Leadbelly wears a suit and plays his guitar, humming and singing "Goodnight, Irene." Next to him sits MARTHA, elegantly dressed, smiling at him.

ANNOUNCER

John Lomax does take the Louisiana Negro convict to be his man. Takes him north to his home in Wilton, Connecticut, where Leadbelly's longtime sweetheart, Martha Promise, is brought up from the South for a jubilant wedding. Then hailed by the Library of Congress' Music Division as its greatest folk song find in twenty-five years, Leadbelly's songs go into the archives of the great national institution.

The interior of the archives is shown, with songbooks, etc., and finally, the original copy of the Declaration of Independence. Leadbelly sings "Goodnight, Irene." Close-up of the Declaration. Scene and music fade out, orchestral music, titles and signature tune. End of newsreel.

The first thing to say about the newsreel is that it is more or less correct on the facts. An itinerant guitarist and sometime farm laborer, Leadbelly had been serving a thirty-year murder sentence at Central State Prison Farm in Sugarland, Texas, when he won parole in 1924 by composing a song begging for a pardon and serenading the state governor. Ten years later, he turned to John Lomax's recording machine to deliver his plea to Governor Allen, and though prison records would later reveal that he was released routinely (under a state law allowing double time off for good behavior), it is clear that Leadbelly believed, or claimed to believe, that John Lomax had set him free. After his release on the first of August, he bombarded his benefactor with offers to drive his car, wash his clothes, and cook his meals. "Dear Sir Just a few lines to let you no iom out and Here in Shreveport La, Looking for you," he wrote. "iom looking for you iom going to work for you Your servan Huddie Ledbetter." On September 22 they met in Lomax's hotel room in Marshall, Texas, where, if we can believe the letter Lomax wrote the next day to his family, Leadbelly showed him his knife and swore his undying loyalty, even insisting that Lomax would never again need to tie his own shoes. Yet for anyone reading that script today, questions of accuracy can only seem academic, overwhelmed as they are by its excruciating depiction of Leadbelly as a hapless, hopeless, mindlessly criminal darky, a part that Lomax seems to have set out for him and in which the singer seems to collude.

Yet it is important to recognize that there are other ways of reading the story. "Dear Mr. Lomax," wrote Zora Neale Hurston in early January 1935, nine months before publishing her landmark folktale collection, *Mules and Men,* and a few days after the news about Leadbelly broke in New York. "I am writing now because I admire your work, and knowing what I am talking about, feel that it is something fine and necessary to American culture and art. May I have the pleasure of talking with both of the Lomaxes as well as listening to Leadbelly?

This is the sort of thing I have been advocating all along." Hurston saw Lomax as a kindred spirit because he shared her passion for the innate, untutored creativity of "the Negro furthest down," the man or woman in the gutter, the singer of rough, unadulterated song. Like Hurston (but unlike many other black intellectuals, W. E. B. Du Bois and Alain Locke among them), Lomax firmly believed that vernacular singers like Leadbelly needed no refinement, no polishing—to do so, indeed, would devitalize what was already consummate art. Whether Lomax responded to Hurston is unknown, but he was clearly pleased by her praise. "A Negro author," he scribbled at the bottom of her letter when preparing his autobiography some years later. "See her excellent book."

As Hurston's admiration makes clear, nothing in the tale of Lomax and Leadbelly is easy to characterize. Most puzzling of all are Lomax's motives in putting the singer in the public eye. Even before he took Leadbelly north, Lomax was convinced that genuine folk singers could not be transplanted. It is "impossible to transport Negro folk-singers from the South and keep them untainted by white musical conventions," he maintained in 1933. "Contact with whites soon brings about cheap imitations of ordinary music and conversations, and the real charm disappears." That very vulnerability made the recording machine essential. Captured on record in their native surroundings, the voices could travel thousands of miles and remain "untainted." By Lomax's own assumptions, to take Leadbelly with him was to court disaster.

That Lomax disregarded such apprehensions owed in part to the rigors of field recording, for taking a "sound photograph" in southern prisons turned out to involve far more than simply turning on the machine. Power supplies could fail, machinery could break down, and wax disks could even warp in the heat. Prison authorities could be uncooperative; sometimes they refused him outright. "I do not think there is a boy in the institution who would remotely dream of using a 'crude' or 'vulgar' song on the grounds," wrote one prison superintendent in response to Lomax's appeal for "the words and tunes of songs and ballads current and popular among prisoners . . . no matter how crude and vulgar they may be." Attempts to help could be even more troublesome, since prison officials rarely understood what he was after. "After a thorough investigation I find that there is at the present time a professional song-writer-journalist imprisoned here, whose term will expire on May 3rd 1935," wrote the head of one penitentiary. "This 'lad' under the name of J. Solomon King, Jordan S. Murphy, and numerous other pseudonyms . . . is the writer of many songs including 'If it Makes Any Difference to You,' 'The Kiss I Can't Forget,' 'Oh! What a Nice Place,' 'Someday Your Heart Will be Broken Like Mine,' 'My Grand-Daddy's Sweetheart,' 'Smiling Through the Rain,' 'I'm Dizzy over Lizzy,' 'If There's a Radio Station in Heaven (Mother Send a Message to Me)'. . . . Trusting that the above information will be of some use to you in your compilation of All American songs."

And then there were the prisoners themselves, who could be sullen or suspicious or lethargic or simply deaf to his needs. A few refused to sing anything but religious music; others were too exhausted from their labors to sing at all. Most vexing were the educated Negroes he met up with from time to time on his journey, the teachers and ministers who attempted to stage-manage his visits to remote black communities to ensure that nothing unseemly made its way onto Lomax's wax disks. Such individuals were "blinding themselves to the power and beauty of the Negro's most significant artistic contribution," Lomax complained. "A bit of shallow instruction has had its inevitable result in a crop of false ideals. These negroes are ashamed of their heritage and make themselves ridiculous (in most cases) when they attempt to ape the whites in the field of music." Maneuvering his way through the black South meant negotiating subtle gradations of class and respectability, an enterprise for which he was ill-prepared. He and Alan may have been born in the region, but they were, nonetheless, outsiders "amid a people we really know little about."

What Lomax needed was an insider, and that was exactly what he found in Leadbelly. Through the autumn of 1934, Leadbelly and Lomax journeyed from Texas to Georgia, through six states and a dozen penitentiaries, and by the end of the first week Lomax saw just how useful his companion could be. Not only was Leadbelly an efficient driver and, much of the time, an exemplary manservant; guitar in hand in the cellblock, he was unrivaled as a demonstrator of what Lomax wanted. "Other singers hearing him became ambitious to show me what they could do," Lomax noted. "I discovered that musicians among the Negro convicts in this prison camp, through Leadbelly's singing, quickly understood what I was looking for."

What Lomax was looking for were "the reels or so-called 'jump-up,' 'made-up,' or 'sinful songs' of the blacks"—secular tunes that, he felt, were richer and more original than even the spirituals. "Negro spirituals abound in idioms and phrases drawn directly from the Bible and from the older white spirituals," he argued. "The secular songs treat of subjects vital to the Negro's life, every day of the week—his hates, his loves, his earthly trials and privations." Because some prisoners deemed such songs "worl'ly" and "sinful," the pair devised a collecting practice designed to allay inmates' suspicions, assure them of the songs' importance, and entice them to contribute as best they could.

At the heart of the practice was a kind of illustrated lecture. They would gather the inmates together, Lomax would speak about the kinds of songs he was after, and then Leadbelly would perform a few samples, the folklorist introducing each one. The results, Lomax maintained, were electric. On their first attempt, at a state penitentiary outside Little Rock,

> We sat at a point in the run-around while the men were crowded inside as close as possible to us, peering out between the iron bars. . . . So eager were they to hear and see Leadbelly that at times some stood on the shoulders of others. When the twanging of his guitar strings rang out, supporting his rich booming voice, silence fell in the rows of cells suddenly and completely. The crap games ceased, the cooncan players dropped their cards, while from dim corners, where groups were mumbling prayers and songs and religious preachments, poured all the worshipers, including the black ministers. For the moment Leadbelly's "sinful songs" became more powerful than the "spirituals."

Lomax owed a tremendous debt to Leadbelly's mediation; by the end of his journey, he had collected well over two hundred disk recordings. In effect, the singer had become his collaborator, a fellow song gatherer, though Lomax never admitted as much: to do so would have confused their roles, and from his perspective it was essential that Leadbelly stay on the correct side of the line. Hefting the machinery, singing into it, was one thing; attempting to operate it was something else. At Cummins Prison Farm in Arkansas, after a particularly raucous illustrated lecture, Lomax found Leadbelly surrounded by inmates, flushed with pride and excitement, jiggling the controls on the sound equipment, eager, as Lomax saw it, to "to 'show off' among his own color." Lomax made clear his irritation and insisted that it should not happen again, but he recounts the incident as an amusing spectacle: the aborigine fingers the machine.

It is worth asking, as Lomax never did, just what Leadbelly would have recorded—and, for that matter, what he would have described had he ever recounted those prison sessions himself. He was a nominally free man spending his days in penitentiary corridors and his nights bunked in with the inmates in the segregated cellblocks. The surroundings were grim, sometimes gruesome. At one penitentiary, seeking a soundproof room for recording, they were directed to the execution chamber, where they elicited songs from the inmates a few feet from the electric chair. Leadbelly himself was an object of extreme curiosity. Far from encountering a fresh start, a new chapter, he found that his history always preceded him. "Before we reached the farm I told Leadbelly that I would not mention, either to the guard or to the prisoners, his penitentiary record," noted Lomax, "but we had not been there an hour before all the Negro convicts knew his story. . . . The same thing happened at every penitentiary we visited together." What Leadbelly did not say directly his growing unhappiness made unmistakable, and ultimately he did speak up. "I'm tired of lookin' at niggers in the penitentshuh," he told Lomax abruptly at the end of October. "I wish we could go somewheres else."

That was the reason, Lomax maintained, that they headed north. Leadbelly was bored and restless and desperate to see

the big city, and Alan (who had spent much of the autumn ill
with malaria but had joined them on the road in late November) was eager to show him the sights. Plus, word of Leadbelly
had begun to spread. Lomax's *American Ballads and Folk
Songs* had been published in late October 1934, and it included many of the songs gathered from convicts and credited
Leadbelly as an important source. The glowing reviews the
book received provoked the head of the Modern Language Association to invite Lomax to unveil his discovery at its annual
convention in Philadelphia in late December. Though Lomax
claimed to be apprehensive—the idea, he said later, "smacked
of sensationalism"—he, Alan, and Leadbelly duly took the
stage with lecture notes and guitar at the evening smoker in
the Crystal Ballroom in the Benjamin Franklin Hotel, billed as
"Negro Folksongs and Ballads, presented by John Lomax and
Alan Lomax, with the assistance of a Negro minstrel from
Louisiana," and sandwiched between a performance of Elizabethan madrigals and a sing-along of sea chanteys.

What followed can only be described as a media circus. In
the first week of January 1935, Lomax unveiled Leadbelly again
and again, to gatherings of publishers, critics, musicians, radio
broadcasters, folk song enthusiasts, socialites, and reporters
from the *Nation,* the *New Yorker, Time,* and what seemed like
every newspaper on the East Coast. The pair fielded offers of
radio broadcasts, concert bookings, a record deal, and a contract for a book of transcriptions of Leadbelly's songs. Though
some of this may have owed to Leadbelly's singing (which was,
wrote the *Brooklyn Daily Eagle,* "infinitely more genuine than
the effete spirituals of Harlem"), to judge by the press coverage, the lurid appeal of the singer himself far outweighed interest in the music. "Murderous Minstrel," the *Time* headline, was

typical. "Lomax Arrives with Leadbelly, Negro Minstrel," trumpeted the *New York Herald Tribune,* adding, "Sweet Singer of the Swamplands Here to Do a Few Tunes Between Homicides." Clearly, what had taken shape on the penitentiary circuit as a sober and educative illustrated lecture was transformed by the press into a vaudevillian freak show.

John Lomax would always claim later that he abhorred such sensationalism, that it was not his doing. It's true that he might not have needed to do much: the simple outlines of Leadbelly's history, his double convictions for violent offenses, conformed to the most hidebound racial typecasting. Yet it would be specious to absolve Lomax of all the blame. Lomax's posture toward journalists—who were not allowed to address Leadbelly directly, lest they interfere with his purity—smacked of the antics of P. T. Barnum. He had set Leadbelly up as a savage curiosity, a kind of homegrown Wild Man of Borneo. Even as he praised the "absolute sincerity" of Leadbelly's singing, he let no one forget his criminal background. Indeed, despite Lomax's claims to the contrary, it is clear that in spotlighting Leadbelly as (in *Time's* phrase) "a black buck," journalists were not simply distorting his words. Back in the autumn, while recording at Atmore Prison in Alabama, Lomax wrote about Leadbelly to a friend in New York, who then passed the letter along to the press.

My chauffeur, while Alan is sick. . . , is a negro who sang so beautifully at Angola, a Louisiana prison farm, that I took one of his records back to Baton Rouge, one hundred miles away. When I played it for the Governor he issued a pardon.

Leadbelly is a nigger to the core of his being. In addition he is a killer. He tells the truth only accidentally. He keeps his promise rarely—when it suits his convenience. He has no sense of loyalty or gratitude. . . . I am thinking of bringing him to New York in January. Then you would have a guest [who] could entertain your crowd.

In bringing Leadbelly north, Lomax set out to create a new kind of celebrity: a flesh-and-blood embodiment of life on the margins, a living, breathing Left Wing Gordon. Yet, almost instantly, he became obsessed with the danger that the experiment raised. Keeping Leadbelly marketable meant keeping him "pure," which meant protecting him from the malign influences in which the city abounded. In New York, that proved almost impossible, since in Lomax's eyes those influences loomed at every step. Since no hotel south of 125th Street would take him, Lomax was forced to house Leadbelly in Harlem, where (though he told Lomax he had sworn off whiskey) he spent his nights touring the bars, eventually making his way to the Cotton Club and befriending its headliner, bandleader and scat singer Cab Calloway. The sight of Leadbelly returning the next morning, drunk, disheveled, and euphoric (he told Lomax that Calloway had offered him a thousand dollars to sit in with the band), convinced Lomax that extreme measures were necessary. Though the press was still clamoring for a glimpse of the singer, Lomax whisked him off to Wilton, Connecticut. In all, the pair's stay in New York lasted less than two weeks.

Even so, Lomax judged, the damage had been done, and the problem ran deeper than simple dissipation. That Leadbelly lied, caroused, and drank to excess was nothing new and indeed nothing more than Lomax expected. It was part of the role he was enacting as Lomax's "boy," his flunky, its script drawn straight from the paternalist traditions of the Deep South. ("Boss, I'se nothin' but a nigger," Lomax reported Leadbelly saying back in November, after one of his periodic disappearances. "There never wus a nigger whut would keep his word—leastwise I never knowed none. I thought you knowed dat.") What distressed Lomax far more was what he began to perceive as a gradual transformation in Leadbelly's stage performances, which accelerated the longer they remained in the North. As their bookings multiplied around the East Coast, Leadbelly turned to new material, introducing songs that he had learned from recordings by the yodeling hillbilly Jimmie Rodgers and Tin Pan Alley standards like "That Silver-Haired Daddy of Mine." With that came what Lomax saw as a new kind of self-consciousness, a studied artifice that the press was quick to decry. "Already the pure nigger in him shows signs of becoming corrupted," carped a reporter for the *Brooklyn Daily Eagle*. "A certain striving for effect is noticeable in his performances, a trick, evidently, that he picked up at Cab Calloway's." What was being played out, as though Lomax had scripted it, was his deep-rooted belief in the vulnerability of the primitive artist, his conviction that mere exposure to commercial music would inevitably result in adulteration. "We (Alan and I) are disturbed and distressed at his beginning tendency to show off in his songs and talk when his money value is to be natural and sincere as he was while in prison," he wrote to his family in mid-January. "Of course, as this tendency grows he will lose his charm and become only an ordinary, low ordinary, Harlem nigger."

Had Leadbelly been corrupted, as Lomax always maintained? Decades on, it is hard to disentangle the facts of these performances from their resonance in Lomax's imagination, but there is reason to believe that the man Lomax met in Angola Penitentiary was never as unsullied as the folklorist made out. From the outset Lomax had heralded Leadbelly for his purity of voice and repertoire. "We saw no printed page of music either in his prison cell or in his home," he maintained. "His eleven years of confinement had cut him off both from the phonograph and from the radio." In actuality, Leadbelly had always enjoyed listening to the radio—he would later record a song titled "Turn Your Radio On"—and his exposure to commercial recordings began well before he arrived in New York. "I learned by listening to other singers once in a while off phonograph records," he later recalled. "I used to look at the sheet music and learn the words of a few popular songs." That openness to all kinds of music would have served him well as an itinerant songster at juke joints and house parties, where he needed a wide-ranging repertoire to play whatever the crowd might demand.

Yet if much of what Lomax labeled Leadbelly's "corruption" was a worldliness that was there from the outset, it is also clear that, to some extent, in the course of their journey, Leadbelly had changed. Back in September they had set out on the road as players in a joint drama, and at the outset they more or less agreed on the script, but exposure to the confident, bustling black world of Harlem made his part increasingly hard to sustain. In Wilton "the most famous nigger in the world," as Lomax described him, returned to his role as valet and house servant (though the arrival of Martha Promise relieved him of cooking the meals and making the beds). In live performance and in recordings, he struggled to negotiate Lomax's confusing demands: that he clean up his diction and slow down his guitar work so that northerners could make out his

lyrics, and that he simultaneously appear wholly unadulterated, as "natural and sincere as he was while in prison." Meanwhile, the folklorist cemented their informal relationship,
signing Leadbelly up to a contract that gave the Lomaxes the
bulk of his earnings. Since he did not trust him with even small
sums, Lomax also insisted on pocketing the coins that Leadbelly earned each night passing his hat.

That Leadbelly grew increasingly truculent could have surprised no one but Lomax himself. As the weeks passed in
Wilton, as the pressures in the household mounted, the singer
disappeared for hours, sometimes days, at a time, stumbling
home morose and sullen, trailing bottles of gin in his wake.
That, at least, was how Lomax described it, a chronicle of
mounting dissipation; a more even-handed interpretation
would have it that Leadbelly had simply had enough. In early
March he and Lomax set off across upstate New York and New
England for a series of concerts on college campuses, and
from the outset Leadbelly flatly refused to be chaperoned. In
Rochester he headed for the city's black district and disappeared for twenty-four hours; in Buffalo he turned down a
room at the "colored" YMCA in favor of what an appalled
Lomax described as "a low, dirty back room. . . down an alley
on Williams Street." Though he passed the hat as usual during
his shows, he refused to hand over the proceeds. "I ain't goin'
to sing no more for you unless I wants to, and I ain't goin'
nowhere unless you bring Marthy along too," he told Lomax.

The climax, as Lomax described it, came on the eighth of
March, the same day that the *March of Time* newsreel was released to theaters across the country. As Lomax read in the
Grosvenor Library at the University of Buffalo, he was confronted by Leadbelly, who had traded his brown overcoat for a

loud green-and-yellow checked suit and abandoned all traces of the old deference. "I wants my money," he announced. When Lomax refused, he reached for his pocket, where he carried a knife. At that moment an acquaintance walked up, and Leadbelly retreated, but Lomax was deeply shaken. "The experience has shattered my nerves temporarily as you can see from this writing," he explained to his family. "I think the main reason I feel about Huddie as I do is that he frightened me. The humiliation of that will be lasting." The man who had approached him in the library was every jumped-up, citified Negro who had ever strutted his way into Lomax's nightmares, and that encounter brought their relationship to an end. "The little drama was played out," Lomax would write one year later in *Negro Folk Songs as Sung by Lead Belly.* "He had been changed by a little prosperity, and possibly through our own mistakes in dealing with him, into an arrogant person, dressed in flashy clothes, a self-confident boaster." Two weeks after the library incident, Lomax put Leadbelly and Martha on a bus back to Shreveport.

A year later, in April 1936, one day after he sent his editors at Macmillan the corrected proofs for the Leadbelly book, Lomax drove from Austin to Central State Prison Farm in Sugarland, Texas, to collect another black convict and set out on the road. James Baker, who went by the nickname of Iron Head, had impressed him on his first recording expedition in 1933 with his wide repertoire of "jumped-up" songs and his rich, resonant voice. Though Lomax had originally thought he was a "triple murderer," Baker was, rather less dramatically, a habitual burglar whose repeat offenses had put him in Sugarland under a sentence of ninety-nine years. In preparation for another trek through southern prisons, Lomax had contacted

Texas's governor James Allred, whom he knew slightly, to arrange to parole Iron Head into his care. He would take charge of the convict for the next four months while they drove across the South making recordings, at the end of which time, if all went well, Lomax would set Iron Head up in his own business weaving rugs from corn shucks (the craft he had learned in prison), and Iron Head would be a free man.

The journey that ensued makes a bizarre coda to the Leadbelly saga, with Lomax apparently acting on a compulsion to repeat the experience in every detail. "Among his own kind," he wrote a few days after his departure, "Iron Head . . . is developing some Leadbelly ego and is beginning to cause me some worry." Taking Leadbelly's place as servant and assistant (though he never learned to drive, so it was Lomax who acted as chauffeur), Iron Head, like his predecessor, grew ever more sullen as he performed for the assembled inmates in prisons from Mississippi to North Carolina, only to have Lomax confiscate the coins he was given each time he passed his hat. When the pair arrived in New York at the end of May, Lomax predicted disaster. "Tell Alan that I drove [Iron Head] to the YMCA at 135ᵗʰ Street yesterday and did everything but tuck him into his bed," he reported. "If I stay up here very long. . . I have decided to send him back home on a bus. In a city he is only in the way. There is nothing for him to do except get into trouble, and he is certain to do that." The journey ended like the one before it: the same one-way bus ticket, the same anger and bitterness, the same perplexity at the convict's ingratitude. Only this time, no one except Lomax's family was listening. The press showed no interest in Iron Head; nor did the New York folk song enthusiasts who had been mesmerized by Leadbelly one year before. When Lomax contacted Mary Elizabeth

Barnicle, the professor of folklore at New York University who had lent him and Leadbelly her house in Connecticut, she at first claimed to be too busy to see him and then turned up for a brief visit, during which she seemed remote and indifferent. "She expressed no interest in Iron Head," he noted with some bewilderment. He did not know, nor did she tell him, that she now had her own folk music project: helping Leadbelly launch a second career.

————

IN A CLIMATE-CONTROLLED ROOM AT THE BARKER CENTER for American History at the University of Texas at Austin are housed the hundreds of boxes and files that comprise the Lomax Family Papers. Here, among photographs, clippings, and family correspondence (much of which, at the time of this writing, is closed to researchers), are the material remains of Lomax's encounter with Leadbelly. I have come to explore the encounter's beginnings, the letters Lomax wrote on the road in 1933, the earliest account of his first prison trek. Though I have come across them already in bits and pieces, quoted in Nolan Porterfield's biography of John Lomax, I am after a first-hand glimpse, in hopes of finding something that might reveal his motives, that might make the man himself come through.

What takes me by surprise is the fact that the evidence consists of love letters. Sometime in the spring of 1933, two years after the death of his wife, Lomax began courting Ruby Terrill, a forty-eight-year-old Latin instructor and dean of women at the University of Texas. Little more than a few dinner dates had passed between them by the time he set out for the South's penitentiaries, but while on the road between June and August he wrote to her regularly, describing the sights and sounds in detail and slipping in his feelings along the way. "Because Alan will drive recklessly and because you are a lovely person, I say now that I love you." Though he claimed to have little hope that she might return his passion, he pleaded for her forbearance. "I have no means of knowing whether my outpourings about this somewhat unusual journey have for you any particular interest, but . . . should it turn out that for any reason you do not care for my letters, will it be quite fair to ask that you do not tell me just now. I am lonely beyond words."

Grieving, lonely, and vulnerable, Lomax wrote in the hopes of showing his beloved that he was capable of heightened emotion, and what provoked that emotion, along with Terrill herself, was the sound of the black convict's voice. The work cries of the prisoners, he told her, were full of "music and mystery and wistful sadness," and the more intense the suffering, the greater the power of the voices that conveyed it. What thrilled him above all was "the simple directness and power of this primitive music, coupled with descriptions of a life where force and other elemental influences are dominating." The sights and sounds of that primal world, he was sure, would haunt him for years to come. "As I think back, and in my dreams, lines of stripe-clad convicts file before me. Down in Tennessee they wore chains and in their singing you can hear the swish of the pick and the clank of the chain."

That John Lomax filled his love letters with the sound of "the swish of the pick and the clank of the chain" may seem incongruous or even perverse, but to Lomax, and apparently to Terrill (who would marry him twelve months later), there was nothing strange about it. What he was responding to in those penitentiaries, what would take him back again and again, was the resonance he heard in those voices. Its visual counterpart can be seen in the photograph he chose in 1934 to illustrate his first published account of his trek, which showed a white prison guard armed with a shotgun overseeing a line of black convicts digging a trench, their backs bent, their heads bowed, without a trace of self-assertion. This was the sound that Lomax was after: a voice of unutterable melancholy, "of hopeless longing, of remoteness, of quiet resignation to the inevitable."

"The truest, the most intimate folk music," Lomax wrote, quoting the music critic Henry Krehbiel, "is that produced by suffering." In an American context, no suffering produced richer, more resonant music than that of African Americans. Such had been an article of faith as far back as the abolitionist movement, but in the hands of Frederick Douglass it had been tied to a political critique of cruelty and injustice. That the slaves could sing as they did demonstrated that they could feel, proof in itself of the monstrousness of a system that made them out to be chattel. Yet even abolitionism contained a kernel of what Lomax was experiencing, this transcendent thrill at the sight of black suffering, at the sound of a black man's pain. Over time, that sensibility would attach itself to the post-emancipation South's convict lease system. The same haunting sound that transfixed John Lomax caught the imaginations of others, like the southern novelist Samuel Derieux, one of Dorothy Scarborough's informants, who wrote of his delight in spending Sunday afternoons lazing in meadows, soaking up the voices of gangs of black convicts singing as they laid down the roads. Howard Odum, too, was mesmerized by the "chain gang songs and jail house blues," with their echoes of "stripes and chains, guards and guns, sometimes cruelty and hardships, sickness and death." The sound that drew them, and that obsessed John Lomax, might be described as the convict pastorale, a song of melancholy yearning, with the black man in prison stripes, laying roads, splitting rails, moaning in anguish, serving as a minor gateway to the sublime.

That experience of the sublime lay at the core of Lomax's love letters. The convicts as Lomax described them were a kind of human landscape, fierce and insensible, but no more aware of their own rugged beauty than were Arctic glaciers or desert crevasses. One night, on the road outside Tuscaloosa, Lomax gazed for a time on Leadbelly's profile in the light of a blood-red moon as he "drove steadily and silently, his black, black face shining like a bronzed statue." No matter how glorious the settings they passed through, scenic grandeur seemed to leave him untouched. "I can find no little feeling for beauty in him," Lomax claimed, little sense of wonder, empathy, or love. "Penitentiary wardens all tell me that I set no value on my life in using him as a traveling companion," he told a friend. "He is as sensual as a goat, and when he sings to me my spine tingles and sometimes the tears come." For Lomax, Leadbelly's sheer animalism made the delicate nuances of his voice all the more haunting, an emotional response so deeply engrained in him that he could not see the questions it was beginning to raise.

Those questions had become national ones in March 1931, when nine black youths, one aged only thirteen, were arrested in Scottsboro, Alabama, on charges of raping two white women on a freight train. Despite flimsy evidence, they were quickly tried, convicted, and sentenced to death, and their convictions withstood appeal after appeal, even after one of the women recanted her story. By the mid-1930s the case of the Scottsboro boys had become an international cause célèbre, and in its wake the American left launched a wholesale critique of southern criminal justice. The radical journalist John Spivak investigated prison conditions in Georgia and saw black convicts treated with a brutality that almost defied description. Spivak photographed prisoners shackled at the wrist and the ankle, left hanging from stocks in 102-degree heat, pulled and stretched along the ground until their arms were nearly wrenched from their sockets. His account, published in 1932 as *Georgia Nigger*, was an impassioned attack on the barbarism and cruelty that bolstered the power of the South's ruling class, and its impact was felt, indirectly, by John Lomax, who reached Georgia with Leadbelly in December 1934, only to find that Spivak's book had preceded him. "The trouble we have had in Georgia has been due to the fact that the hospitality of the Prison Board has been shamefully abused by visitors from the North who have come here and invented, after having been the guests of these gentlemen, horrors and cruelties even worse than those practiced in the Dark Ages," he wrote in disgust to Ruby Terrill. "It took me nearly three days to break down the opposition."

Clearly, for Lomax, Spivak's critique was wholly unfounded, and over the years he would take great care in his own writing to avoid the appearance of an exposé. At times he rewrote his field notes accordingly. In one of his earliest letters to Ruby Terrill, he described a song relating the "terrible story of the fear of a negro as he sees the 'Captain' riding up with the bull-whip in his hand to punish the black for an offense. Here the chorus was made up by the line 'Great God Almighty!,' uttered in a voice that mingled terror with . . . [a] horrible shrinking from physical pain." As set out in Lomax's original letter, the song spoke of current prison practices, punishments carried out in the here and now. Six months later, however, when Lomax published an account of his trek in the *Musical Quarterly,* that song had become an historical artifact, describing the days long gone "when convicts were leased by the State to owners of large cotton and cane plantations," a song of past sufferings to which the prisoners listened in "awed and reminiscent silence."

Had Lomax been asked, he would doubtless have replied that such alterations did not amount to whitewashing. Southern penitentiaries housed hardened lawbreakers who had been convicted fairly and were treated humanely; those few who were innocent and had been imprisoned unjustly were generally "Negroes who have been convicted on Negro evidence only. Negroes do 'gang up' on each other." The melancholy voices of black prisoners resulted not from ill-treatment, but from an essential restlessness—"the Negro's desire, as one said, 'to git away f'om here. I jis don' nachly like dis place.'" Even though Lomax listed "the injustice of the white man" as one of the subjects of black prisoners' songs, that referred simply to the misfortune borne out of the heritage of slavery, not to the continuing and systematic oppression of the present day. Yet even as Lomax dismissed it, the left critique of southern criminal justice would eventually have a profound impact on him, particularly by the end of the decade, when Leadbelly returned to the public eye.

The comeback began inauspiciously. At the end of 1935, Leadbelly had moved from Shreveport to Dallas, where he washed cars in a filling station and saw a few lawyers. From them he discovered that Lomax claimed to be entitled to two-thirds of the money earned by his performances; he also claimed to hold full copyright on his songs (which would prevent Leadbelly from performing them himself). In response,

Leadbelly embarked on a legal battle that would last, in fits and starts, for two years, even as he hatched plans to return to New York, convinced that there was an audience for his music and determined to show Lomax that he could manage without his help. By a stroke of luck, the gas station manager nursed his own dreams of adventure. When he realized who Ledbetter was, he sold his business, rented his house, and drove Leadbelly back to Manhattan, booking him for a week's engagement at the Apollo Theatre in Harlem. The show they devised was a singing and dancing extravaganza with two lines of chorus girls, a jazz pianist, and Leadbelly in convict stripes reenacting the pardon story. But within a few days the show folded; black New Yorkers, as Leadbelly's biographers put it, "stayed away in droves." The African American press was no kinder. "The advance publicity stated that this man had been in two jails under murder charges and that the wardens, on hearing him work out on the guitar and vocally, set him free," wrote the music critic of the *New York Age*. "Maybe they did, but after hearing the man myself, I'm not so sure that musical excellence prompted the two governors' actions. It may have been that both they and other inmates wanted some peace during their quiet hours."

In despair, with no money coming his way, he turned to Mary Elizabeth Barnicle. A mainstay of New York's radical circles, Barnicle was a onetime suffragist born and bred in New England, who moved to New York after World War I and took part in labor and civil rights struggles. As a folklorist, she focused on political, occupational, and sexual lore, encouraging her students to see folk music not as a quaint "survival," a remnant from an archaic time, but as a vital form of communication and protest. Though at first she had regarded John Lomax as a kindred spirit, she had grown to detest his treatment of his protégé and had said as much to the singer himself. Within weeks of Leadbelly's return to New York, she was paying him to perform for her classes and serving as his unofficial manager, guiding him into the radical folk-singing circles that she saw as his natural home.

Those circles were large and thriving in the mid-1930s, the heyday of the Popular Front, when all shades of left opinion united to oppose fascism abroad and racial and class oppression at home. For many, folk songs became a key tool in the struggle, a voice of popular resistance, a music that spoke the people's language, fostering a feeling of shared identity and purpose. In the same year that Leadbelly returned to New York, the American Music League, a collective of musicians and music lovers affiliated with the Communist Party, announced its intention "to collect, study, and popularize American folk music and its traditions." With Barnicle's help, Leadbelly soon joined Woody Guthrie and Aunt Molly Jackson (a miner's wife from Kentucky whose career was also managed by Barnicle) in a new pantheon of left icons, revered as living incarnations of American vernacular song's essential radicalism.

Just how that would affect John Lomax became clear in August 1937, when Leadbelly was profiled in the *Daily Worker* by the African American novelist and Mississippi native Richard Wright. A member of the Communist Party since the early 1930s, Wright had befriended Leadbelly that summer after moving to New York from Chicago, while at work on what became *Uncle Tom's Children,* the short story collection that would make his name.

Wright's article in the *Daily Worker* amounted to a radical revision of the Leadbelly saga. Under the headline "Huddie

Ledbetter, Famous Negro Folk Artist, Sings the Songs of Scottsboro and His People," Wright described Leadbelly as an "embodiment" of "the entire folk culture of the American Negro," who composed songs born of his life experience "of dodging white mobs, of wandering at night to save his life. . . , and of seeing black men drop dead from the heat of southern suns in the cotton fields." John Lomax was the story's archvillain, a calculating bully who, contrary to legend, played no part in Leadbelly's release. "When Ledbetter won himself a pardon for a second time out of a southern prison by composing folk songs, the southern landlords exploited him, robbed him of his self-made culture and then turned him loose on the streets of northern cities to starve," Wright argued. "John A. Lomax, collector of American folk songs for the Library of Congress, heard of Ledbetter and went to see him in prison. And here begins one of the most amazing cultural swindles in American history." "Beguil[ing] the singer with sugary promises," persuading him he would make him rich, Lomax used Leadbelly's singing talent to manipulate prisoners into "confid[ing] their folk culture in him." In New York he "gave out a vicious tirade of publicity to the nation's leading newspapers," depicting Leadbelly "as a half sex-mad, knife-toting, black buck from Texas." Swindled out of his songs, exploited and vilified, Leadbelly was then cast aside. Only his rediscovery by the left kept him alive and believing in himself. "The folks in the Workers' Alliance [a Popular Front organization] are the finest I've ever known," Wright quoted Leadbelly as saying. "I feel happy when I am with the boys in the Workers' Alliance. They are different from those Southern white men."

Owing in large part to Wright's article, by the end of the decade Leadbelly had become a left cause célèbre. Whether the singer himself would have told the same story is open to debate. Much evidence suggests that the welcome he found in radical circles was not as wholehearted as Wright made out, that he was occasionally met with incomprehension from comrades whose ideas of authentic black folksong were no more elastic than those of John Lomax. The composer Earl Robinson described inviting Leadbelly to sing at Camp Unity, a Communist Party summer retreat, where he performed "Ella Speed" and "Frankie and Albert," sensational ballads of murder and sex. "The camp was in an uproar," recalled Robinson. "Arguments raged over whether to censure him, or me, or both of us." Leadbelly placated the crowd the next night by performing "Bourgeois Blues," an attack on segregation in Washington, but the matter was not always settled so easily. Even his most broad-minded comrades could be dismayed by his love for the song creations of Tin Pan Alley and his desire to spice up his sets and recording sessions with songs by movie cowboy Gene Autry, yodeling hillbilly Jimmie Rodgers, and the latest Bing Crosby hit.

Nonetheless, what remains indisputable is that the left brought Leadbelly an eager audience, more respect than John Lomax could ever have given him, and influential friends who were prepared to fight battles on his behalf. Wright was one; another was Lawrence Gellert, an activist and folk song hunter who befriended the singer in the late 1930s, advising him on his legal wrangles, helping him to engage a lawyer, and providing invaluable moral support. Gellert was a longtime critic of John Lomax's song-gathering practices. Late in 1934, after the publication of *American Ballads and Folk Songs* and as news circulated of his discovery of Leadbelly, Gellert unleashed a scathing attack on the folklorist in the letters column of the radical journal *New Masses*. In sharp contrast to the publicity sensationalizing Leadbelly's criminal record, Gellert turned the spotlight on Lomax, in his eyes an archetypal racist driven by a reactionary nostalgia for the shuffling Sambo of southern lore.

Gellert knew field recording, and the South, firsthand. Born in Budapest in 1898, he emigrated to America at the age of nine and grew up on New York's Lower East Side, where he found his way into radical circles through his older brother Hugo, an artist and political cartoonist. Failing health in the early 1920s sent him south to Tryon, North Carolina, where he moved into the town's black section, got involved with a black woman, and, inspired by the singing he heard in his neighborhood, acquired a cylinder recorder and began documenting African American song. In contrast to Lomax, who sought in black music sounds of "primitive purity" and "wistful sadness," Gellert was after (as he put it) "propaganda," music "as a weapon" in political struggles. He shared the Communist Party's conviction that America's oppressed black masses formed a potential revolutionary vanguard, and he believed that those political sympathies allowed his black subjects to drop their guard and perform songs that few white people were ever in a position to hear. What he captured on disk, he believed, made a sharp contrast to Lomax's recordings: not "the nonsensical jingles served up for the white man's amusement," but the songs of resistance and rage that black people sang among themselves.

With those who made claims for Lomax's humanitarianism in championing an obscure black convict, Gellert bluntly disagreed. "Getting 'our niggers' out of difficulties with the Law when we need them to work or to entertain our crowd is a time honored custom with the Southern landlords," he argued. "Along with Jim Crowism, the whole vicious system of share-cropping, lynching, and the oppression of the millions in the Black Belt, the practice is rooted in the feudal traditions that still dominate the Gentlemen's South." "Our niggers" were those who broke the rules in acceptable ways, drinking or carousing or pulling a knife in a juke joint on a Saturday night. Those lawbreakers it was easy to tolerate: they confirmed the white southern conviction that Negroes were amoral and ani-malistic. In essence, they legitimated segregation, demonstrat-ing through their sheer dissolution that white southerners needed it to protect themselves.

The Lomaxes of the world were nowhere to be found when it came to those black convicts whose cases raised awkward questions. They were silent on the case of Angelo Herndon, a nineteen-year-old party activist from Georgia, sentenced to twenty years in prison for distributing communist leaflets. And they had nothing to say about the Scottsboro boys, the case that in Gellert's eyes demonstrated the true face of the South. Seen against that backdrop, Lomax's sponsorship of Leadbelly revealed itself as nothing more than racist paternalism. "Imag-ine Ben Davis Jr., editor of the *Negro Liberator*, going to Gov-ernor Talmadge of Georgia with [a record] sung by Angelo Herndon and getting a pardon for him! Or ditto Governor Miller of Alabama with a record sung by nine Scottsboro boys in chorus!"

It is a measure of the potency of Gellert's critique that, though he surely did not know it, the recording that he mock-ingly envisioned had actually been within Lomax's grasp. In late October 1934, at the peak of international outrage over the Scottsboro verdicts, Lomax arrived at Alabama's Kilby

Prison to hunt for songs among the inmates. There he had his first significant dispute with Leadbelly, who fought with him over money and disappeared for two days, leaving Lomax the arduous task of recording at Kilby on his own. Two years later Lomax would describe this stop at length in the Leadbelly book, yet nowhere did he note the presence of Clarence Norris and Heywood Patterson, the leading Scottsboro defendants, who were interned at Kilby on death row that same week. (In a further twist to the tale, it seems that at least one of the Scottsboro boys had heard of Lomax's prison recording project and would have been a willing participant. Sometime in 1936, the twenty-three-year-old defendant Olen Montgomery began writing blues songs from his prison cell. After the lyrics to his "Lonesome Jailhouse Blues" were published in the *Labor Defender*, he attempted to get hold of an eight-string guitar. He had heard about inmates making records in jail, and he thought it could bring him a new career and a new reputation. "If I live," he wrote to his lawyer, "I am going to Be the Blues King.")

Clearly, there were limits to what Lomax would capture in his "sound photographs." Voices that challenged, that expressed resistance, he could not acknowledge, could not even hear. As the decade wore on, as Scottsboro continued at stalemate, Popular Front folklorists took up Gellert's contention that what Lomax recorded was not true and unmediated and that, on the contrary, the machine could lie. The authentic black voice as they heard it was the voice of resistance, and no such voice would reveal itself to John Lomax, who "embodies the master-slave relationship intact." What he had captured on those prison recordings had been shaped by his plantation mentality, and, most likely, by coercion and fear. Gellert, for one, had no doubts about the tactics that Lomax must have employed. "On southern chain gang and jail, where Mr. Lomax got many of his songs, officials are perverts, sadists and murderers, with a hatred and ill-will towards their charges unequalled anywhere outside of Fascist Germany," he argued. "I'll wager that many a work-tired negro in dirty bedraggled stripes was yanked off a rock-pile by bribed plug ugly guards and ordered to 'sing for the gentlemen.'"

As it happens, Lomax himself could have provided the evidence to enable Gellert to claim his bet. Late in the 1930s he wrote to a friend reminiscing about his first penitentiary recording tour, the same one on which he met Leadbelly, and fondly recalled an occasion when an inmate refused to cooperate.

Some time ago when I was recording Negro work songs in the Nashville Penitentiary I found an enormous Negro man, Black Sampson by name, who had been a section hand, a levy camp worker, a steamboat roustabout, and a laborer in a Railroad construction gang. He could sing many of the songs used by the negroes in all sorts of gang work. Moreover he had a wonderful, rhythmic, baritone voice. But he would not sing the negro songs of labor because he had "got religion" in the penitentiary and had been told by his pastor that these songs were "sinful." For two days he tantalized me by singing these songs, always where the microphone could not catch his voice.

The last afternoon of my stay the Warden of the penitentiary came by and asked if I had got everything I wanted. I told him of Black Sampson's refusal to sing for me. "Go bring Black Sampson here," he said to one of the guards. Soon the big black man, frightened but smiling ingratiatingly, came into the room. "Black Sampson," said the Warden, "stand up before the microphone and sing whatever this white man tells you." Black Sampson shambled up to the microphone. I started the machinery whirling for the recording, but Black Sampson did not sing. He prayed, "Oh Lawd, you see what a fix yo po black man is in. Heah he is down in de world where he has to do ev'ything this white man tells him to, but Oh Lawd, I hope you will understand and forgive me for de sin I is about to commit and not charge it up against a po negro who caint hep hissef. For Jesus sake, Amen," and then he sang some beautiful work songs. Meanwhile our machine had recorded both the prayer and the songs. I call this my prize record.

———

FOR WHAT MAY PERHAPS BE OBVIOUS REASONS, HISTORY HAS not been kind to John Lomax. He swaggers through the pages of recent accounts of the blues much as Wright and Gellert depicted him, all bluster and bombast and self-satisfaction, treating his black subjects with a high-handedness so monumental it is almost disarming. What emerges is a portrait of a ruthless, exploitative tyrant who paraded Leadbelly onstage in convict stripes and enriched himself on his humiliation. In the end the depiction resembles nothing so much as Dorothea Lange's famous 1936 photograph of a white plantation owner in the Mississippi Delta, a burly, suspender-clad patriarch with one foot on his car bumper, exuding unassailable confidence in his authority as three ragged black men sit hunched and cowed on the porch steps behind.

Yet that portrait, with all its harsh outlines, simplifies far more than it illuminates. It certainly cannot account for the warmer recollections of many of those who knew and worked with him, even some whose politics differed sharply from his own. "Now Mr. Lomax, my god he hated old Roosevelt, hated the whole damn New Deal, he was very very conservative in his politics," recalled the song collector John Henry Faulk, a left activist who would later fall victim to a McCarthy-era blacklist. "But he was such a dear old soul. You would delight in his stories and accounts of people." Asked why a man of such engrained limitations would devote himself to black musicians, Faulk pointed to a sheer breadth of vision that his backward racial opinions made all the more remarkable. "Because Lomax was unquestionably a genius," he explained. "He was a man of a magnificent mind but he never put two and two together. He would just say, 'These [crimes against blacks] are aberrations of lawless people.'" Those who watched him in the field testified to his extraordinary ear for exceptional voices and his capacity to treat black informants with sensitivity and tact. Harold Spivacke, head of the Library of Congress's Music Division, accompanied him to a segregated prison in Virginia and watched him sit for hours with a blind banjo player, singing songs and swapping life stories, leaving his recording machine untouched in the car. When Spivacke recorded the man the next day, so comfortable was he before the microphone that "all I had to do was turn over the records." As a song gatherer, he came to realize, Lomax was "a consummate artist," a view with which John Henry Faulk concurred: at coaxing songs from shy and unforthcoming people, Lomax was "the best I ever met."

In his hidebound racial attitudes Lomax was a man of his time and place, worse than some and better than many. Although he never stopped believing that the South treated

African Americans justly and fairly, he could also speak up to demand that it accord with its professed ideals. Threaded through his correspondence are letters he wrote to southern governors, urging them to investigate prison conditions and free any convicts unjustly interned. In the summer of 1941 he wrote to the governor of South Carolina to protest what he had seen at a convict road camp, "a hundred negroes resting in their quarters, all fastened together on a single long chain."

> In making my reports to the Library of Congress I have found so much unjust criticism and misinformation about the treatment of Negro convicts in the South that a year or so ago I wrote a news article explaining the widely misunderstood term "chain gang." In this story I stated that I had never seen two convicts chained together. (As a matter of fact no instance of physical brutality in all my experiences have come under my personal notice.) I can no longer make this claim. . . . I do not know of the special reasons that make it necessary for these men to be chained together on their rest day. I only know that I have never before seen a practice which seemed to me so unnecessarily inhumane.

Unquestionably, as Faulk himself noted, Lomax "never questioned the system," never believed that it should be changed. (Indeed, even in this letter he muted his criticism: his own correspondence reveals that he saw prisoners in chains on his penitentiary recording tour of 1933.) Yet by his standards he was acting magnanimously, championing the cause of Negro prisoners to whom no one else was attending, "the forgotten ones who have no influential friends," no radical lawyers or New York folk musicians raising money on their be-

half. That such actions should brand him a racist left him bewildered and angry, and the more it happened, the more infu-
riated he became.

What was most frustrating was being dismissed as some
kind of throwback when he, more than anyone, could see just
how innovative and influential his work had been. Even
though Depression-era radical folklorists recoiled from his reactionary nostalgia, they were swept up by the romance that
he wove around the recording machine. Lawrence Gellert,
for example, began making disk recordings of black song in
the mid-1920s, but in none of his early accounts did he reveal
the means by which the songs were acquired. His articles in
the *New Masses* in 1930 and 1931 posed his song collecting as
a process of eavesdropping and chance, and he presented his
findings as overheard treasures carried along on the southern
breeze: "I heard a washerwoman striding along the road with
a bundle of laundry balanced on her head sing this"; "a tray
boy in an Asheville, N.C., sanatorium sang this one." Compare that to his introduction to *Negro Songs of Protest*, published in 1936:

> For more than a dozen years I lived alternately in Tryon, NC,
> and Greenville, SC. I enjoyed the friendship and protection
> of influential whites. And with impunity I haunted the Negro
> quarters. Long and painstakingly I cultivated and cemented
> confidences with individual Negroes without which any at-
> tempt to get to the core of the living folk lore is foredoomed
> to failure.
>
> Repeatedly from these vantage points I invaded the Black
> Belt. Armed with a mechanical phonograph, a sawed off
> megaphone and a bundle of blank aluminum records (my

recording outfit) I trekked, railroaded and hitch-hiked the
length and breadth of the deep South. . . . I slept on dirty
floor pallets in miserable ghetto hovels or ramshackles half
disappeared in malarial swamps. . . . Through GA, the Caroli-
nas, way over the Mississippi and Louisiana even, in city
slums, on isolated farms out in the sticks, on chain gangs,
lumber and turpentine work camps, I gathered more than
300 songs of the black folk—songs that reveal for the first
time the full heroic stature of the Negro dwarfing for all time
the traditional mean estimate of him.

Here the machine—"my recording outfit"—gives the passage
a gritty power that it would not otherwise have. Gellert vests
his authority in the fact that he "armed" himself with this
equipment and carried it "the length and breadth of the deep
South." Though he despised what he saw as Lomax's colonial-
ism, knowingly or not he paid homage to his influence, echoing his sense of song gathering as rugged adventure, charged
with the excitement of a guerrilla ambush or a wilderness trek.

The historian William Stott has written suggestively of the
1930s "documentary spirit," the heroic resonance that attached itself to the mechanical reproduction of sound and image, most famously to the photographs of Walker Evans and
Dorothea Lange. Used properly, the camera could go beyond
art and artifice to capture (in James Agee's phrase) "a portion
of unimagined existence," hidden truths of a hidden America
that had gone unnoticed for too long. In Lomax's hands, sound
technology carried those same connotations, and over the
course of the decade, his ambition to capture forgotten voices
(combined with the macho thrill of hefting the equipment)
caught the imagination of the left. By 1940 left-liberal folk-

lorists like Herbert Halpert and Benjamin Botkin had taken recording machines beyond the Archive of Folk Song, into the Federal Theatre Project, the Federal Music Project, and the Federal Writers Project, where they documented everything from children's rhymes to occupational lore to (in a project that Lomax himself helped initiate) the life histories of African Americans who had been born as slaves. Underlying these recording efforts was a commitment to a broadly inclusive American culture, a celebration of those voices of resistance and struggle that the powerful would prefer to drown out. That celebration owed a great deal to John Lomax's innovations and influence, for embedded in his search for authentic folk voices on the American margins was an expansive energy whose radical potential Lomax himself could never really acknowledge, and perhaps could not altogether perceive.

OF ALL THE FALLOUT FROM LOMAX'S COLLISION WITH Leadbelly, all the invective and accusations, none of it was as painful to him as the drama that played out with his son Alan. From the beginning, and even as tensions had mounted, Alan had always been close to the singer, who seemed genuinely fond of the "Little Boss," and Leadbelly's return to Shreveport left Alan (as Lomax put it) "cut up," torn, and deeply upset. In the aftermath, Lomax wanted his son's life to get back to normal. Above all, he wanted him to return to his studies at the University of Texas. Alan had enrolled there in 1933 after spending a year at Harvard, but since then their song-gathering treks had disrupted his studies. Lomax had great hopes for his son's academic achievements, believing him capable of taking folklore to a new pinnacle of scholarly renown. Alan,

Alan Lomax.
Courtesy of the Alan
Lomax Archive.

however, had plans of his own, and eventually Lomax assented: he would return to the university in the autumn, but first he would head out on the road, collecting songs in Florida and Georgia with Mary Elizabeth Barnicle and Zora Neale Hurston.

The third of Lomax's four children, Alan was his father's favorite, like him bright and quick-witted, gregarious and charming, prickly and pugnacious. Nearly everyone who met him agreed that there was something special about him. Spotting him on the street in Austin, Lomax's friend Roy Bedichek discerned a figure straight out of Walt Whitman, "bare-throated, bearded, rough, but clean inside and out," "as picturesque and belligerent a vagabond as I ever saw." To

Carl Sandburg, he seemed "intensely American and flagrantly and vagrantly modern, somewhat of my own trend except that I could never begin to catch him in certain areas of mental efficiency." From early on, his sharp mind and winning manner made him the focus of his father's sense of thwarted ambition. On the road in 1933, as they battled heat, mosquitoes, recurrent malaria, and a disk recorder that continually broke down, Lomax watched with pride and satisfaction as Alan threw himself into the work. That trek convinced him that, if nothing else, his son was a natural folklorist. "We did well for so short a stay," he wrote to Ruby Terrill from Galveston, Texas, "thanks to the fine impression Alan makes by his earnest sincerity."

For all the pleasures of that journey, one source of tension still simmered between them. Back in 1932, while an undergraduate at Harvard, Alan had been arrested for taking part in a political demonstration demanding the release of Edith Berkman, a Communist Party activist and union organizer who was facing deportation. That incident, which prompted him to withdraw from the university, left John Lomax angry and distraught. "It distressed my father very, very much," Alan would recall. "I had to defend my righteous position, and he couldn't understand me and I couldn't understand him. It made a lot of unhappiness for the two of us because he loved Harvard and wanted me to be a great success there." In the months that followed, arguments raged between them about Alan's "communistic activities" and "communist friends." Indeed, in taking Alan out on the road, Lomax may well have hoped to ease the tensions that had grown up between them, as well as to get him away from unhealthy influences. "He needs to build himself up physically," he wrote to Ruby Terrill, "and he will also benefit from the breaking of associations with extreme radicals and rebels against society (the most of them Jews) that he has consorted with at the University."

Faced in 1935 with the prospect of Alan's trek south, at the outset he did not put "Miss Barnicle" (as he always called her) in that category. For all their political differences, he considered her a friend, delighting in her flattery (she once introduced him to her class at New York University as "a ballad in himself"), her merry disposition, her silvery laugh, and her "generosity to me and mine," which he deemed "quite past understanding." Barnicle had lent him her house in Wilton, introduced him to New York literati, and lifted his spirits during the darkest days with Leadbelly. "I am quite satisfied to have Alan under her influence," he wrote to Ruby Terrill as the summer trek loomed. "For many of her judgments I am in disagreement. She is, however, wholesome and honest and seems fond of Alan and he of her. I know she would save him from harm even as you and I. Then he must go his own way some time."

The journey began in June. While Lomax traveled back to Austin, Alan, Barnicle, and Hurston headed to St. Simon's Island off the coast of Georgia, equipped with a recording machine provided by the Library of Congress. The result, Alan wrote in August, was "the most exciting field trip I have made," an adventure whose story "really can only be told in a long, rambling novel." With Hurston's help they rented "a little Negro shantey" in an isolated island community and found themselves "on such friendly terms with the Negroes as I had never experienced before." Issuing a call for folksingers, on the first night they found their front yard jammed with musicians, and in a week's time they had made forty recordings of spirituals, work songs, ring shouts, and "jook" music. Then they moved on to Hurston's hometown of Eatonville, Florida, and to Lake Okeechobee in the Everglades, where "folk-songs are thick as marsh mosquitoes." After that, "for various reasons," Hurston went back to New York, but he and Barnicle sailed on to the Bahamas. "Here we came and here we have remained ever since, bewitched by these fairy islands and busy recording the livest [*sic*] and most varied folk-culture we had yet run into." At the end of the summer, the pair traveled back to New York, having gathered some two hundred disks for deposit at the Archive of Folk Song. Back in Texas, Lomax read his son's letters with pride and pleasure, then waited impatiently for his return.

The first inkling he had that anything was amiss came in mid-September, when he received an indignant letter from Hurston.

My dear Mr. Lomax,

I thought once that this letter would not be necessary, but what I heard two nights ago make me feel that it is.

Miss Barnicle is not the generous disinterested friend of yours that you think. If she has her wish, Allan [*sic*] will not be back with you for years to come, if ever. She is trying to get him something to do so that he will not return to college this year, but will stay here in New York. For one thing she has a certain attachment for the boy and the next, she is trying to build herself a reputation as a folklorist thru the name of Lomax.

When she proposed that I go on this trip with them one of the things she earnestly urged upon me was that I must help her to get this lovely young man out of his stifling atmosphere.

He had a backward father who was smothering Allan with fogy ideas both of mind and body. I heard how you took that gentle poet and artist Leadbelly and dogged him around and only her sympathetic attitude and talks with him (when you were not present, of course) kept the poor fellow alive and believing in himself. Leadbelly got no ideas of persecution from the Negroes in the [V]illage as you supposed. He got them right there in the house in Wilton. Why? She was attracted to him as a man by her own admission. And next, she like all other Communists are making a play of being the friend of the Negro at present and stopping at nothing, *absolutely nothing* to accomplish their ends. . . .

One of the things that she is working hardest for is that Allan shall not return to Texas this fall. She says he does not need the schooling and he needs New York and freedom. I promised that I would help all I could to persuade him to that end. But Mr. Lomax when I met Allan and he told me his plans and talked about you in the way he did, I just could not find it in my heart to destroy the boy. That is what it would amount to in the end. . . . When I left Allan in early August he was in the notion of doing what you wished. Saturday night he came here and told me that [he] did not intend to return to Texas unless he couldn't find anything to do here. That you had written to him urging him to come home as soon as possible but that he wasn't going if he could help it. So you see, what she said was her objective on this trip south seems accomplished. I have not mentioned details and incidents because that would be too tiresome but I do know what I'm talking about. And none of it would add to your happiness. She knows that I see thru her and do not approve. She has used a great deal of sophistry on Allan to cover up and I have merely let him know that I do not think that she is clean. He is so terribly young and men are dumb for the most part before the tricks of women anyway.

At the core of Hurston's long, furious letter was an accusation: that Barnicle and the other "Reds" with whom Alan was associating were intent on turning him against his father, and that the crux of their indictment was his treatment of Leadbelly. Just how Lomax responded to Hurston's letter is hard to gauge. What evidence there is suggests that, at least at first, he ignored it. At that point Barnicle was still writing him warm and effusive letters, and he continued to like and trust her. (That, Hurston had written, was precisely the response the other woman was counting on: "She knows that I know, Oh God, just too much, but I am certain that she feels sure of you to the extent that you would never believe a word against her. Further you are a white southerner and I am a Negro and so I am certain that she feels that. . . you would never believe me.") In any case, whatever fears he had about Alan soon abated when his son returned to the University of Texas, where he received a degree in philosophy in 1936.

Yet in the long run, Lomax may well have cast his mind back to Hurston's warnings. Over the next few years, as Barnicle staked out a career as Leadbelly's manager, she and Alan maintained a close friendship, and as Alan became a fixture of New York's radical folk music circles, his ideas about folklore collecting aligned themselves ever-more pointedly with the left. In 1937 he replaced his father as assistant curator at the Archive of Folk Song, and in the ensuing years he filled the archive's shelves with material that John Lomax would never have countenanced, from proletarian folk songs by Woody Guthrie to militant union tunes by Aunt Molly Jackson to an eight-hour interview with Jelly Roll Morton, an attempt to document the "folk roots" of jazz, a music that his father detested. He even pushed for the accession of commercial recordings. In 1939 he spent several weeks surveying the output of the race and hillbilly labels, ultimately drawing up a "List of American Folk Songs on Commercial Records," which the archive made available to all who requested it. That process convinced him that folklorists' obsession with salvaging pristine rural purity had deafened them to what was most vibrant. What was most stunning was the sheer variety of those recorded voices: some rough and primitive, some urbane and sophisticated, but all revealing hidden currents of feeling, songs of love and lust and longing, of anger and fear and hard times. "The commercial recording companies have done a broader and more interesting job of recording American folk music than the folklorists," he told Harold Spivacke. "Every single item of recorded American rural, race, and popular material that they have in their current lists and plan to release in the future should be in our files."

Underlying all these initiatives was a new, politicized vision of what constituted folklore, a vision that was sweeping through the radical left. Material that his father (and, indeed, Hurston) would have dismissed as purely a product of urban corruption seemed to Alan to be authentic and vital, part of what his friend Benjamin Botkin termed "living lore." Unlike the folk song John Lomax searched for, living lore was not confined to prisons or similarly isolated rural enclaves. As "folklore in the making," it proliferated in the metropolis: in the songs and tales of seamstresses, construction workers, bus drivers, street peddlers, and the "symphony" of urban nightlife—"taxi dance halls, night clubs, honky tonks." That such songs were sometimes recorded commercially did not place them outside the category. As Botkin explained, the authenticity of living lore lay in something recording did not eradicate: its audible, palpable social dynamics. It was music that grew out of the rhythms of the workplace, whose lyrics spoke of everyday delights and frustrations, and sometimes of struggle and injustice. Like "the blues and reels and the work songs and 'hollers' of the Black South," it was a direct "expression of social change and culture conflict."

It was that vision of living lore, that search for social change and cultural conflict, that led Alan to what would become his best-remembered expedition. In 1941 he and the musicologist John Work and the sociologist Lewis Jones, both African American academics from Fisk University, launched a two-year survey of black music in Coahoma County, Mississippi, based in the county seat of Clarksdale. Though the region was overwhelmingly rural, this was no search for preindustrial musical relics: the aim, instead, as Alan put it, was "to explore objectively and exhaustively the musical habits of a single Negro community in the Delta, to find out and describe the function of music in the community, to ascertain the history of music in the community, and to document adequately the cultural and social backgrounds for music in the community." Far from using the phonograph to escape from the phonograph, they were out to trace the phonograph's influence: the records to be found on local jukeboxes, the recordings to be found in people's homes, and the recording artists who influenced the repertoire of local musicians. Of particular interest were local guitarists like McKinley Morganfield (whom the locals called Muddy Waters), who described their collections of phonograph records, or like Son House and Willie Brown, who had made commercial recordings themselves. Those aims marked the study as a direct assault on folkloric nostalgia. "It is a folklorist's illusion that folklore communities are pure, that the pure old tradition is the one most worth studying," Alan observed in his field notebook. Above all, he sought testimony of the music's relation to broader patterns of social life, including the racial injustices that his father had downplayed or denied.

For John Lomax, watching from the sidelines, all this seemed horribly misguided, and by the early 1940s he was writing to Alan weekly, sometimes daily, to tell him so. The task of a folklorist, he reminded his son, was "to record what you find, regardless of its import," not to seek support for a political dogma, which simply meant distorting the truth. The problem with "advanced Negroes" like the scholars from Fisk was that they set out to rewrite history, to present their people as they wished they were, in defiance of the unvarnished facts. Privately he feared that Alan had become "hopelessly involved in the slimy toils of Communism," and nothing he did seemed capable of extricating him. Alan wrote a few brief replies to his letters, but more often than not he left them unanswered. In that silence Lomax felt himself repudiated as a reactionary embarrassment, "a bourgeois southerner (I am so branded in your mind by Miss Barnicle)."

Although none of these developments owed directly to the debacle with Leadbelly, the memory of that encounter loomed over them, for as Alan became a folklorist in his own right, he brought Leadbelly along with him. Once the singer reconstituted himself as proletarian folk artist and began performing in New York under Barnicle's management, Alan helped to support him, recording him again for the Library of Congress and lending him money when his fortunes flagged. In 1938 Leadbelly and Martha stayed with Alan in his apartment in Washington and were thrown out of the building by Alan's racist landlord, an incident that Leadbelly commemorated in his song "Bourgeois Blues." One year later, when Leadbelly was involved in a stabbing and arrested on murder charges, Alan put up the money for his bail and then dropped out of Columbia (where he had begun a doctorate in anthropology) to help raise funds for his defense. Once Leadbelly was released from Riker's Island, Alan became his most ardent promoter. In March 1940 they appeared together at a "Grapes of Wrath" evening at New York's Town Hall, a benefit performance for migrant farm workers, and throughout that spring and summer he featured the singer on a radio series on American folk song that he wrote and directed for CBS. Listening to the broadcasts from Austin, John Lomax declared Leadbelly bereft of any appeal (though more listenable than another regular artist, "the Oklahoma Dust Bowl man," Woody Guthrie, whom he judged "an absolute zero on any program at any time"). Meanwhile, Lomax was acutely aware of how he himself was figuring in the evolving Leadbelly legend. That same summer he had a bruising encounter with Mary Elizabeth Barnicle, who no longer made any pretense of civility and brusquely told him that all of New York condemned him for his treatment of the singer.

In response, Lomax's own estimation of Leadbelly turned increasingly caustic. "Save for being a triple murderer, a drunkard, a congenital liar, and a super double super hypocrite Leadbelly is a most excellent guitar picker," he told a journalist in 1944. "He quickly spoiled his singing by adopting the patter of the city slicker." By then it had become clear that his relationship with his son had irrevocably changed. Although Alan never criticized him in public, never expressed anything other than pride in his father's achievements, in his actions he had quietly, remorselessly distanced himself. Once, it had seemed

as though their shared love for folklore would act as a bond between them, as it had when Alan was a small, sickly child,
when his father carried him outdoors on hot Texas nights and
sang him folk songs to lull him to sleep, and as it had on their
penitentiary trek in the summer of 1933, when he watched
Alan fiddle with the controls on the disk recorder to hide the
tears welling up in his eyes. In his son, Lomax wrote in a moment of anguish in 1940, he had invested "the core and center
of my being." Small wonder, then, that in Leadbelly's renown
he saw the gulf that had grown up between them, all the ways
in which his favorite child had gone astray.

IN THE FINAL YEARS OF HIS LIFE, THE LEFT'S FOCUS ON
living lore steadily pushed John Lomax to the sidelines, and he
watched with growing bitterness as his vision of field recording
was harnessed to a politics that he abhorred. Briefly employed
as a kind of éminence grise as folklore editor on the Federal
Writers Project, he was soon replaced by Benjamin Botkin,
and when he returned to the field with a disk recorder, the
Library of Congress showed polite but perfunctory interest. In
response, Lomax devoted himself to battling what he saw as
the left's distortions. He was outraged late in 1938 when the
poet Sterling Brown, who headed the collection of Negro folklore for the Federal Writers Project, alleged (inaccurately) that
Bessie Smith had bled to death in a car crash in the Mississippi
Delta because white ambulance staff had refused to respond
to the call. The tale instantly entered left mythology, and Lomax threw himself into its refutation, amassing a pile of letters
from Mississippi health care officials to document their timely
response. Brown's accusation, Lomax fumed to Alan, was "an

outrageous slander on the Southern white man." What was at stake here was the region's essential decency and justice, a belief that not even Lomax's tour through southern penitentiaries could shake.

In February 1947, eleven months before the heart attack that killed him, he published his autobiography, *Adventures of a Ballad Hunter*. The original manuscript contained a lengthy account of his travails with Leadbelly, clearly an attempt to get the last word, to set out the definitive story and free himself from lingering charges of exploitation and racism. His publisher, however, thought its inclusion "unwise." Lomax based his account on extracts from his letters to Ruby Terrill, which revealed more than he realized of his convoluted racial assumptions. Though Lomax could not see that—he felt sure that any sensible reader could see that he had behaved with complete justification—his editor insisted that the chapter's inclusion might provoke a lawsuit. In the end, Lomax deleted the chapter entirely and mentioned Leadbelly only in passing.

Instead, he told the story of his friendship, at the age of nine, with a neighbor's eighteen-year-old black servant, Nat Blythe. It was Nat, he explained, who inspired his interest in African American music. He had taught Nat to read and given him lessons in history, geography, and math, and in return Nat taught Lomax about black song and dance. "From Nat I learned my sense of rhythm. He danced rather than walked," moving with "such enthusiastic abandon that all of us would join in the patting and dancing." Three years after they met, Nat received a thousand dollars from his master and set out for the city to seek his fortune. "I have never since seen or heard of him," he concluded. "His Negro friends think he was murdered for his money, and his body, bound with baling wire and weighted down with scrap iron, thrown into the Bosque River. As I have traveled up and down the South these recent years, I find myself always looking for Nat, the dear friend and companion of long ago. I loved him as I have loved few people."

Lomax asks us to see the sum of his journeys across the South as a prolonged search to recover an intimacy lost in childhood. Perhaps this story reveals more than he intended, not just about his attempts to befriend Leadbelly and Iron Head, but about how at some level he needed them to go wrong. Nat Blythe, he suggests, was killed not by whites but by fellow Negroes en route to the city, like him seduced by the false promises of the modern age. Lomax's spectacular ruptures with his black protégés allowed him to relive the pain of that loss, to reassure himself that the intimacy he had cherished could not be recaptured, to persuade himself that it was modernity, not southern injustice, that had destroyed that beautiful dream.

$\backsim$ *five* $\backsim$

Been Here and Gone

W HEN THEY LOOKED BACK TO THE BEGINNING, FRED-
eric Ramsey, Charles Edward Smith, and William Russell remembered the rundown building on the corner of U
Street in Washington, D.C., with a hamburger joint on the
ground floor and no indication of anything else. It was the late
1930s, they were white, and this was a segregated black neighborhood, but still they opened the door alongside the burger
shop and climbed the rickety stairs. On the top floor was a
large, dingy room; the dank, chill air was barely affected by the
coal-black iron stove. Only the bar, the jukebox, and the battered piano indicated that it was a nightclub, which for a time
had been called the Music Box but now had been rechristened
the Jungle Inn. Behind the bar, mixing a drink for a customer,
was a light-skinned black man of uncertain age, thin, slow-
moving (in retrospect they realized he was sick), and the look
he gave them was somber and grave. At first he did not seem
to believe that they were interested in hearing his music, the

hits he had generated on the Victor label before his fortunes turned sour in the Depression. But eventually he unplugged the jukebox and sat down at the piano, and before he played, when he flashed them a brief, wary smile, the light glinted on a diamond in his front tooth.

So incandescent was that introduction to Jelly Roll Morton that the three men would later downplay the long quest that had led to it: years spent listening to race records and foraging tirelessly for those they could not easily find. Ramsey's passion for Morton's recordings had hit him in the early 1930s when he was a student at Princeton, around the same time that it overtook Charles Edward Smith. But it was William Russell who had heard him first. Back in 1929, when he was teaching music composition at a high school on Staten Island, Russell had asked his students to bring in some of their parents' records from home. As a classically trained violinist, he expected the exercise would demonstrate the supremacy of the European tradition, but among the disks brought in was "Shoeshiners' Drag" by Jelly Roll Morton and His Red Hot Peppers. From the first bars Russell was hooked. The sheer complexity of the music was what was most immediately striking—the dazzling, rich, polyphonic rhythms, as intricate as anything Arnold Schoenberg had devised but even more vital and free. Since childhood Russell had nurtured ambitions to be a composer, but what he was hearing was so much more imaginative, so much more sophisticated, than anything he could possibly write.

In the years that followed, Russell made it a mission to acquire all of Morton's recordings. The expense was not an issue: no one else seemed to want them, and you could buy the records in bulk for as little as thirty-five cents a box. The prob-

Charles Edward Smith, William Russell, and Frederic Ramsey,
July 1941, the day after Jelly Roll Morton died.
Courtesy of the Historic New Orleans Collection.

lem was finding them. Morton had recorded his sides for Victor and Gennett in the early 1920s, and since then black consumers had consigned him to the margins. Finding his recordings meant devising strategies to unearth what African American listeners regarded as outdated, obsolete rubbish.

Occasionally Russell got lucky and found a cache of old Mortons in music stores in midtown Manhattan. More often, he took the subway up to Harlem and combed dime stores and junk shops and the Salvation Army. In 1934 he took a job as an accompanist for a theater troupe and began crisscrossing the country, and during his travels he rummaged for old records in St. Louis and Detroit and on the South Side of Chicago. Eventually, he helped to set up a trading post for old records in Manhattan, the Hot Record Exchange, in 1936, and there he crossed paths with Ramsey and Smith. They made an odd trio—Russell an eccentric, close-mouthed, balding curmudgeon; Ramsey a suave, garrulous, six-foot-five patrician; Smith a boyish, earnest, resolute Marxist who wrote jazz criticism for the *Daily Worker*—but they learned to share the labor between them, trading tips and comparing finds and canvassing the country for records the others wanted.

Still, for all that the quest for old records consumed them, Morton himself seemed fated to exist only as an evocative name on a faded label, a genius whom the undiscerning had forgotten and no one knew how to track down. Then in 1937 Charles Edward Smith moved to Washington, D.C., to work for the Federal Writers Project, and that spring he read a single, astonishing sentence in the jazz magazine *Down Beat:* "To many who have wondered what has become of 'Jelly Roll' Morton, this may be good news—Morton is featured at the Jungle Inn, local sepia spot, where he is billed as 'The Originator of Jazz and Swing.'"

Within weeks Smith had become a club regular, as were Ramsey and Russell when they were in town, and soon Morton's presence was well-enough known that a coterie gathered around him. Apart from the poet Sterling Brown (who sometimes joined Morton at the keyboard), most of the enthusiasts were white record collectors who discouraged Morton from composing new material (he occasionally dreamed of writing pop songs for jukeboxes). Sitting around, asking him questions, they found that it was easy to get him to talk, and so they urged him to tell stories and spin out the numbers he remembered from old New Orleans.

In a short time, those collectors' enthusiasm had stoked Morton's latent desires to claim a formative place in jazz history. Late in March 1938, Morton tuned in to one of his favorite radio programs, "Ripley's Believe It or Not," and heard an interview with the composer W. C. Handy, who was introduced as the father of blues and jazz. Neglected by record buyers, forgotten by jazz fans, his songs reworked and his royalties stolen by younger composers, Morton felt insulted beyond endurance, and in response he unleashed a four-thousand-word letter to the jazz and African American press.

> Dear Mr. Ripley:
>
> For many years I have been a constant reader of your cartoon. I have listened to your broadcast with keen interest. I frankly believe your broadcast is a great contribution to natural science.
>
> In your broadcast of March 26, 1938, you introduced W. C. Handy as the originator of jazz, stomps, and blues. By this announcement you have done me a great injustice and you have almost misled many of your fans. . . .
>
> It is evidently known, beyond contradiction, that New Orleans is the cradle of jazz, and I, myself, happened to be the creator in the year 1902. . . . In the year 1908 . . . I met Handy in Memphis. He was introduced to me as Prof. Handy. Who ever heard of anyone wearing the name of a professor advocate Ragtime, Jazz, Stomps, Blues, etc?. . . Of course, Handy could not play any of these types and I can assure you has not learned them yet. . . .
>
> Mr. Handy cannot prove anything in music that he has created. He has possibly taken advantage of some unprotected material that floats around. . . . This very minute, you have confronting the world all kinds of Kings, Czars, Dukes, Princes and Originators of Swing (*swing* is just another name for *jazz*) and they know that the titles are deceiving. . . . I would like to put a lie tester on many of these make-believe stalwarts of originality. Mr. Ripley, these untruthful statements

Mr. Handy has made, or caused you to make, will maybe
cause him to be branded the most dastardly impostor in the
history of music.

. . . Music is such a tremendous proposition that it probably needs government supervision. . . . There are many who
enjoy glory plus financial gains and abundance, even in the
millions, who should be digging ditches or sweeping the
streets. Lack of proper protection causes this. . . . I only give
you facts that you may force your pal to his rightful position in
fair life. Lord protect us from more Hitlers and Mussolinis.

Very truly yours,

Jelly Roll Morton
Originator of Jazz and Stomps
Victor Artist
World's Greatest Hot Tune Writer

As Morton began devising a narrative of his role in jazz history, he formulated it on a mythic scale, and for that reason
Smith recommended him to Alan Lomax. Though Lomax was
not a jazz fan, he and Smith both frequented the watering
holes of Washington's radical left, and Smith knew of Lomax's
desire to create a new, progressive canon of American folk
song, a more expansive sense of who "the people" could be.
Perhaps Lomax even told him of a book he had been reading,
Howard Odum's *Rainbow Round My Shoulder,* which had gotten him thinking about new uses for recording equipment,
how it could capture not only songs but the sound and flavor of
vernacular speech. What had enchanted him about Odum's
book was the sheer musicality of Left Wing Gordon's reminiscences, the way he moved back and forth between speaking
and singing and seemed to make no real distinction between

them. That Morton could prove just as eloquent a memoirist Smith could not have doubted. Morton was an unparalleled raconteur. Since he had begun his career in New Orleans at the turn of the century, he could provide a kind of folk history that folklorists had roundly neglected, of African American secular song in its earliest, seediest, most disreputable days.

Lomax was intrigued enough by Morton to book the Coolidge Auditorium at the Library of Congress for several recording sessions from late May until the middle of June. "[Morton] will trace by piano and narrative the trend of popular American music from the standard sentimental songs, through ragtime and up to jazz," explained the *Washington Daily News.* "The man Jelly Roll, also a singer of real caliber, will tell stories into his records, old song legends of the South, particularly New Orleans. The piano as a secondary medium will illustrate the stories. In short, history illustrated with music."

Ramsey, Smith, and Russell expected great things from the sessions, but once they heard the copies of the recordings that Lomax dubbed for them, they were astonished beyond their wildest expectations at how extraordinary a source the man had turned out to be. All Lomax had needed to do was sit Morton at the piano, turn on the machine, ask a few questions, and keep the glass of whiskey brimming, and Morton would unleash a flood of remembered melody and anecdote. Lomax asked him about the men and women he had known in his early days in New Orleans, and Morton told him about the great musicians like Tony Jackson, a "sissy-man" and a fabulous composer and one of the greatest pianists who ever lived, and Buddy Bolden, "the blowingest man ever lived since Gabriel," who blew his brains out through his trumpet and ended up in the crazy house. He remembered the Broadway

Swells, the gang of toughs he used to run with and sing with and march with in the Mardi Gras parades. They were musicians and pimps—sweetback men, Morton called them—who lived off the earnings of fifth-rate whores; Morton had been bewitched by their sense of style, their red-flannel undershirts and jackets with turned-up collars and cork-soled shoes with gambler designs on the toes, and by the moseying walk they called "shooting the agate," their hands at their sides, their index fingers extended, moving in a slow, deliberate strut. He told Lomax about the rough camaraderie of the honky-tonks, where St. Charles millionaires rubbed shoulders with longshoremen and guys from the levee who didn't bathe more than once in six months. Some of them were gamblers with names like Chicken Dick and Boar Hog and Sheep Bite, men so mean and heartless they could chew up pig iron and spit out razor blades. He demonstrated how they played cards, the game they called Georgia Skin, slapping his hand on the piano bench to mimic the sound of the card hitting the table. As he played, his heel thumped out the beat and his speaking voice itself became music, soft and guttural and melodic by turns.

There could be no question that the recordings were poetry, all nine hours of them, but one moment stood out above all. It came in the last session, on June 12, in which Morton was re-creating the soundscape of Storyville, the city's red-light district, where music poured out of all the houses and everyone was wild about the blues. All you had to do was walk down Basin Street and you would hear it through the open windows, from the small-time cribs where they charged fifty cents to the mansions like Lulu White's, where the mirror alone cost thirty thousand dollars. Women sang blues in the doorways to tout for business and to convey every imaginable shade of feeling, and when Morton started playing piano in the district, he learned to sing them too. By then he had picked up the name of Sweet Pappa Jelly Roll, and he wore a Stetson hat and a peacock-blue coat and eighteen-dollar striped trousers that fit as tight as a sausage casing, and all the women who saw him were just dying to turn his damper down.

Then Morton paused and in a soft voice recalled the first blues he had ever heard. One day as a young boy, visiting his godmother in the Garden District, he heard music drifting from the house next door, home to a singer and prostitute named Mamie Desdoumes. "On her right hand she had her two middle fingers between her forefingers cut off," he remembered, "and she played with the three, cause she played a blues like this, all day long when she first would get up in the morning." And as his own fingers teased out a few halting, stumbling notes, he sang:

> I stood on the corner, my feet was dripping wet
> I stood on the corner, my feet was dripping wet
> I asked every man I met.
>
> Can't give me a dollar, give me a lousy dime
> Can't give me a dollar, give me a lousy dime
> Just to feed that hungry man of mine.
>
> I got a husband and I got a kid man too
> I got a husband and I got a kid man too
> My husband can't do what my kid man can do
>
> I like the way he cooks my cabbage for me
> I like the way he cooks my cabbage for me
> Looks like he sets my natural soul free

The song ended there, Morton's lilting, feminine vocal sub-merged beneath the hiss of the needle on vinyl, but that melody, those lyrics, in their sheer mournful magic they lingered on.

It would be another twelve months before they heard the song again, during a recording session of New Orleans greats that Smith and Russell assembled in New York City, Morton playing that hesitant three-fingered piano as Sidney Bechet and Frederic Ramsey listened in, and more years still before Ramsey went to New Orleans and tracked down Mamie's house on Toledano Street. But from that moment they were caught in its echoes, intent on recapturing the world it evoked: the vanished enclave of Storyville, where the air smelled of sex and blood and longing, and where pimps and whores sang the blues.

———

TODAY, SOME SEVENTY YEARS AFTER HE SAT DOWN AT THE piano in the Coolidge Auditorium, Jelly Roll Morton's Library of Congress interview has become the stuff of legend: a set of recordings of unparalleled frankness and vigor, so obscene in places that some of the sessions remained buried in the library vaults for a full fifty years. Yet what has been forgotten is the singular context out of which they emerged, the community that pushed Morton forward and that, in the wake of the interviews, determined to build on Lomax's initiative.

In the autumn of 1938, weeks after the Library of Congress sessions had been completed, Smith, Ramsey, and Russell secured a book contract for what they envisioned as a new kind of jazz history, for which they would track down every New Orleans musician who might have memories of the music's beginnings. The result, published in October 1939, was *Jazzmen,* the first history of jazz by American writers and the first anywhere to be based on research. Its rhapsodic portrait of the music of Storyville created an international sensation and helped to generate what became a New Orleans revival, an attempt to recapture what jazz fans imagined as black music at its most authentic and vital, the sound of the turn-of-the-century red-light district, of New Orleans in its glory days.

If Smith, Ramsey, and Russell are remembered at all since then, it is as reactionary antiquarians, "moldy figs" opposed to musical innovation in any form. Jazz historians tend to scorn them, and blues aficionados ignore them entirely. No books chronicling blues history give *Jazzmen* so much as a mention: it is a minor footnote to a different story, a brief flurry in the development of a different musical form.

That blues and jazz are separate, distinct musics has been an axiom of blues history since the 1960s. Going back to the interwar years, one finds the matter is not so simple. Throughout his interview with Alan Lomax, Morton used the words "jazz" and "blues" more or less interchangeably, as did race record advertisements in the African American press, where the term "blues," like "jazz," signified simply "black popular music," whether or not it had the so-called blues chord progression or an AAB rhyming scheme.

No less than Dorothy Scarborough or John Lomax, the *Jazzmen* cohort were visionaries and dreamers obsessed with uncovering uncorrupted black music, yet they envisioned that purity in the red-light district, in the terrain of urban dissipation that the likes of Scarborough feared most. That they found authenticity in the metropolis to some extent comes down to their politics. The 1930s saw the emergence of a vibrant circle of jazz aficionados who understood jazz as an urban music and whose romance with its collective improvisations was infused with the politics of the Popular Front. Yet, though the *Jazzmen* writers were on the left (Ramsey a pacifist, Russell a New Deal liberal, Smith, some claim, a Communist Party member), politics alone does not explain the lure that Storyville held out for them. Whereas conventional folklorists had been driven by nostalgia for music heard in live performance, the *Jazzmen* set were impelled by commercial recordings—records by Jelly Roll Morton and Joseph "King" Oliver that were manufactured in the 1920s and that sometime in the early 1930s Smith, Russell, and Ramsey began to collect.

"There is a world of difference between the blues as collectors know them and the folk stuff [that the Lomaxes] waxed for the Archive," Smith explained in 1939. The latter was simply anachronistic, the product of folklorists' imaginations, while the real blues, the blues that mattered, was the product of the modern world. "Most of us" (he was writing to his fellow collectors) "think that folk music went into a decline in the last century to make way for a few bright blasts on a golden horn."

That horn first sounded in Storyville. It signaled the rise of a blues that was very different from that sought by John Lomax. It was urban, sexual, and proletarian, and in collectors' imaginations it was first voiced by prostitutes touting for business and echoed by the rough, dirty melodies blown out of Buddy Bolden's cornet, "Kid" Ory's trombone, and Sidney Bechet's saxophone.

———

BEHIND THE PUBLICATION OF *JAZZMEN* LAY A DEVELOPMENT that no one anticipated: the mass production of popular music

generated a vast amount of waste matter, unsold and discarded
recordings, some of which could have a second life. That res-
urrection began in the early 1930s, and it proved no less startling to the musicians whose recordings aficionados were after.
One young enthusiast, Kenneth Hulsizer, found as much when
he tracked down Jelly Roll Morton at the Jungle Inn and began bombarding him with questions about the supporting
players—the "personnels," in the argot of collectors—on his
1920s recordings.

Though to Hulsizer's delight Morton "looked much like his
pictures in the old Victor Race Catalogues," he was by then
poor, embittered, and bewildered by Hulsizer's interest. It
took some time for Hulsizer to convince him that he was neither a talent scout nor an FBI agent but simply in search of information about wax platters that Morton had forgotten about
long ago.

> He had never heard of a record collector. I was the first one
> he had ever met. When I asked him if he had any of his old
> records, he laughed and said, "No, what would anyone want
> of those old things." Records were merely something made to
> get a little money and to spread his name. A profitable sort of
> publicity device. The only music that counted was the music
> that you played directly to people who applauded and paid to
> hear you.

Though Morton's dismissal of phonograph records
stemmed in part from his roots in New Orleans jazz, whose improvisations the recording process curtailed, his bewilderment
when confronted by a record collector appears to have been
broadly shared. What seemed inexplicable was the urge to

hoard a manufactured product whose makers intended it to be ephemeral. Pressed by the thousands in factories, sold for small change over the counter, recordings in the 1930s had an exceptionally brief shelf life. With the coming of the Great Depression, race labels of the 1920s like OKeh and Electrobeam Gennett had been forced out of business and replaced by new, larger recording conglomerates that supplied recorded music for jukeboxes and the radio, generating a steady stream of popular hits. Radio and jukeboxes placed a premium upon novelty, playing recordings for a few weeks or months before replacing them with others more freshly pressed. Collectors amassed paintings, ceramics, exotic plant specimens, unique items of enduring cultural value—surely not mass-produced commodities designed to be discarded fast.

Yet it was precisely in the 1930s, as their shelf life contracted, that race records became collectable objects. That was when the passion first hit Frederic Ramsey. Born in 1915 in Pennsylvania, Ramsey had grown up in a hothouse of art and ideas. His father, Charles Frederic Ramsey, himself the son of an artist, was an abstract painter who had served as the director of the Minneapolis School of Art until he was dismissed because of his socialist leanings. The family resettled in New Hope, Pennsylvania, where they found a community of dissident intellectuals (including a pair of Quaker social scientists, Edward and Emily Mead, whose daughter Margaret was Fred's babysitter).

From early on, the younger Ramsey displayed a flair for the written word. Valedictorian of his class at Solebury School, he enrolled at Princeton to study modern languages and represented the university on a goodwill trip to France, where he researched an essay by interviewing James Joyce, a feat considered so audacious it was reported by the *New York Times.* His senior thesis on the fictional techniques of Rabelais won him the Prix France-Amérique for sensitivity to European culture. When he moved to New York to take a job in publishing, his teachers and acquaintances expected great things.

All of which made what happened next seem inconceivable. While he was at Princeton, Ramsey had begun amassing disused recordings by King Oliver and Kid Ory and Jelly Roll Morton, black musicians whose names did not figure on the Hit Parade. Occasionally he could find the disks at the record store across from the university library, but mostly it meant making trips to New York, scavenging through junk shops in midtown, or going up to Harlem and making the rounds of the general stores.

On the eve of his move to New York, in the summer of 1936, Ramsay had a letter read out on the WABC radio broadcast "World of Swing," in which he identified himself as a record collector. Among those who responded was the show's scriptwriter, Charles Edward Smith. "I liked your letter for its emphasis upon the good jazz of other years," Smith wrote. "It's worth while skimping on current stuff to get together a worth while collection of the best men of the past."

That shared quest to find disks by "the best men of the past" cemented Ramsey's friendships in New York with a group of like-minded enthusiasts: Smith, John Hammond, Marshall Stearns, Stephen Smith, Charles Payne Rogers, and William Russell (with whom Ramsey found an apartment). By the time Ramsey moved to New York, those scattered aficionados had already coalesced into a subculture. In 1934, Smith had published an article called "Collecting Hot" in the men's magazine *Esquire,* and abruptly what had been a pastime or an interest had an identity attached to it. As Smith explained it, collectors were defined by their passionate commitment, driven at once by the sound of the music and, not inconsiderably, by the thrill of the chase. Race record sales in the 1920s had depended on mail order and on stores in black neighborhoods, and the most unlikely outlets would stock them, from pharmacies to funeral parlors. Finding those disks several years after their release meant canvassing the black sections of cities for commodities long ago discarded or forgotten.

William Russell, a classically trained composer and violinist whose passion for the recordings of Jelly Roll Morton led him to abandon composing entirely, learned to go door-to-door in Harlem and on the South Side of Chicago, where the Depression had transformed streets like Cottage Grove Avenue into "one solid row of junk shops . . . [with] victrola records stowed away in every corner." "Make out a want list of all the things you would take in any kind of 'beat up' condition," he wrote to Frederic Ramsey on the eve of one such expedition. "Just list the things you don't have, which you can hardly expect to find new, and would be willing to take even badly worn, or else mark 'good condition only' after title." While finding mint-condition recordings was best, scratches could be welcomed as badges of honor, physical evidence of the collector's discernment, his capacity to reclaim material that undiscriminating consumers had consigned to the rubbish heap.

Behind that capacity for discrimination lay a kind of ad hoc training and a self-confidence honed in the Ivy League. Most of the early collectors, like the Princeton graduate Ramsey, were products of elite universities, where they nurtured their passion for music in campus clubs devoted to the appreciation of "hot jazz." In 1935 Stearns and Hammond, both Yale gradu-

ates, founded the United Hot Clubs of America, a campus network committed to advancing the jazz recording as "a worthy
cultural object of study." Hot Clubs functioned as an informal
tutorial in taste and aesthetics, dedicated to the practice of
studious listening, of applying intellectual effort to mass-
produced objects, and learning to distinguish the fake stuff
from the real.

Making those kinds of judgments did not require aesthetic
training (apart from William Russell, few collectors had a formal education in music). More important was a talent for argument—though the collectors thrived on an atmosphere of
tribal commitment, they did not generate a party line. Indeed,
to read the bits of journalism and criticism produced by the
likes of Smith, Stearns, and Hammond is to enter a world of
intense antagonisms, of passionately sectarian schisms over
which performers and which recordings most fully embodied
the true spirit of jazz.

For Smith, Russell, and Ramsey, the answer was clear: the
true spirit of jazz could best be discerned on a set of recordings made in the 1920s for the Gennett and Victor labels by
Jelly Roll Morton, King Oliver, Kid Ory, and Louis Armstrong—all black natives of New Orleans. The intensity with
which they held to this view was only in part a response to the
music. Just as centrally, they were challenging the underlying
assumptions that informed both collectors' circles and writing
in the popular press: that, although jazz was undeniably black
in its origins, only white musicians, with their greater capacity
for creative thinking, had transformed it into art.

"There will always be wayward, instinctive, and primitive
geniuses who will affect us directly, without interposition of
the intellect," Gilbert Seldes had written in 1923. "[Yet] the

greatest art is likely to be that in which an uncorrupted sensibility is *worked* by a creative intelligence. So far in their music the negroes have given their response to the world with an exceptional naivete, a directness of expression which has interested our minds as well as touched our emotions; they have shown comparatively little evidence of the functioning of their intelligence." Fifteen years later, that attitude persisted. Ramsey and his cohort discerned it above all in the popular fascination with Bix Beiderbecke, the white Chicago cornetist who played beautifully, lived dangerously, and died young of alcoholism in 1931. That fascination—which reached a peak in 1938 with the publication of Dorothy Baker's novel, *Young Man with a Horn*—posed Beiderbecke as jazz incarnate, a self-willed outsider in thrall to primitive sounds that by sheer creative brilliance he raised to the status of art.

By the late 1930s, Ramsey lamented, even in collectors' circles "everyone was talking Bix and Chicago." To do so, as they saw it, was to buy into a story that pushed black creativity to the margins. Even while Bix fans lauded jazz as a kind of outsider art, they replicated the racism of the Hit Parade, in which white musicians like Paul Whiteman and Benny Goodman were propelled to the foreground, while brilliant black innovators like Johnny Dodds and Tommy Ladnier were left to die in obscurity and want. The more they argued with their fellow collectors, the more Smith and Ramsey longed for some new kind of jazz chronicle—not yet another piece of jazz criticism, but a different sort of story that would put the focus on black creativity, where it rightfully belonged.

Then in the autumn of 1938, a few months after Jelly Roll Morton completed his interviews at the Library of Congress, Frederic Ramsey was approached by an editor at Harcourt

Brace, where he worked as a clerk in the sales department, and asked to comment on a manuscript on jazz. He returned it the next morning with the margins full of invective. It was a miserable book, as miserable as virtually everything written on jazz, all uninformed claims and superficial opinion, with no sense of where the music had come from or why. Smith had told him about Morton and his sessions with Lomax, so he knew that a deeper and more vibrant story was out there, and reading this manuscript convinced him that it had to be told. He knew about the writers and photographers Smith was meeting in Washington, D.C., Alan Lomax and Benjamin Botkin among them, who were forging new, progressive forms of documentation that pushed the experience of marginal peoples to the foreground and gave them space to speak for themselves. Jazz needed that kind of story: a definitive account of its origins, which could only come from the mouths of the musicians who had created it. Most importantly, he knew the men who could uncover the tale. He and his friends, he told the editor, "could do a better book."

—•—

OPEN THE COVER OF *JAZZMEN* AND TURN TO THE FRON-tispiece, and you see what was designed to distinguish this book from everything published on jazz until that point.

> Now here is the list about that Jazz Playing. King Bolden and myself were the first men that began playing jazz in the city of dear old New Orleans and his band had the whole of New Orleans real crazy and running wild behind it. Now that was all you could hear in New Orleans, that King Bolden's band, and I was with him and that was between 1895 and 1896 and

they did not have any dixie land Jazz Band in those days. . . .
So you tell them that Bunk and King Bolden's Band was the
first ones that started Jazz in the City or any place else. And
now you are able to go ahead with your Book.

The quote came from a letter to Ramsey and William Russell from William Geary "Bunk" Johnson, an elderly trumpet
player whom they found picking sugarcane in New Iberia,
Louisiana. Ramsey and Russell had been steered to Johnson
by Louis Armstrong and a few other New Orleans musicians,
who thought they remembered "someone called Bunk" playing in the city in the early days.

Johnson's claims to have been there at the beginning,
which he would ultimately parlay into recording sessions and
concert appearances, were central to the sensation that
Jazzmen created and to the ridicule that has enveloped the
book ever since. For a generation of jazz enthusiasts, *Jazzmen*
became a kind of Bible. Its racy, lyrical portraits of the music's
beginnings gave it a readership that never seemed to diminish:
the book would go through multiple reprints (including a
pocket-sized edition marketed to soldiers during World War
II). Yet Bunk, its key source, although a consummate talker,
was quickly revealed to be unreliable: ten years younger than
he claimed, Johnson had never been a member of Bolden's ensemble. That Ramsey and Russell swallowed his tales has led
many historians to dismiss them as credulous dupes and to
write off the value of the book altogether.

Yet to lambaste *Jazzmen* for its failure to distinguish fact
from fiction is to misconstrue what the book is about. Steeped
in the methods and ethos of the New Deal's Federal Writers
Project, the authors had set out to compile (in the phrase of

the period) a "folk history," whose value lay in the sheer vigor of the testimony of the people themselves. The introduction emphasized the importance of firsthand accounts of jazz's beginnings, of gathering memories of participants and witnesses and getting them down in their subjects' exact words. "One or another of the authors has interviewed every living jazz musician who could contribute factual material," they noted. "In some cases, their remarks were directly transcribed in shorthand; in others, careful notes were taken. The sum-total of information obtained in this manner was then typed and made available to all the contributors." They presented the book, in other words, as a collaboration between the (mostly) white interviewers and their (mostly) black subjects. The truth they aspired to was poetic, not literal, conveyed not by solid nuggets of information independently verified by outside authorities, but by color, by atmosphere, by the quality of feeling that the tales evoked.

Nowhere were those tales more vivid, more atmospheric, than in the accounts of Storyville, a region of thirty-eight blocks bounded by Canal, Basin, North Robertson, and St. Louis Streets, which were turned over entirely to brothels, cabarets, and saloons. In William Russell's phrase, it was "the most glamorous, as well as the most notorious center of legalized vice in history." Established in 1898 (and taking its name from the alderman whose city ordinance created it), it flourished until 1917, when it was shut down by the federal government.

By the late 1930s, when *Jazzmen* was published, Storyville had already been the subject of mythologizing, most notably in the culminating chapter in the popular 1936 book *The French Quarter,* journalist Herbert Asbury's "informal history of the

New Orleans underworld." Like his best-selling 1928 *The Gangs of New York*, *The French Quarter* was a rambling compendium of scabrous rumor and salacious anecdote drawn from police blotters, old newspapers, and interviews with elderly crooks. Asbury emphasized the vice and dissipation that had shaped the city from its beginnings, the voodoo rites and gambling dens and weird African dancing in Congo Square. Although he notes the city's racial dynamics, he does not object to them—they feature in the story largely as atmosphere. In Asbury's narrative, the rise of the racially mixed district of Storyville figures as both climax and turning point: the moment when prostitution gained unprecedented visibility, but also when it began to decline, for as Asbury concludes with blasé, man-of-the-world irony, middle-class girls are now as loose as prostitutes, and Americans as a whole have embraced the wickedness they once felt compelled to segregate.

There is one mention of jazz in *The French Quarter*, though it does not figure in the index and is so fleeting that it is easy to miss. Midway through a discussion of the décor of the brothels on North Basin Street, Asbury turns to the entertainment that the brothels relied upon, the "groups of itinerant musicians" they sometimes employed, in whom he spied the origins of the modern jazz band.

> One of the most popular of these combinations. . . was a company of boys, from twelve to fifteen years old, who called themselves the Spasm Band. They were the real creators of jazz, and the Spasm Band was the original jazz band. There were seven members besides the manager and principal organizer, Harry Gregson, who was the singer of the outfit— he crooned the popular songs of the day through a piece of

gas-pipe, since he couldn't afford a proper megaphone. The musicians were Emile Lacomb, otherwise Stalebread Charley, who played a fiddle made out of a cigar-box; Willie Bussey, better known as Cajun, who performed entrancingly upon the harmonica; Charley Stein, who manipulated an old kettle, a cow-bell, a gourd filled with pebbles, and other traps and in later life became a famous drummer; Chinee, who smote the bull fiddle, at first half a barrel and later a coffin-shaped contraption built by the boys; Warm Gravy; Emile Benrod, called Whisky; and Frank Bussey, known as Monk. . . . Cajun Bussey and Stalebread Charley could play tunes upon the harmonica and the fiddle, and the others contributed whatever sounds chanced to come from their instruments. These they played with the horns in hats, standing upon their heads, and interrupting themselves occasionally with lugubrious howls. In short, they apparently originated practically all of the antics with which the virtuosi of modern jazz provoke the hotcha spirit, and sometimes downright nausea.

If nothing else, Asbury's account is intriguing in its sheer brevity—clearly, in 1936 to speak of the "New Orleans underworld" did not require him to speak of jazz. (Compare his account to Al Rose's 1974 book *Storyville, New Orleans;* even though denying that jazz began in Storyville, the author nonetheless felt obliged to devote a full chapter to the subject.) Just as clearly, to speak of jazz's origins did not require Asbury to speak of black musicians. Asbury's account does not mention race, but the fact that (as he explains in a footnote) Harry Gregson was now "a Captain of Detectives in the Police Department" makes it almost certain that the Spasm Band's members were white. For Asbury, such an ensemble was the origin of the Hit Parade swing of the 1930s, which he disdained as merely "antics," cheap, mass-market amusement not particularly marked by the race of its musicians.

As connoisseurs of race records, the *Jazzmen* writers had a different story to tell. They were out to authenticate those Mortons and Olivers, to flesh out the purity that they heard in the music, and that meant establishing a place of germination and a line of transmission. While Asbury's Storyville was simply a vice district, *Jazzmen*'s Storyville was a community, a black proletarian haven where outcasts and the disreputable expressed resistance, found training and fellowship, and created a new art form. From the outset, Smith and Ramsey were aware of a potential danger in their project: they could be seen as catering to the voyeuristic taste for "slumming" most famously associated with Carl Van Vechten, the Jazz Age music critic and Harlem habitué who had celebrated Bessie Smith as an "elemental conjure woman" with a "plangent African voice." Van Vechten's passion for Negro arts (as well as his willingness to wield money and influence on artists' behalf) had helped many black artists but repelled many others, given Van Vechten's vociferous championing of black artists and writers as "primitive" and "exotic." Both Ramsey and Smith (they were less sure about Russell) disliked that sort of rhetoric and were determined to avoid any parallels.

Ultimately, Smith sought advice on their project from the black poet Sterling Brown, whom he had gotten to know at the Federal Writers Project and at the Jungle Inn. "I said we were trying to avoid the Van Vechtian line, etc.," Smith reported to Ramsey. "I was glad I did, for Sterling told me his feeling about how the Negro should be discussed racially, and it's the same as ours. That is, where heritage is legitimate, such as pentatonic scale, ok, but don't try to explain his hot virtues by his savage breast—in other words, environment shapes us. I agree with him, and I'm sure you do, and I learned from him that this is a very very important issue with Negroes, that they do not care to be set apart anthropologically even when this is supposed to be a compliment." In the end, Brown was sufficiently impressed with their project to offer them his poem "Ma Rainey," and Smith urged Ramsey to go through the manuscript with its inclusion in mind. "I hope, in view of this, you'll go through the stuff once again (especially Russell's) and cut out—just DELETE—all adjectives or phrases or comparisons that are AFRICAN—'like an African dancer'—'His African voodoo ancestors,' etc. Sterling, I know, would not have any part of a book that had any trace of that in it and, believe me, he is representative of the most progressive Negro thought."

Aligning their book with "the most progressive Negro thought" meant framing their black protagonists as creative geniuses. At the center of their story, the starting point in their line of transmission, was the tortured artist Buddy Bolden. Though Ramsey, Russell, and Smith seem to have assumed that they were the first to write about him, Bolden had in fact been discussed in the New Orleans black press back in 1933, in an article entitled "Excavating Local Jazz" by an African American journalist named E. Belfield Spriggins. Spriggins had interviewed Bolden's trombonist Willie Cornish, and he described the "sensation" "King Bolden" created "many years ago . . . [in] popular dance halls around the city" with a number since labeled "Buddy Bolden's Blues" (or "Funky Butt"). For Spriggins, Bolden was one name among many, and he mattered simply as the creator of the first local jazz hit. But listening to the stories they were told by Bunk Johnson, Willie Cornish, and Jelly Roll Morton, the *Jazzmen* authors seized upon Bolden as the music incarnate: battered by poverty, disdain, and racism but able to fight back through "an innate power of invention," an intuitive, untutored brilliance that had all New Orleans running wild before it finally drove him mad.

Though Bolden was, in their eyes, a genius, his talent flourished because of his surroundings, the low-life barrelhouses and honky-tonks of Storyville. This, to Ramsey, Smith, and Russell, was the side of the red-light district that mattered: not the lavish pleasure houses Asbury dwelled upon, where blacks entertained but were kept out as customers, but the gutbucket dives like Pete Lala's or the Big 25, where black musicians played after hours. It was a common mistake, Charles Edward Smith once remarked, to assume "that the musicians found no appreciative audience in dives and didn't play their best there." On the contrary: "jammed every night with river rowdies, card sharks, roughnecks, pimps, and all varieties of male parasites," clubs like Pete Lala's brought performers and spectators together in a kind of ecstatic fusion, the musicians "dragging out the blues with a slow beat and fierce intensity" as the rough-edged audience egged them on. Hustlers and roustabouts were there to relax, and whores were there to drum up business, and together they set the tone. "Inside the low, smoky room, the musicians sweated for their bread, delivering 'gully-low' stomps and blues, the kind that the respectable 'dicty' people pretended to hate, but yelled for as soon as they had a few drinks under their belts," wrote Ramsey. And if a few, like Johnny Dodds, "hated the long hours, the low pay, the sweat, the obese, waving back-sides," others, like Bolden, found it exhilarating, playing louder and louder to send the dancing crowd into a frenzy, then dropping the volume to take inspiration from the sound of their shuffling feet.

For the *Jazzmen* writers, black popular music was born in that atmosphere of underworld communion, and with Bolden as its guiding spirit, what followed took the shape of a fall from grace. Storyville figures in the book as a ribald, plebeian Garden of Eden, and its closure in 1917 amounts to an expulsion from paradise. Traveling to New York and Chicago, the musicians were hit by the virulent racism from which the Storyville community had partially sheltered them, and on top of that exploitation by the commercial record companies. Over the course of the 1920s, great artists like Oliver and Morton were recorded by the Victor and Gennett labels, run by men with little knowledge of music and even less concern for art, who used them for a time and then let them go. So Jelly Roll Morton ended up mixing drinks at the Jungle Inn; Kid Ory worked on a chicken ranch; King Oliver sold apples on street corners and pushed a broom in a pool hall before dying of a broken heart. Most telling of all, Bunk Johnson, "the ideal successor to the throne of King Bolden. . . .[with] an unprecedented sense of swing and feeling for the low-down blues and gutbucket style," had never been deemed worth recording. The conclusion was clear: the history of jazz on records was one of cheapening and adulteration, with brilliant black innovators either ignored entirely or cavalierly discarded, the credit for their innovations assigned to white imitators while the innovators themselves descended into poverty.

That fulmination against commercial recording might seem an odd conclusion to a history written by record collectors, yet the *Jazzmen* writers' attitude toward their collections had always been ambivalent. On the one hand, and in marked contrast to traditional folklorists, they welcomed the recording process, regarding commercial disks as (in Smith's phrase) "a transcribed history," artifacts that contained forgotten echoes of a marginalized, rejuvenating national heritage. As the writing of *Jazzmen* itself proved, commercial recordings could prompt curiosity, debate, and historical research and investigation, and they kept echoes of New Orleans alive. Yet that process was blighted by acquisitive, racist recording executives and (they implied) by the record-buying masses, who were fickle and undiscerning at best. It was due to that sheer lack of discernment that hot jazz was not and would never be popular. The nature of the popular market meant record companies would always be loath to record it, preferring a music of "shallow emotionalism," music that, as Smith put it, "plucked at the surface emotions with a monotonous persistence."

There was, however, one recording that they hoped would tell a different story. Throughout their research for *Jazzmen*, Ramsey and Smith kept hearing rumors of a wax cylinder made sometime in the mid-1890s by Buddy Bolden. The story sounded plausible: the 1890s had been the decade when phonograph companies first got off the ground, and some had made recordings of local musicians for their salesmen to use when demonstrating the technology. Bolden's trombone player, Willie Cornish, told Smith that he thought he remembered the band being employed by some "white company" to perform in front of a bank of recording phonographs, and while he did not have any of the resulting cylinders, he knew a woman in New Orleans who might have hung onto some.

Smith would never find the recording; when he tracked down the woman, she apologized. She had indeed owned a box of old cylinders that might well have included something by Bolden, but she hadn't listened to them for decades. For the past forty years they had been stored in her living room just a few feet from where they were standing—"just sitting there," she said, gathering dust—but finally she had tired of looking at them. About one year earlier she had thrown them out.

In a sense, that tale of the Bolden cylinder loomed over the New Orleans revival. It accounts at once for the frenzied hopes that animated their searches for old recordings—who knew what one might unearth at the local Salvation Army?—and for their wistful near-disappointment with those recordings that they actually found. Much as they loved those Mortons and Olivers, they inevitably ran a poor second to the sound that collectors imagined: African American music at its purest, in the rough democracy of Storyville, where they liked their blues "mean and dirty" and where Bolden would call out to his band:

> Way down, way down low
> So I can hear those whores
> Drag their feet across the floor.

TODAY LITTLE REMAINS OF WHAT ONCE WAS STORYVILLE. Long before the environs of Iberville and Basin Streets had been engulfed by the waters unleashed by Hurricane Katrina, the buildings that housed the 101 Ranch and Pete Lala's Cafe had fallen victim to urban renewal. Even as Smith, Ramsey, and Russell were writing, New Orleans was calling on the newly created U.S. Housing Authority to pull down the old buildings and construct public housing for low-income families, and in the process erase the physical remnants of a place and a period the city now deemed an embarrassment. Some of the most famous street names were changed: Franklin Street, where Pete Lala's had stood, became Crozat; Basin Street, for a time, became North Saratoga. In 1942, William Russell wandered around with a camera and captured the transformations in progress, the broken glass, the "No Trespassing" notices, the boarded-up facades of the cribs and dance halls.

Perhaps the steady, relentless disappearance of those final bits of material evidence helps explain the lush romance of the revivalist portrait, an aura that rapidly intensified. In the years that followed the publication of *Jazzmen,* as the city fathers be-latedly realized that the jazz heritage constituted a potential tourist attraction, enthusiasts who came to the city in search of the remains of the old dives and barrelhouses found that they had to rely entirely on their imaginations. The saloons on Bour-bon Street seemed a poor substitute, with their crowds of drunken college students and sailors on furlough, and the most avid collectors lamented the passing of a place that had created great art, forged a community, and invested pleasure with rau-cous protest. "The barrelhouse was the refuge of the tragically destitute, the blindly rebellious, the abjectly sodden," explained the critic Rudi Blesh in "Jazz Begins," part of a 1946 collection of essays that he helped to edit with Frederic Ramsey. "For this was the haunt of the blues, music of tragedy, dull despair, flam-ing revolt. Through the foul, smoky air loud with the clatter of cups, the shrill-edged laughter, rowdy shouting, and drunken snores and weeping, rang incessantly, day and night, the stark, simple blues." And as important as the music, in this portrait, was the man who created it.

In a dark corner, hunched over the battered upright piano,
the aged, rosewood "box," sat the "beater," a lonely figure,
"stacking the blues," tapping his foot, humming in a rough
voice the bare and melancholy phrases, the dark words:

> Got to keep movin'
> Blues fallin' down like hail
> I got to keep movin'
> Blues fallin' down like hail
> I can't keep no money
> For a hellhound on my trail
> Hellhound on my trail

Reading that passage now, over half a century after Blesh
wrote it, is disconcerting. Abruptly, bizarrely, the role of the
forlorn brothel pianist is being performed by the wrong actor,
and that foul, rowdy, ghetto barrelhouse has a soundtrack entirely out of sync with the script. But that reaction to Robert
Johnson's "Hellhound on My Trail" is of our time, not of
Blesh's. As it happens, the jazz collectors who celebrated Storyville lionized Robert Johnson too. As early as the late 1930s,
Johnson's recordings were circulating among a small but ardent group of New Orleans enthusiasts, Frederic Ramsey,
Charles Edward Smith, and John Hammond among them. (In
1939, Hammond loaned his copies to Alan Lomax, who included eight Johnson titles on his "List of American Folk
Songs on Commercial Records.") What captured their imaginations in Johnson's music was the same kind of magic they
heard in Morton: a music as "dry on the ear as some wine may
be on the tongue," infused with "an unquenchable power...,

a power direct and unornamented, completely unmixed with cloying sweetness, languor, or sentimentality."

In their attempts to account for that power, to find a story of origins with which to make sense of it, the record collectors who generated the New Orleans revival were the first blues historians. To dismiss them for finding the wrong story is to overlook the work such tales perform. In purporting to reveal a music's beginnings—the moment of emergence, when we can see it in its pure, unadulterated, natural state—stories of musical origins are always social and political fables. For the aficionados of old New Orleans, purity took the form of a lonely man "stacking the blues" at a battered brothel piano, a proletarian soothsayer, an underworld bard telling stories of longing and lust. Just what vision and values that figure connoted depended on who was conjuring him. The historian Eric Hobsbawm, who participated in the revival, has described how for revivalists, "New Orleans became a multiple myth and symbol: anti-commercial, anti-racist, proletarian populist, New Deal radical, or just anti-respectable and anti-parental, depending on taste." Some clearly found the raunchy, disreputable setting enticing, and not all were as scrupulous as Smith and Ramsey about steering clear of "the Van Vechtian line." The best that can be said, and it is not inconsiderable, is that (unlike the New Orleans city fathers and the U.S. Housing Authority) aficionados of New Orleans jazz felt no need to pathologize Storyville, that they were bewitched, not by the threat but by the promise of black urban life.

For a time, Storyville would even cast that spell upon Alan Lomax. On the face of it, Lomax played little part in the revival (apart from producing the recordings that, in a sense, started it all), but in truth he had never stopped thinking about the tales that Morton had told him. They simmered in his imagination even in the Mississippi Delta, where in 1942 he spent a fruitless afternoon trying to coax stories of the red-light district and examples of "that early blues" out of an elderly brothel pianist named Jaybird Jones, who unlike Morton was a man of terse, sometimes monosyllabic replies.

In 1949, seven years after Morton's death and three years after Rudi Blesh worked out a deal with his estate to issue a selection of the Library of Congress recordings, Lomax went to New Orleans to look for the traces Morton left behind. He had been there with his father fifteen years earlier, trawling the dance halls (with a brace of detectives in tow) in a quest for uncorrupted singers, and then he couldn't get away quickly enough—the younger Negroes, he wrote, "were on the whole ignorant of the songs we wanted and interested only in the blues and in jazz." But this time the city seemed different, as he heard Jelly Roll's stories confirmed by other musicians like Johnny St. Cyr and Omer Simeon, and as he wandered around the Iberville Housing Project and imagined the streets as they once had been, the cribs and the dives and the sweet hot music pouring out of every window. The result of his visit, published in June 1950, was an elegiac celebration of New Orleans jazz titled *Mister Jelly Roll.*

In many ways *Mister Jelly Roll* marked the culmination of the New Orleans revival, as well as the gospel of living lore that had shaped Lomax's folkloric practice. In Morton's account of his Storyville past, Lomax found social change and cultural conflict in abundance: a music "of protest and of pride," created in a polyglot city by a fractious mix of Creoles and darker-skinned, working-class blacks. With its "streets thronging with pimps, chippies, rotten police, and Babbitts on a binge," Storyville had given birth to "a truly fresh stream of culture," a "lusty and life-giving proletarian art." In its sexual robustness, Lomax heard a full-blooded contrast to the sentimental tones of the "sweet" music generated by "the marketplace of Tin Pan Alley." Even though jazz was "a marvel that has spawned a monster—a monster entertainment industry. . . whose million orifices pour out each week the stuff of our bartered dreams," Morton showed its utopian beginnings, commercial black music as it might have been. In his Storyville blues Lomax heard what Ramsey, Smith, and Russell had heard: "a rich evocation of underground America," a rough-edged, egalitarian world where pimps and whores could double as artists, exulting in the "ecstasy" of cultural creativity, in the germination of a new art form.

IRONICALLY, HOWEVER, EVEN AS *MISTER JELLY ROLL* HIT THE bookstores, the New Orleans revival was beginning to flag, and with it the rhapsodic tale of the red-light district as the birthplace of black proletarian art. The reasons for that are complex, but in part they come down, again, to politics. From the outset, the revival's vision of New Orleans jazz as "a music of protest and of pride" had been steeped in the politics of the Popular Front, that coalition of liberal, left, and radical opinion that fused solidarity with the laboring masses with an impassioned commitment to racial justice. As Lomax and Ramsey and Smith envisioned it, New Orleans jazz was a music that "did not draw a color line," whose defiantly black and working-class roots affirmed the creative vitality of black urban life.

Yet those allegiances, and even that language, came under fire in the Red Scare that followed World War II. Among the casualties was Lomax himself. In September 1950, a group calling itself Counter-attack, made up of onetime FBI agents, published a pamphlet entitled *Red Channels: The Report of Communist Influence in Radio and Television.* It urged the blacklisting of 151 allegedly subversive writers and artists, including Langston Hughes, Lena Horne, Pete Seeger, Orson Welles, Dorothy Parker, and "Alan Lomax. Author, *Mister Jelly Roll.*" In response, Lomax sailed to London, where he remained for the next ten years.

The collapse of the *Jazzmen* collective was less dramatic. None of its three main contributors fled the country, and none were jailed or blacklisted, but in the absence of a vibrant political impetus in the shape of the Popular Front, the energy and collectivism had gone out of the enterprise, and all of them fell on hard times. Only William Russell continued to devote himself to the gospel of Dixieland jazz. In 1944 he had founded a record label, American Music, to record Bunk Johnson and other New Orleans jazz artists, but the enterprise never really made money, and eventually he had to give it up.

Charles Edward Smith retreated from jazz research altogether, though in his case that retreat was forced upon him. In 1950 he stepped off a curb in Manhattan and into the path of a speeding car. The accident, which nearly killed him, left him sick, depressed, and penniless. Eventually, he moved to a one-room New York apartment and put all of his papers and records in storage, but he could not keep up the payments on the storage space. Ultimately it all disappeared, all his records, all his photographs, all his research for his planned books on Storyville, jazz, and Jelly Roll Morton.

In a sense, those individual stories were symptomatic, for by the early 1950s it was unmistakable that the romance of

Storyville had decidedly palled. Those years saw a new generation of folk music enthusiasts, based by and large on university
campuses, who were enchanted with the power and purity of
rural American cultures. In concerts at coffeehouses and music festivals across the United States, that enchantment gave
birth to a folk revival. But in a climate of Cold War reaction,
this folk-song movement had a different tone from its predecessor in the late 1930s, when such songs were taken up as
"living lore," for their illumination of class and ethnic struggle.
"For those of us whose revival began around 1958," writes
Robert Cantwell, then a young college student entranced with
the banjo, such political associations "would have been, in our
naive and compliant youth, a barrier to any enthusiasm for
folksongs."

Nor did the folk revival have room for the sounds of the
metropolis, what Benjamin Botkin had called the symphony of
urban nightlife. The aftermath of World War II had seen a
massive increase in black migration to cities, and with it rising
rates of male unemployment and families headed by women.
That in turn encouraged the growth of a virulent critique of
black social "pathology," as liberal social scientists argued that
the city's vicious leisure pastimes and "matriarchal" families
were creating a society of damaged black men.

Even as early as the late 1940s, that sense of black city life
as somehow pathological was trickling into the work of jazz
critics, beginning to qualify their celebration of the vitality of
the African American urban experience. Even Rudi Blesh expressed something of it in his 1946 book *Shining Trumpets*,
denouncing the pernicious influence on race recordings of un-
scrupulous black entertainers who had been "corrupted by city
ways." Such musicians, he suggested, were effectively pervert-

ing black musical traditions, hearing in the blues simply a "lascivious song," echoing with "drunken snores in the barrelhouse, the snarl of the hop-head, prostitutes' shrill laughter." Although the music, he maintained, did "have all these things in it," such listeners missed the underlying tone of lament: the fact that, "in all of this, a lost race is searching for home." The core of the blues, Blesh suggested, was a spirit of alienation. In the years that followed, as more white writers latched onto the music, that claim would become an article of faith. But few of them would make room for the barrelhouse, for the laughter of prostitutes or the snarl of hopheads. The world they depicted would be pastoral and, with barely a woman in sight, singularly free from the disorganization so evident in the black urban world.

THERE IS NO MORE DRAMATIC EXAMPLE OF THIS CRITICAL about-face than the work of Frederic Ramsey. Since his earliest days as a record collector, Ramsey had preached the gospel of New Orleans, and no one had been more pivotal in pulling the *Jazzmen* project together. He had been enchanted by the vision of the music's plebeian beginnings in the dives of Storyville. Yet the postwar critique of black urban pathology would take its toll even on him, and by the 1950s he began casting about for a new origins tale.

In the years following World War II, his interest in New Orleans jazz slowly diminished. He got married, had a child, and moved to a remote, hilly corner of New Jersey, where he built a rambling wooden house with big windows and unfinished walls, grew his own vegetables, and brewed his own beer. Though still a passionate fan of black music, he was nonetheless ready to leave New York. As early as the mid-1940s, he had stopped going to Harlem to collect race records—there were, he told a friend, too many muggings, and the whole experience of being there now felt exhausting.

Besides, he had stumbled upon a singer who became his new obsession. One night after the war and before his marriage, when he was strolling through Greenwich Village, he wandered into the Village Vanguard and found Charles Edward Smith deep in conversation with the nightclub's featured entertainer, Leadbelly. Until then, Ramsey had never been particularly drawn to Leadbelly's music, but now hearing it left him transfixed. Leadbelly's voice "was rough and grainy, and some of its raw tones came up as if scraped out of his throat," he recalled eight years later. "It rang out with intensity because he often shouted with violence. . . . The hollers he yelled out were almost impossible of notation in our occidental music scale." Above all, what made him exceptional was "his extraordinary ability to tell a story." Leadbelly spoke and reminisced as he sang, and his songs themselves formed a narrative, as he moved from blues to work songs to cowboy tunes to reels, like a "record collector who, with a large library to choose from, spends an evening pulling out his favorite disks in a sequence both varied and suggestive." What that sequence suggested was a tale that none of his recordings had captured.

In 1948, with the help of a wartime innovation, the tape recorder, Ramsey spent three days in Leadbelly's apartment, as the singer re-created the stories and songs of his youthful wanderings through the cotton fields and timberlands of Texas and Louisiana. Though Leadbelly was weak and his playing sometimes faltered, Ramsey was mesmerized by what resulted, a tale of picaresque adventure. "Rambling," Ramsey concluded, "was strong in Leadbelly's blood."

Eventually, Ramsey took to rambling too. In 1951 he and a friend, the photographer John Vachon, drove from New Jersey to North Carolina and across the South to Louisiana, drinking in the sight of crumbling levees and tumbledown cabins and black women picking cotton in headscarves. Two years later, with a letter of support from Sterling Brown, he received a Guggenheim Fellowship for a project on "jazz backgrounds," aiming to dig further into the southern landscape, taking photographs and making recordings. In February 1954 he, his wife Amelia, and his three-year-old son Loch left home in their battered 1941 Chevrolet coupe for a six-month trek across the rural South. The trunk of the car held two cameras, a Rolleiflex and a small unobtrusive Leica, and two tape recorders that Moses Asch of Folkways Records had loaned him: a state-of-the-art, two-speed, high-fidelity model and a Magnemite Portable, hand-cranked and battery-operated, for sites with no ready source of electricity.

Late in March, the couple drove into the Talladega National Forest in the northeastern corner of Alabama. The land there was thin and worn and had long ago been given over to sharecroppers, and with the roads and hills so often impassable, little seemed to have changed for the last eighty years. "Life in the country extremely old—mud chimneys, small old cabins, a hog on every farm, jugs on poles for martin nests," he reported to Asch. "The mule and the wagon are the principal modes of transportation." They settled into a tourist cabin, the only white faces within miles, and while Amelia befriended the landlady and Loch rode his tricycle in the dirt tracks, Ramsey

Fred and Amelia Ramsey, 1950.
Courtesy of Martha Ramsey.

made the rounds of the front porches, asking for people who sang "old-timey" songs. Everything about it enchanted him: the decrepit cabins, the lined faces, the quavery voices. At first he kept his cameras and tape recorders in his bag, but soon he simply stopped putting them away. Everything seemed to demand to be photographed; everyone had a story to tell.

The result of Ramsey's quest was a ten-volume LP anthology, *Music of the South,* issued on Folkways Records, and a book-length photographic essay entitled *Been Here and Gone.* The book makes a startling contrast to *Jazzmen,* setting out a new kind of blues origins story, rooting the music not in the swirling urban underworld, but in a region where time had stopped. Mechanization, he explains, has not reached these lands: "here, hands are still striving to accomplish tasks set almost a hundred years ago." The landscape still bears the imprint of slavery: "Nearly everything that is lived in, or that houses livestock or farm implements, was built long ago."

At the center of that primeval landscape, the emotional core of the book, is the figure that Leadbelly had got him imagining, that of the wandering blues singer. He is, Ramsey explains, a dying breed, for these "men who carried the devil on their backs, the box pickers and songsters who were the vagrants, easy riders and drifters of a period just past, are hardly ever to be encountered along southern highways today." The book sets out to track down the last of them, these sharecroppers, ditchdiggers, loggers, and mule skinners who took to the highway in despair of their lot. The music they produced, as Ramsey presents it, bears little resemblance to the rough, dirty blues of Morton's New Orleans. The blues of the wanderers is a song of melancholy, growing organically out of the pain and privation of their experience. Their feelings of torment infuse the blues verses that thread through the text, placing the voice of the wandering bluesman in a melancholy counterpoint with Ramsey's own.

> I got the blues so bad, it hurts my feet to walk,
> It has settled on my brain, and it hurts my tongue to talk.

Been Here and Gone paints a stark portrait, a world of poverty, hopelessness, and degradation. Yet the tones of the portrait render it more than just pitiable, making it enticing and attractive as well. Time and again Ramsey suggests that this rural world is alive in ways the modern, urban world is not, rich in a musical form—the blues—that is intensely personal and infused with passion. The cabins in Ramsey's photographs here are held together with junk, with chicken wire and bits of scrap metal, and yet the lives led within them contain subtler, more substantive forms of abundance: music that, like all else, is made by hand and permeates daily work and pleasures. In the mouths of the men he encountered, music became "a personal expression. The music that was everywhere had been welded to a way of life."

Suffusing Ramsey's text is a deep sense of longing for that way of life. As he paints it, this is a world of direct connections, unlike our own, where the stuff of life is swamped by the glut of commodities, drowned out by the din of mass-market pop. Preserving that world, or at least commemorating it, was for him an urgent mission—far more urgent, it would seem, than making an open stand against racial injustice. Though he wrote in the midst of the civil rights movement, the words "racism" and "segregation" do not appear in his text. *Been Here and Gone* is permeated with a sense of loss, a sense of a way of life and a people about to vanish, a disappearance that Ramsey attributes to an inevitable process of modernization: "tractors will replace mules, automobiles and trucks will push aside wagons. Machines to plow and cultivate and harvest will do the work of men and women in the fields." There's no mention of the contemporary battles over civil rights and desegregation, the political turmoil that was pushing young people out of the rural South, no acknowledgment that, in truth, many of the people in his photographs might welcome seeing some of the old ways go.

In a Cold War culture in which radicalism had been forcibly terrorized into the social margins, Ramsey had come

to recoil from the politicized vision that had guided the folklore narratives of the Popular Front. Looking back on his time
with Leadbelly, he was filled with disgust at the way the left
had exploited the singer, taking a gentle, humanitarian soul
and forcing him to parrot the party line. "I had looked vainly
[in previous studies]," he explained, "for accurate and convinc-
ing accounts of the persons who were making [black] music."
In *Been Here and Gone* he sought a new kind of accuracy, one
that distanced itself from what was fast being deemed, in dis-
paraging tones, the "sociological" thrust of interwar writing on
black song. Stripping away that distorting framework, he
sought to capture the truth of the music: not its politics or its
social dynamics but its heartfelt poetry, its rich emotion, which
could only be corrupted by the invasive forces of the urban
world. As he explained to the *New Yorker*, the soullessness of
modern mass culture was infecting even the most remote corners of Alabama and Mississippi: "The kids down South,
more's the pity, would rather listen to some juke box cutting
loose with rhythm and blues than learn the good old music."

That sense of longing for the purity of a black rural idyll
had never been present in *Jazzmen,* but Ramsey had come to
feel that his earlier enthusiasm had been misplaced. "It is beginning to be evident that perhaps as high as eighty per cent of
all New Orleans jazz musicians either come from the country,
or spring from families moved in from the country," he wrote
to Moses Asch. "Again, don't let Charles worry that I'm trying
to *take away* from New Orleans. I think I'm adding to it by
digging origins, showing how the lusty, hard-working families
came in and brought their strength with them—their march-
ing strength, their blowing and dancing strength. The music
took shape here, but it, like many cultures that have flowered

in many cities, had deep country roots. Roots in the country ways, roots in country ruggedness. Roots in the singing in the churches, and roots in the plantation blues."

For Ramsey, uncovering the truth of black secular music now meant uncovering those "deep country roots." As he wrote, he steadily chipped away at the portrait of black music he had helped draw in *Jazzmen*, disentangling the blues from jazz to imagine it as a discrete musical form, a hermetically sealed harmonic landscape cut off from the taint of modernity. It was, as he put it, the "plantation blues," and his photographs enveloped it in the sepia-tinged aura that phrase suggests. Ramsey's archetypal bluesman could have stepped out of the mid-nineteenth century; indeed, he exists out of time altogether. His hands toughened by labor, his face free from artifice or contrivance, he stares unflinchingly into the camera, a man among men, a heroic wanderer, a hard-bitten loner with a guitar.

six

The Real Negro Blues

I F YOU HAD BEEN WALKING PAST THE BUILDING ON THAT night in January 1944, you might have heard a raspy voice, a guitar, and the crackle of scratched vinyl, and perhaps you would have looked up. At first, your gaze might have dwelled on the crest over the doorway, the inverted triangle bearing the words "Spirit Mind Body," but finding the sound would have meant looking still higher, at the row of small anonymous windows on the fourth or fifth or sixth floor. Perhaps curiosity would have impelled you to slip inside the building, past the distracted young man at the reception desk, past the sailors loitering in the lobby, up the staircase, down the dark hallway, until you could crouch outside the door. Then, if you peered through the keyhole, you would have seen the revolving disk, the cardboard boxes full of records, and the angular man kneeling by the turntable, his eyes closed, his face taut with the absorption of a monk in prayer.

You might have formed the impression that few other people entered that room. Maybe it was the Spartan décor—the narrow iron bedstead, the battered desk, the bedside table holding a half-empty bottle of whiskey and a single clouded glass. Maybe it was the air of preoccupation conveyed by the sheer number of records and the tattered copies of the *Record Changer* stacked at the foot of the bed. Most likely, though, it was the man's thin, intense face, the gravity conveyed by the graying hair at his temples, the fierce self-containment of his gaze. But had you felt emboldened and knocked and told him you had been drawn by the music, he might have surprised you. For though he would not have said much about himself—he might not even have revealed his name—he would have rif-fled through the cardboard boxes and shown you the treasures of his collection, battered records by obscure musicians whose names you would certainly never have heard.

He estimated that these boxes housed about three hundred records in total. Not nearly as many as other collectors, not nearly as many, indeed, as he wanted—he was currently draft-ing a want list that comprised, at last count, about thirteen hundred items—yet, modest as his collection might be, every item in it was choice. If a record did not thrill him, he would not buy it (or if he had, inadvertently, he would not keep it long), even if it came recommended by the few collectors whose taste he respected. Owning a complete set of an artist's recordings, collecting master numbers in sequence, acquiring unissued pressings simply for their obscurity: such motives might compel other collectors, but none appealed to him. What he was after were magical sounds, by their nature rare and elusive. He prided himself on tolerating no junk.

He had made that rule ever since the day late in the 1930s when he had wandered into a Salvation Army warehouse in search of cheap books and noticed a battered disk with the word "sardana" printed on a green Columbia label. From his research into Old World folk dances (he had been reading up on the subject for a couple of years at that point), he knew the *sardana* was a circle dance native to Catalonia, revived in the nineteenth century and now a kind of national emblem. That it had made its way onto a phonograph record surprised and intrigued him, so he started looking for other examples, and soon what began as a casual hobby became something far more impassioned. There were simply *so many* records to trawl through. Ever since the radio had replaced the phonograph as the main source of music in most people's homes, junk shops and general stores and furniture retailers had been inundated with disks, some of them used, some still in their packing crates, for sale for as little as a dollar per box.

By the early 1940s more resources had appeared: trading magazines like the *Record Changer* and stores wholly devoted to secondhand records, like Fichtelberg's at Sixth Avenue and West 44th Street, or the shop a few blocks farther north that all the collectors called Indian Joe's. Suddenly he was finding all kinds of extraordinary examples of Spanish and South American folk music recorded in the 1920s on Victor and Columbia's foreign-language labels, *gardanas* and *munieras,* melodies he had only imagined, and the more he unearthed, the more he coveted (he still hoped to find a *zamacueca,* a dance of the Indians of the Chilean uplands). But beyond that, he sometimes thought, he had been bewitched by the disks themselves, by the unrevealing black surfaces, the gaudy green-and-purple

labels, the spiral grooves that, when set in motion, released peculiar, exotic, primitive sounds.

Somehow, at some indefinable point, he had crossed a
threshold from buying to collecting. The odd thing was that,
until then, he had never been drawn to recorded music—certainly not the treacly big band standards that dominated the
jukeboxes by the early 1940s, nor the recordings he'd heard a
decade earlier, when he spent several months immersed in the
stuff. The summer after he graduated from high school, he
had worked for a family friend in a record shop in a black
neighborhood. Day after day, he stood at the counter playing
customer requests, disks by Bessie Smith, Ma Rainey, Victoria
Spivey, and Lonnie Johnson, all of which struck him as cheap
and tawdry, and that gut-level aversion to race records stuck
with him for the next ten years. He cringed to recall that, only
two years ago in 1942, the owner of one of his regular haunts,
the Central General Store on Long Island, had sent him a list
of mint-condition Paramounts, two great unopened boxes that
he had unearthed at the back of the store. None of the disks
had ever sat on a turntable, and he could have had them for a
dollar apiece, but at that point he still dismissed as worthless
anything with the word "blues" in the title. So he forwarded
the list to a friend and record-collecting correspondent, a West
Coast folk music aficionado named Harry Smith, who
promptly bought up every last one.

It took him another few months to discover that there was
blues and then there was *the blues*. Late in 1942, at Smith's
suggestion, he sent away to the Library of Congress for the
nineteen-page "List of American Folk Songs on Commercial
Records" compiled by Alan Lomax at the end of the 1930s.
What he read there confounded everything he had ever as-

sumed about race records. The dizzying variety of musical styles, the sheer oddity of the song titles, the abundance of fire-and-brimstone sermons ("Babylon Is Falling Down" by the Reverend F. W. McGee, "Black Diamond Express to Hell" by the Reverend A. Nix): it all hinted at sounds richer and stranger than anything he had encountered before. Most intriguing of all were Lomax's mentions of blues recordings, for if many sounded predictably urbane and sophisticated ("De7069, 'Chain Gang Blues' by Kokomo Arnold, mod[ern] t[ext] m[elody] and s[tyle], sings in Chicago night clubs"), a few promised something undiluted and raw. "Co11420-D, 'Depot Blues,' Charley Lincoln, completely authentic rural blues, primitive g[uitar] s[tyle]"; "PA12752, 'Good Times Blues,' Ramblin' Thomas, authentic rural blues, simple, v[ery] f[ine]"; "Pe7–05–81, 'Cross Road Blues,' Robert Johnson, individual composition v[ery] f[ine], traces of voodoo." A few weeks of digging and writing to dealers brought him a copy of the Robert Johnson, and then his curiosity became an obsession. By January 1943, he had compiled a sixteen-page "want list," as collectors called it, that he sent to record traders across the country, and soon he acquired enough blues recordings to file them in their own cardboard box.

What mesmerized him about these disks was something he found hard to describe, harder, at least, than with the Spanish folk music, where he had listened for a certain simplicity in the accompaniment, a way of handling the guitar and Galician bagpipe that evoked what he imagined to be the rural vigor of the Spanish landscape. With the blues he was after a particular and elusive quality of voice. He heard it in Six Cylinder Smith on Paramount 12698, "Oh, Oh, Lonesome Blues," in the way he would lift his voice at the end of each line, then abruptly drop it again. And in Ed Bell on Paramount 12546, "Frisco Whistle Blues," in which the singer careened from a growling bass to a high-pitched wail. And in Ishman Bracey on Paramount 12970, "Woman Woman Blues," in which the bluesman repeated every third line with his choked, broken falsetto until the effect was hypnotic.

Back in the early 1930s, when he clerked in the record store, he had encountered nothing as compelling as this. Blind Lemon Jefferson had been perhaps the closest, "a real old-fashioned singer" as the ads had billed him, whose recordings practically flew off the shelves, but by comparison he sounded tame and prosaic, with a taste for crude double entendres that probably accounted for his appeal to the store's customers, onetime rural Negroes who had taken on city ways. The voices he was hearing now had nothing jocular or sophisticated about them.

The greatest of those singers were swamp primitives, barely civilized, like Bullet Williams, or Jelly Jaw Short, who threw his voice around like a voodoo doctor, shouting and mumbling and growling and wailing, or Tommy Johnson, whose eerie rolling guitar set off his singing's naked emotion, passionate and yet wholly artless. They had none of the ersatz folkishness of a Leadbelly, straining for dramatic effects.

After one year, he could choose songs by instinct, or such a finely tuned sense of labels and master numbers that it amounted to the same thing. He knew now that label color distinguished the early Vocalions from the later issues, that OKeh reached its peak with its 05000–06000 series, and that high-numbered Paramounts were almost always worth hearing, since the best singers seemed to have been recorded just before the company went out of business. And sometimes he searched for recordings whose existence he simply imagined. In the most recent *Record Changer*, he had placed the following ad:

BL. ON BL.-LABEL VOCALION
ANY WITH S. A. MASTER #'S

"Blues on black label Vocalion, any with San Antonio master number"—in other words, any Vocalion blues made in the same studio that had recorded Robert Johnson. One such extraordinary voice, he reasoned, must have been followed by others just as exceptional. Guesswork was the best he could do in the face of the mysteries these disks presented, these singers whom no one remembered, who seemed to have come out of nowhere and then vanished without leaving a trace.

On the face of it, it might seem odd that the recordings he sought proved so elusive. Since the United States had entered World War II, the supply of used records had never been greater; government scrap drives encouraged people to hoard far more shellac than the war effort needed, and boxes upon boxes of disks turned up in junk shops, great groaning masses of them. Blind Lemon Jefferson could be found everywhere, but the titles he sought had never sold very widely and probably had not been pressed in large numbers to start with. Furthermore, few other collectors bothered to buy them, so even though he doggedly continued to advertise in the *Record Changer*, his efforts largely proved pointless. And while he still made his weekly pilgrimages to Fichtelberg's, the Central General, and Indian Joe's, he usually came home with nothing.

Lately, he had experimented with bypassing the regular sales channels entirely. Six months ago, in the summer of 1943,

he had struck up a correspondence with Ellis Horne, the clar-
inet player in Lu Watters's band, who agreed to look out for
the disks on his want list and send them to him in exchange for
New Orleans jazz rarities. A month ago he had traveled to
Camden, New Jersey, where Victors and Bluebirds had been
manufactured, in the hopes of finding former employees who
had taken test pressings home. And just last week he journeyed south and knocked on doors in the black section of
Charlotte, North Carolina, where cabins were lit by kerosene
lamps and records played on hand-wound Victrolas, but at one
house a dog attacked him and at another a man pulled a knife.
After that he decided to stick to the shops.

On this day in January, though, he had been lucky. At Indian Joe's north of Times Square, near the back of a bin
marked "miscellany," he found a record in a sleeve so tattered
he almost flicked past it, until something about the name
caught his eye. It was Paramount 13110, "Some These Days
I'll Be Gone," sung by an artist called Charley Patton. Alan Lomax, he recalled, had listed a couple of disks of religious music
by a duo called Patton and Lee—"street singers," Lomax had
called them—but those had appeared on Vocalion, so it might
not be the same man. The record itself had so many scratches
it looked to be almost unplayable. Normally he'd have tried it
out in the shop, but the phonograph was mobbed by Stan Ken-
ton and Glenn Miller fans engaged in their interminable
three-minute playbacks, so he went to the counter where Joe
was dozing and paid a dollar for it and headed back to his
room.

And it was there, in his cell-like room surrounded by collector's paraphernalia, that he picked up the Patton, slipped it
out of its sleeve, and put it on the turntable. At first he heard

nothing but hisses and crackles, but then came a rumbling, growling voice, deep and sepulchral, welling up within the surface noise as though echoing from another world. So thick and slurred was the delivery that at first he strained to make out the lyrics. But as he listened, with his back straight and his brow furrowed, as though every pore in his body were absorbing the music, he began to nod and smile, and even before he replaced the tonearm and turned up the volume and his neighbor began to pound on the walls, he realized that he had found it, the voice he'd been searching for all along.

———

THERE IS A HISTORIC LANDMARK IN THE BOROUGH OF Brooklyn, New York, that has been forgotten. In the early twentieth century, the neighborhood known as Williamsburg was home to a polyglot population: Italian and Polish immigrant families pushed out of overcrowded Manhattan; Irish families who'd been there a bit longer; and single men of various ethnicities attached to the nearby Navy Yard. To cater to the latter, in 1904 the Young Men's Christian Association opened a lodging house at 179 Marcy Avenue, near a stop on the BMT subway line and a few blocks in from the Williamsburg Bridge. And it was there at the Williamsburg YMCA, in a single room sometime in the mid-1940s, that the Delta blues was born.

It was born, that is, in the imagination of one of the YMCA's long-term residents, an impassioned record collector named James McKune. Born sometime around 1910, McKune was the driving force behind the cohort of music enthusiasts who powered the blues revival of the 1960s, when white Americans found new meanings in old recordings that

African Americans had long ago cast aside. Based in and around New York and calling themselves the Blues Mafia, McKune's coterie set up record labels, issued LP anthologies, and wrote liner notes, articles, and books of blues history that framed the blues as we now know it, a music of pain and alienation, a cry of African American despair. Giving life to that tale were the rough, ragged voices of Delta loners like Charley Patton and Robert Johnson, the prized items in their collections of 78s, which they invested with the mystical passion that John Lomax had invested in Leadbelly, hearing in them voices that were untainted by contact with the modern world.

Understanding the blues revival means untangling that perception, and doing so means looking at James McKune. The facts of his life remain extremely hazy. My suggestion that he began with an obsession with Old World folk dances, that his first collected disk was a Spanish folk recording, that he discovered the blues through Alan Lomax's list—all that is simply a plausible story based on speculation and inference. In the memories of revivalists he looms as a figure of legend, a mysterious loner whose ear for the blues shaped the tastes of a generation, an eccentric iconoclast who took many guises—a wizard, a prophet, a lunatic. Friends, or rather disciples, clustered around him, but no one knew him very well, and only the barest facts emerge from their stories, many of them sketchy and confused. McKune came from Baltimore, or Albany, or North Carolina; he moved to New York City some time in the 1930s, or perhaps it was during World War II. His personal life was shadowy, at least to his blues acolytes. "I don't know if this should be mentioned, but he was like a closet homosexual," claimed his fellow record collector Pete Whelan. "I didn't know but [another collector] Bill Givens spotted it right

James McKune's high school graduation photo, ca. 1928.
Courtesy of Pete Whelan.

away." What they spotted, all of them, was that he drank more and more heavily as time went on. By the late 1950s, his job as a *New York Times* subeditor had been long abandoned; for a while he worked as a desk clerk at a men's hostel and sorted letters in a Brooklyn post office, but eventually he lost those jobs too.

By 1965 McKune had moved out of the single room at the Williamsburg YMCA that he had lived in for twenty-five years and could be seen wandering the streets of Lower Manhattan, "sockless," one collector remembers, "and seemingly brain-damaged from alcohol." In September 1971 his unclothed body was found bound and gagged in a welfare hotel on the Lower East Side. Police detectives surmised that he had been killed by a stranger whom he picked up for sex.

Out of the fog of half-remembered facts of the unconventional life and the ugly death, one thing remains clear in all his friends' minds: the magnificence of his record collection, the pioneering brilliance of his taste in blues. "There was a guy called Jim McKune who was murdered who was like a grand doyen, if you will, and he was a real mentor," recalls record collector and blues historian Lawrence Cohn. "I mean, he was listening to Charley Patton before any of us even knew who Brownie McGhee was." Pete Whelan remembers: "He lived in one room in the YMCA and he had all his records in cardboard boxes under his bed. And he would pull out one and say 'here's the greatest blues singer in the world' [and] I'd say 'Oh yeah?' 'cause I had just discovered this guy, Sam Collins, who was great. . . . Jim pulls out this Paramount by Charley Patton. I said 'Oh yeah, sure,' and, of course, he was right!"

No one knows why or how James McKune came to collect blues records. McKune left only scraps of evidence behind him, too few for any biographer to draw conclusions about his impulses and motives and too elliptical for any historian to sustain a narrative with him at center stage. The best we can do is to follow the trail of the disks he pursued with such obsessive intensity. As a neophyte collector in the early 1940s, he stepped into the network of trading in old recordings that Frederic Ramsey, Charles Edward Smith, and William Russell had helped to create in the previous decade, a subterranean world with customs, traditions, even an argot all its own. What made him unique and, in time, influential, was the sensibility that he developed, which would ultimately transform the collector's subculture, enveloping the mass-produced disk in an aura of rarefied art. Telling the story of his life means making a virtue of his unknowability and imagining him as best we can, a backroom aesthete orchestrating the blues revival from behind the scenes—poring through the bins in used record stores, trading tips with other collectors, and listening alone in his single room at the Y, conjuring up ghostly, gritty voices from the battered 78s that he stored in a cardboard box under his bed.

THE ONE HUNDRED BLOCK OF WEST 47TH STREET NEAR Times Square in Manhattan is now dominated by an anonymous, glass-fronted office building surrounded by one of those windswept plazas that feel permanently empty of human life. But had you looked in the 1940s, you would have found at number 107, sandwiched between a luggage store and a pipe and tobacco shop, an entranceway opening onto a flight of stairs. To the right of the entrance, bold vertical capitals spelled out the legend "RECORDS," and the stairs were blazoned with invitations:

HOT JAZZ RECORDS.
RECORDS 4 FOR $1.00.
STEP UP SAVE A BUCK.

That was the Jazz Record Center, or "Indian Joe's," founded around 1940 by Big Joe Clauberg, a chain-smoking Native American giant and onetime circus strongman who turned to more prosaic work when the Depression hit and the circus trade dried up. In 1938 he and a friend rented the premises near Times Square and set up a used magazine and bookstore, which they used as a base for publishing the *Hobo News,* a tabloid directed at the growing population of homeless. Since each issue was laden with risqué jokes and cartoons, no regular distributor would take it, so every other week Big Joe loaded copies of the paper into his truck and delivered them to points west and south. One of his customers was a jukebox operator who offered him used records at a very low price. Big Joe hated driving back to Manhattan with an empty truck, and, besides, his store had lots of free space. Over time, he increased his stock until those bins of used records took over the shop.

Almost immediately, the store was inundated with customers, men by and large, endowed with obsessive enthusiasms and seemingly endless time to browse. Business peaked on Saturday nights, when collectors squeezed in to rummage for records while rubbing shoulders with Big Joe's colorful cronies—circus performers, grizzled sea captains, and a permanently inebriated bookie whose habit of sleeping on the shop floor earned him the nickname of Horizontal Abe. Clauberg's advertisements urged customers to "come up—play records—chew the fat," and record enthusiasts took him up on the offer. Collector Pete Kaufman remembered: "We paced about the store, played records, discussed a variety of subjects, and took care to avoid stepping on Horizontal Abe, while Big Joe dozed intermittently at his large desk in the back of the store." Boasting "the completest Jazz Stock in the East," "Everything from Bunk to Monk," the Jazz Record Center soon became the prime resource, hangout, and pilgrimage site for record collectors up and down the East Coast.

Setting up the Jazz Record Center with that truckload of jukebox discards, Big Joe stumbled upon what had become, in the ten years since Frederic Ramsey first began collecting, a thriving subterranean world. Although Ramsey, Smith, and their comrades had mostly made up the practice as they went along, the habitués of Indian Joe's encountered a whole range of institutions available for the enthusiast, to help them find disks, make friends, and cultivate tastes.

Secondhand shops were only part of the story. Just as important were the specialist magazines that began springing up in the 1940s, like *Record Changer*, first published in 1942, in which collectors could offer items for sale or trade and put out requests for the recordings they sought. Such publications offered neophytes a sense of belonging, along with a wealth of practical tips, from storing and cleaning records to packing lunches for trips to junk shops ("bananas are the ideal collector's food because they can be peeled and eaten without being touched by the hands"). (Perhaps that practical imperative explains the legendary diet of record collector William Russell, who claimed to subsist only on bananas, raisins, almonds, shredded coconut, and the occasional bowl of cornflakes.)

By the mid-1940s, to be a collector was to immerse oneself in an arcane private language rooted in the process of standardized manufacturing. Label names and master numbers formed the core of that subcultural lingo, echoed by the Byzantine system of grading used disks (N, E, VG, G, F, P, with half and quarter stops in between) that remains in use to this day. Part of the pleasure of the collector's practice lay in mastering that insider's vocabulary and manipulating the trading resources, developing convoluted webs of exchange. "Only last night I gave a lady $2.00 for Br. 3457 Melancholy/Wild Man by Dodds, an OKeh Miff Mole, 10 Whitemans with Bix and or Bing on them, 3 OKeh Armstrongs, and about 15 other items of various types," explained one aficionado in 1945.

> Multiply this by 15 or 20 and one has a wonderful batch of trading material. . . . I have in my files about 150 want lists so that when I do pick up an item I can always tell just about who I can send it to. . . . The guy that has say a Blind Willie

Johnson that you want needs only about 12 rare items by Bing Crosby for completion. I dig around in all my correspondence and back issues of record magazines til I find one of those Crosbys for disposition. Then the guy that has it will be interested in nothing I have to offer and will not sell the Crosby except for say $15.00 but will trade it for Lillie Delk Christian's Ok Too Busy. I trade a guy two Bessies for the Lillie Delk and the sailing is easy from then on. Often it is more complicated than this.

Yet merely talking the talk and trading the disks was not enough to place one at the top of the hierarchy—and by the mid-1940s, record collecting had become an intensely hierarchical world. The most prominent members of what had become known as "the collecting fraternity"—Ramsey, Smith, Russell, Marshall Stearns, John Hammond, Charles Payne Rogers, Stephen Smith—made it clear that a genuinely reputable collecting practice raised issues of knowledge, tradition, and taste. "There are collectors, and then there are Collectors," Rogers explained.

The first-named, lower-case bunch are those who merely collect, seizing upon the current thing in popular music, be it swing, bop, or juke-box, with never a glance at jazz tradition or background. . . . They are the blindly crusading devotees, the faddist espousers of "the latest." Some may be a little more panoramic in their approach, a little more catholic in their tastes, due to the influence of a slight smattering of jazz history picked up from the trade magazines. But this leads them to collect everything in sight, even the eight bars of Bix embedded in the sticky morass of some mickey-mouse arrangement.

The true Collectors, a relatively small (but expanding) group are far more discriminating. No snobs, they are those whose collections show the selective processes that have been at work in evaluating the whole azimuth of jazz. Your upper-case Collector is himself more musically grounded and is possessed of a more enlightened viewpoint, enabling him to discern the finer jazz performances at will, as they are issued on records. Since his approach is historical, unlike the first group he experiences no particular blush of shame in according some tardily discovered jazz figure his proper proportion of importance.

As Rogers saw it, "Collectors" distinguished themselves from mere consumers by their rejection of mindless, market-driven buying. Instead, they employed powers of discrimination honed by years of studious listening, immersing themselves in disused recordings that provided a rich sense of the musical past. To be a "true Collector," in other words, was to have acquired a sense of history. With that came "an enlightened viewpoint," a capacity "to discern the finer jazz performances at will," to serve at once as historian and critic, mapping jazz traditions and hierarchies that flew in the face of popular taste.

At the cutting edge of the collecting fraternity, that sense of discernment fused with politics. Men like Hammond, Ramsey, and Smith partook of the Popular Front's jazz-inflected imagination, seizing upon recordings of Dixieland jazz as (in Smith's phrase) "a transcribed history," artifacts full of tantalizing echoes of the sound of New Orleans in its glory days. To collect those recordings and explore that history was to them a political act. It meant training the spotlight on a distinctly black, defiantly proletarian art form in an era when, as they saw it, jazz had been tamed, sweetened, and commodified, with white performers like Benny Goodman and Paul Whiteman praised as its consummate practitioners.

Still, for all that the romance of New Orleans jazz guided the tastes of the collecting fraternity, by 1950 signs were afoot that its appeal was beginning to wane. The changing political climate that affected the likes of Frederic Ramsey was part of the story, along with changes in recording industry sales practices. The late 1930s had seen the establishment of the first reissue labels—small enterprises, mostly run by collectors (*Jazzmen* contributor Stephen Smith was among them), that made deals with the major record companies to issue new pressings of their back catalogues. Once the viability of the experiment had been proven, the major labels themselves followed suit. Over the course of the 1940s, the collector's market was flooded with new pressings of vintage recordings by King Oliver, Louis Armstrong, and other sought-after New Orleans greats. Prices of 78s nosedived. In 1952, a major auction of choice jazz rarities held by the record trader Francis Wolfe collapsed when the recordings failed to make their minimum bids. Although a few collectors held out for the original disks, most were content with the new reproductions and poured scorn on (as one collector put it) "the jerks who pay ten bucks for an original Louis that's available on a dozen private labels at 79 cents."

Yet for some, the problem was not reissues but the cult of New Orleans itself. Taking up collecting in New York City, where he moved after World War II, Pete Whelan felt that the gospel of Dixieland had hardened into an orthodoxy, arid, dog-matic, and stultifying, with the collector's Bible, the *Record Changer*, little more than "a propaganda machine." Though he had loved the music of Morton and Oliver when he heard it on the radio as a boy in New Jersey, he began casting about for music with more luster about it. Sifting through boxes in junk shops, thumbing through the bins at Indian Joe's, he searched for something singular, something magical, without a clear sense of what that something might sound like.

———

IT WAS THIS WORLD OF ODDBALLS AND OBSESSIVES THAT James McKune entered in the early 1940s, a nondescript man of indeterminate age who turned up in Indian Joe's every Saturday night. He was extremely thin, of medium height, with sandy hair graying at the temples, dressed in a white button-down shirt, black trousers, white socks, and black shoes, by all appearances his lone set of clothes. Engaging him in conversation was risky. "McKune had this way of talking," one acquaintance remembers. "He'd make these abrupt gestures, he was very intense, and everybody that he was talking to would be backing up against the wall, because he'd be, not pushing you back, but you'd be afraid of the hands and elbows coming at you." In his pocket he carried a want list that he distributed to used record traders: thirteen hundred 78s recorded in the 1920s and 1930s on the most obscure labels by performers of whom no other collectors had heard.

Late in 1943, McKune ran his first ad in the *Record Changer*, and by the end of the decade, the peculiarity of his wants had drawn him a circle of acolytes. Henry Renard, Ron Lubin, and Pete Kaufman were intrigued enough to write to him (his advertisements gave his address in Brooklyn), and soon they were meeting regularly, along with Stephen Calt, Lawrence Cohn, Ben Kaplan, Nick Perls, Bernie Klatzko, and Pete Whelan, who first encountered McKune in the aisles of Indian Joe's. Most of the men were ten years McKune's junior, and unlike the eminences of the "collecting fraternity," were not products of the Ivy League. Pete Kaufman ran a liquor store, Pete Whelan wrote ad copy for a railway magazine, Henry Renard clerked for one of Indian Joe's competitors, Ron Lubin drove a truck for a photographer, and none of them had a lot of money to spend.

In McKune, all these men found a mentor. He introduced them to the sites of collector's mythology, the places where the *Jazzmen* set got their start: the furniture stores under the subway tracks in Queens where Charles Edward Smith unearthed boxes of untouched OKehs and Vocalions; the Polish Music Shop on 14th Street, where John Hammond found all his Paramounts and Victors; even, incongruously, Bloomingdale's, in whose basement William Russell uncovered a stock of mint-condition Paramounts.

Saturday afternoons they met at Indian Joe's, where they thumbed through the bins in between swigs from the bottles of muscatel that Pete Kaufman brought along from his store, suspending their searches briefly at three, when a man called Bob turned up with a suitcase of pornographic books. One night each week they convened at each others' apartments and debated the merits of their latest finds. In all this, McKune took the lead. In July 1950 Kaufman ran an ad in the *Record Changer* offering the substantial sum of three dollars, more than most collectors offered for the most prized 78s, for a copy of "McKune's Comprehensive Want List of 1943." By then, a small coterie of aficionados had come to revere him as a collector's collector, a connoisseur with an unusually discerning ear.

At the heart of his allure lay the alternative his tastes provided to that of the collecting mainstream, for from the outset the romance of Dixieland left him cold. Most irritating, as he saw it, was the obsession with the music's history and social significance, the endless speculation about its underworld beginnings, the relentless celebration of its collective improvisations as an inherently progressive form. "I have read with enthusiasm two books in which you have had a hand, *The Jazz Record Book* and *Jazzmen*," he wrote to Frederic Ramsey in 1944 from his room at the YMCA. "But I failed to find in either book information which I had sought therein, namely, how the record collector may find out in what year a particular record was made (or issued), and how he may find out the personnel of the recording group when only the leader's (or vocalist's) name is given on the label." That Ramsey never replied to the letter only heightened his conviction that the *Jazzmen* cohort had missed the point: they were weirdly indifferent to the actual recordings, the mysteries of the recorded disk.

Untangling those mysteries was the self-appointed task of McKune and his circle, who by the mid-1950s had dubbed themselves the Blues Mafia. As that name implied, they were a brotherhood, united by their disaffection for the cult of New Orleans and their devotion to authentic blues, a music known only to the cognoscenti, secret, occult, and obscure. Having traded away more recordings than most people would hear in a lifetime, McKune was the grand old man of the group, and he surrounded himself with an air of inscrutability that made his tastes seem all the more pristine and refined.

"On principle," Whelan recalls, McKune would not pay more than three dollars for any record. To hand over more substantial sums would tarnish what ought to be a radical act of salvage, of rummaging through rubbish and finding treasures ignored by the masses and overlooked by a record collecting fraternity whose tastes were too often blinkered and staid. McKune had nothing but scorn for collectors like used record trader Jake Schneider, who became famous among aficionados for amassing nearly half a million recordings.

That McKune's room at the YMCA housed a comparatively modest collection owed partly to practicalities—only so many disks could fit under that bed—but more importantly to his fastidiousness: only three hundred disks, Whelan remembers, but "all of them choice." He was contemptuous of the "treacle fanciers," as he called them, the bobby-soxers who occasionally ventured into the Jazz Record Center in search of bargain Glenn Miller, and he had no more time for the jumped-up sounds of Louis Jordan and Muddy Waters that were dominating the postwar African American soundscape. Nor did he enjoy "people's music," the proletarian folk song purveyed by Leadbelly and Woody Guthrie under the aegis of the Popular Front. The recordings that he salvaged came from the bottom of the discard pile, the dross that everyone else had rejected, records that, as one collector later put it, were "considered worthless by everyone but [McKune] himself."

It had been in 1944, a year after he took up collecting, that McKune unearthed his greatest discarded treasure, a scratched, worn copy of "Some These Days I'll Be Gone," recorded in 1929 by Charley Patton, a singer about whom he knew nothing and whom no other collectors were after. On first hearing, Patton's voice sounded almost too primitive, but

after that initial shock, McKune was transfixed. What overwhelmed him was Patton's artistry, his inventiveness with his
materials, the way his rough-edged voice conveyed a breath-
taking delicacy of technique. "He tells a story only in part,"
McKune explained, "singing the same phrases again and again,
varying his voice, almost making the guitar part of his voice."
On the flip side was the old blues standard "Frankie and Albert," which he sang "as it probably has never been sung before. . . . His is a tale quietly yet passionately told. At the end
you are shaken. You play it again and you forget that anyone
else ever sang it." What McKune heard in Patton's voice was a
transcendent, mystical power: "only the great religious singers
have ever effected me similarly." The only appropriate response to such artistry was to listen "silently. In awe."

Patton became McKune's archetypal blues voice, the
model that he impressed upon the Blues Mafia, that he had
them listening out for in those weekly sessions hunched over
the phonograph in each others' apartments. McKune had
mixed feelings about those evenings: too often, he complained, they deteriorated into loud boozy chatter, "conditions
not conducive to good listening," when what was needed was
the reverent silence in which vocal greatness could make itself
heard.

Even in that group of obsessive enthusiasts, McKune distinguished himself by the sheer intensity he brought to the
quest. The discographer Dick Spottswood learned as much in
1952, when he was a fifteen-year-old collecting novice and, by
some kind of beginner's luck, managed to unearth two Skip
James 78s, "Hard Time Killing Floor Blues" and "If You
Haven't Any Hay Get on Down the Road," recordings so rare
that not even the Blues Mafia had been able to find them.

Though they were barely acquainted, McKune telephoned him to announce that he would be coming to Spottswood's house to hear them, which meant traveling 250 miles to the suburbs of Washington, D.C.

> I said, "Are you sure? That's a long ways" because he lived in the Williamsburg section of Brooklyn in New York. And that's what he did. He got on the Greyhound bus, he came down to Washington, he took whatever local conveyance he could—I couldn't help him, because I wasn't old enough to drive!—and came all the way down to my house in Bethesda. He listened to those Skip James records once, maybe twice, I don't know. I know he wasn't there an hour, even. He turned around and went back home to Brooklyn, having heard the records that he had come to hear.

THE BLUES MAFIA MIGHT HAVE RUMBLED ON FOREVER, honing their tastes, refining their want lists, had it not been for an upstart collector who affronted their sensibilities and provoked them to move into the public eye. The offending party was Samuel Barclay Charters IV, a thirty-year-old jazz aficionado and aspiring Beat poet who moved to New Orleans in the early 1950s and began casting around for new sounds after the Dixieland revival dried up. Like McKune, Charters would turn his attention to forgotten voices from discarded race records. Yet he would invest that process of rediscovery with a sense of social purpose that was utterly contrary to McKune's aestheticism, and the fallout from his intervention would transform the blues collecting world.

Equipped with magnetic tape and a contract from Moses Asch, Charters spent much of the 1950s scouring Alabama for skiffle bands, the streets of New Orleans for Mardi Gras Indians, and the Bahamas for calypso musicians, including the brilliant guitarist Joseph Spence. In New Orleans he got to know Frederic Ramsey, who was in the midst of the southern treks that would result in *Been Here and Gone*. One glance at Ramsey's photographs fired Charters's imagination and led to a book and an LP issued in 1959 on Folkways Records, both entitled *The Country Blues*.

At heart, *The Country Blues* was a work of advocacy. In sharp contrast to *Been Here and Gone*, published one year later, which scrupulously detached music from social commentary, Charters posed African American music as at least implicitly political, a music rooted in hardship and struggle. His experiences in New Orleans in the 1950s, as the civil rights movement intensified, had alienated him from what he saw as a racist, conformist mainstream, and that sense of disaffection would intensify in the following decade, when he aligned himself with the New Left, wrote poetry protesting the Vietnam War, and ultimately left the United States altogether. In 1975, he reflected on his motives in writing the book.

> In simple terms I was trying to effect a change in the American consciousness by presenting an alternative consciousness. I felt that much of what was stifling America was its racism, and what it desperately needed was to be forced to see that the hypocrisy of its racial attitudes was warping the nation's outlook on nearly every other major problem it was facing. And I also felt that the black culture

itself was a necessary element in the society. The white culture had developed the same kind of defensive hypocrisy toward so many elements of its life, from sexuality to personal mores. In the black expression I found a directness, an openness, and an immediacy I didn't find in the white. The texts of the blues were strong and honest, using language in a way the white culture hadn't used it for hundreds of years. . . . I found that the awareness of the real sources of power in the society, the consciousness of social inequalities, and the direct expression of sexuality in the black culture was so much closer to the American reality that I felt I somehow had to make people conscious of what these other voices were saying.

To that end, Charters set out to uncover the "country blues," an intensely personal music that "became the emotional outlet for Negro singers in every part of the South." The term itself he appears to have lit upon in consultation with Ramsey, who used it in liner notes in the mid-1950s, but Charters gave it a new kind of prominence, raising it to the level of a brand name. At a fairly late stage in preparing his manuscript, he seems to have met up with Pete Whelan and other Blues Mafiosi to listen to some of their rare recordings. But he was not really interested in rarities; his aim was to "keep the focus where the black audience put it," and so he put most of his effort into recovering sales figures from the files of record companies and the industry trade press. The book that resulted barely mentioned Charley Patton, gave a bit more attention to Robert Johnson, but put the spotlight on Lonnie Johnson, Leroy Carr, and Big Bill Broonzy, the musicians whose recordings black Americans of the 1930s had bought.

When the book was published to glowing reviews, with Charters lionized for recovering a forgotten art form, McKune was incensed. As he saw it, Charters understood nothing about country blues: he had chronicled the wrong musicians entirely, not even mentioning the singers who had raised the music to an art form. In response, McKune contacted Trevor Benwell, publisher of the British-based collectors magazine *VJM Palaver* (one of the few collectors magazines to survive the 1950s), and offered to write a riposte. The result was a column pointedly entitled "The Great Country Blues Singers," which would run intermittently until 1965. Its first installment is as close as McKune ever got to issuing a manifesto. In its sheer manic fury, it is worth quoting at length.

> Collectors of the Negro country blues singers should read this. Or they should have it pinned on them by others who read it.
>
> This essay makes up for what Sam Charters did not say, or did not say fully enough, in his book *The Country Blues.*
>
> At the end of his book Charters acknowledged that he had been helped by listening to the blues records of Pete Whelan, Pete Kaufman, Ben Kaplan. But nowhere did he admit that his book was disappointing to Whelan and to me, or that it might be disappointing to other fanciers of primitive Negro blues.
>
> Do not think me only querulous. What Charters did for the authentic country blues singers, he did well. But he wrote many pages upon the popular blues singers, Blind Lemon Jefferson, Leroy Carr, Lonnie Johnson, Bill Broonzy, Brownie McGhee, Lightning Hopkins.

Jefferson is a country blues singer. He made many Paramount records. I have heard all but five. In my estimation, formed by listening to blues records since 1943, Jefferson made only one record I can call *great*. That is "Jack o' diamonds/Chock House Blues," on Pm 12373.

Lightning Hopkins is a country blues singer today. But I doubt that his most fervent admirers would claim that he was Blind Lemon's equal. The other singers, above, extolled by Charters, *regardless of their sales,* are not country singers.

Charters wrote his book on the basis of record sales. This would, or might, be all right if his book were published for those Negroes, fifty years old or older, who could thereafter read all about the singers they listened to thirty years ago.

Few of these people have bought Charters' book. It has been bought mostly, I should guess, by blues collectors or by students of Negro folkways, *who might become blues collectors.*

This is my important point. I know twenty men who collect the Negro country blues. All of us have been interested in knowing who the *great* country blues singers are, not in who sold best.

On his own basis, best-selling blues singers, Charters may be all right. But I write for those who want a different basis for evaluating blues singers. This basis is their relative greatness, or competence, as country blues singers.

In obvious ways the column was an extended fit of pique. In McKune's eyes Charters was little more than an opportunist, a Johnny-come-lately jazz enthusiast with no real knowledge of blues. Not even the visit to Whelan had helped, since (McKune claimed) Charters turned up only once his book was largely written, too late to incorporate anything he might learn.

Beneath the wounded pride, the aggrieved territoriality, lay McKune's distaste for the whole premise of Charters's project: his decision to use the tastes of African American record buyers as a kind of aesthetic guide. McKune took it as given that the masses could not discriminate, and in his eyes it did not matter whether those masses were white or black. To think otherwise was to resurrect the most philistine brand of left-wing populism, to confuse solidarity with connoisseurship, to pose the appreciation of black music as in itself a political act. Whereas Charters insisted on mining every moan or wail for its social significance ("hours in the hot sun, scraping at the earth, singing to make the hours pass"), the whole point of McKune's *VJM Palaver* columns was to evaluate the singers purely as artists. That, he insisted, was what would-be collectors of country blues needed: advice from experts who had been "listening to blues records since 1943" and who possessed the training, the cultivation to understand "greatness," to distinguish the pedestrian from the artful, the ersatz from the real.

To display that training and cultivation (and to expose Charters's mistakes), the Blues Mafia set out to make the truly great voices public. Sometime around 1960, Pete Whelan canvassed his fellow enthusiasts for the least-battered copies of their most treasured 78s, hired a tape engineer and a partner with money, and set about making taped reproductions. The long-playing albums that resulted began appearing in 1961 on an independent label that Whelan dubbed the Origins Jazz Library. As the name suggested, Whelan envisioned the LPs as a kind of reference collection of primordial sounds, the soil from which jazz sprang, primitive music as an art form in its own right.

The glaring omissions and misconceptions in Charters's book were spotlighted by the new label's first two releases: OJL–1, devoted to Charley Patton, whom Charters had wholly neglected; and OJL–2, an anthology of blues greats pointedly titled *Really! The Country Blues*. Wasn't Charters's country blues real? an interviewer asked Whelan twenty years later. "It was real," he responded. "Just not real enough."

The "realness" of this "country blues" lay in its rough-hewn sound, its heated, primal emotion, and the primitive character of the song form. As one fan of the OJL releases explained: "The voice is dark and heavy, often thick and congested, with a peculiar crying quality. . . . and suffused throughout with an emotional intensity that is all but overpowering (the words seem almost torn from the singer's throat)." These were barely songs at all—more a rhythmic wail of anguish, in which "monosyllabic cries" expressing "strong, uncontrollable feelings" often "carr[ied] far greater meaning than do the song's words."

Those criteria for blues authenticity McKune had spent two decades honing. Alone in his room at the YMCA, playing his 78s at a low volume so as not to penetrate the building's thin walls, he listened for spare, sparse music; oblique, poetic lyrics; and rough-hewn voices that were supercharged with raw emotion. Politics was absent from those recordings, at least on the surface. As he explained, "After you've listened to the real Negro blues for a long time, you know at once that the protest of the blues is. . . [in the] accompanying piano or guitar," not in anything as unsubtle as lyrics. "Real Negro blues" could be recognized by its inimitable vocal: searing, primitive, yet wholly artless, marked by "an intensity devoid of dramatic effects." From voices like that McKune assembled a pantheon of "great country blues singers"—anguished loners and wanderers like Skip James, Son House, Charley Patton, and Robert Johnson, their very obscurity a testament to their ferocious integrity, the rough, ragged intensity of the songs that they sang.

Issuing these voices on LP could conceivably end that obscurity, but none of the Blues Mafiosi really expected the albums to sell. Origins Jazz Library was an attempt to preach to the near-converted, to guide the tastes of what they assumed would be a discerning few. Hence the forbidding title for the label, with the word "Library" guaranteed to scare off the frivolous. Stephen Calt later estimated that about half of OJL's customers were Europeans, the other half a mix of seasoned collectors and young guitarists eager to broaden their repertoires. For OJL–2, *Really! The Country Blues*, Whelan ordered only five hundred pressings, and it would take over two years for sales to exhaust that first batch.

Still, it was enough. Almost immediately, the OJL recordings became the Bible of new, younger blues enthusiasts like John Fahey, people who were often musicians themselves and entranced by the rough-hewn voices, the scratched, grainy sound, and the sense of acquiring secret knowledge, of eschewing Charters's easy answers and participating in a vanguard.

In time the impact of the reissues would stretch still further, to critics and chroniclers who would write the country blues into history and establish its credentials as an art form. For the future *Deep Blues* author Robert Palmer, who encountered the albums as a musician in Memphis, they were "the definitive country blues anthologies," a view held as well by Jeff Todd Titon, whose exposure to the albums would lead him to study ethnomusicology and write the influential book *Early*

Downhome Blues. Other fans included a young historian named Lawrence Levine, just completing his graduate work at Columbia and beginning the investigations into African American folk songs that would result in a foundational work of African American cultural history, *Black Culture and Black Consciousness;* Greil Marcus, who discovered the albums at his local record store in Berkeley; and veteran jazz collector Marshall Stearns, an English professor turned musicologist and director of Rutgers University's Institute for Jazz Studies, which he had helped to establish in 1953.

So intense was the curiosity surrounding country blues that even the Library of Congress took notice. In 1962 it released *Negro Blues and Hollers,* an LP compilation of the field recordings made by Alan Lomax, John Work, and Lewis Jones in the Mississippi Delta in 1941 and 1942. To write the liner notes, library staff turned to Stearns, who approached the task with professorial gravitas, an air of establishing scholarly orthodoxy in a field thick with debate. "The kind of blues on the present recording, made in the early forties before they disappeared, have come to be called 'country' blues—a name which has led to endless argument," he began. "Literature on the country blues is hard to come by," he noted— Samuel Charters, though raising the form's public profile, had made only "a beginning." "To get to the heart of the matter, one has to dig deeper": to the Origins Jazz Library reissues of country blues rarities, and to the "unique articles" in *VJM Palaver* by "James McCune [*sic*], the dean of country-blues fanciers." The value of McKune's articles lay in his having dispensed with sociology in order to focus solely on the form's "artistic merits." Country blues recordings as he defined them were "archaic in the best sense. . . gnarled, rough-hewn, and eminently uncommercial." In them one heard a music "fixed in time and space," unaffected by technology or the market, "tied down to—and unerringly reflect[ing]—the geographic area, the local manners, and the exact vernacular of a specific place." That specific place was the Mississippi Delta, which thanks to McKune could now be identified as the land where the blues was born.

Stearns's liner notes brought McKune momentarily into the limelight, the closest he would ever come to public recognition as a country blues expert. Yet they also contained the seeds of what would become a rebranding. By the late 1960s, the phrase "country blues" being, it seems, too tainted by Charters's misapprehensions, aficionados relabeled the music "Delta blues." The phrase took on an added luster in 1963 when Columbia reissued Robert Johnson's recordings on an LP entitled *King of the Delta Blues Singers.*

Soon the idea that the Delta was the original home of the blues, that it generated a uniquely pure form of black music, came to seem incontestable; in time, even Samuel Charters agreed. Nowhere else in the South, he wrote in 1965, could have bred a music so raw, so primal, for nowhere else was so cut off from the currents of modern life. And nowhere else did racial oppression rule with such ferocity. In the Delta time had effectively stopped—it remained a quasi-feudal region still stuck in the dynamics of slavery. Those circumstances shaped the blues in its natural state, a music of peculiar power and purity, an intensely emotive, deeply personal song form permeated by alienation and pain.

At the heart of this story lay the venerable vision of an untainted black voice. That it could be found at its purest in the Mississippi Delta had never occurred even to as recent a blues enthusiast as Frederic Ramsey, whose vision of a raw, archaic "plantation blues" targeted the rural South as a whole. ("Don't know what the Delta along the way will hold," he wrote to Moses Asch of Folkways Records as he prepared to travel there in 1954. "Probably at least one good blues singer.")

Nor did that tale of a "Delta blues" emerge readily from what Lomax, Work, and Jones found in the region in 1941, three years after the murder of Robert Johnson. The residents they interviewed uniformly attested that the region felt modern to those who lived in it, fast-paced and worldly, particularly in contrast to "the Hills," the mountainous counties to the east, where families had deep roots in the soil and traditional mores seemed fully in force. In the Delta no one stayed in one place for long, and its young people were flouting tradition—moving around in search of better wages, scorning the church, experimenting with sex, immersing themselves in a mass-marketed world of automobiles, motion pictures, and recorded music. Surveying the black bars of Clarksdale, Lewis Jones found no recordings by local musicians; the most popular tracks were those by Louis Jordan, Count Basie, Fats Waller, no different from Harlem or the South Side of Chicago. Lomax himself found modernity in the most unlikely places. Late one night outside the small hamlet of Friars Point, he stumbled across a juke joint on the edge of a cotton field and opened the door to find a blaring jukebox and a roomful of people jitterbugging to Duke Ellington.

The revivalist vision of Delta blues could accommodate none of these accounts. Still less could it accommodate Lewis Jones's conclusion that the Delta was home not to a premodern "folk" or a tyrannized "caste" but a "rural proletariat." With its suggestions of black resistance and echoes of Popular Front radicalism, that phrase had no place in the revival. "Pure blues," for the likes of McKune, took the form of voices that were searing, personal, and apolitical. That would become one of the keynotes of the blues revival: real, authentic blues was not protest music. On this score, in time, even Samuel Charters came around. "If the blues simply mirrored the protest of the moment they would finally have little more than an historical interest, like the songs of the suffragettes or the Grange movement," he wrote in the wake of the OJL reissues. Instead, the Negro turned to the blues "as the expression of his personal and immediate experience." The result was "a poetic language" that spoke of "a larger human reality," timeless truths of alienation and loss.

———

WHEN JAMES MCKUNE UNCOVERED HIS FORGOTTEN VOICES, he took it for granted that all these singers were dead. His friend Harry Smith made the same assumption, and so did most of those who bought his *Anthology of American Folk Music,* issued on Folkways Records in 1952. "All those guys on that Harry Smith Anthology were dead. *Had* to be," one fan of the anthology remembers believing. Had to be, because those voices had been so fully appropriated, so thoroughly brought back to life. The country bluesman as McKune envisioned him was a man of fierce integrity, a heroic loner. That he could be encountered only on vinyl guaranteed that he would remain uncorrupted. After all, voices on record cannot talk back.

As it happened, however, they could. In June 1964, veteran Mafiosi Nick Perls made an astounding discovery: Son House was alive, aged somewhere in his seventies, living alone in a housing project in Rochester, New York. Within days, three other collectors uncovered the aged Skip James, alive, though not well, in Mississippi. Soon other elderly bluesmen emerged from the woodwork, and the Blues Mafia swung into action to engineer, publicize, and manage their comebacks, setting up dates in the recording studio and tours on the coffeehouse and folk festival circuit.

In what seemed like an instant, the Delta blues acquired living, breathing embodiments. Record collectors had fleshed out Delta blues as an unvarnished music "of almost archaeo-logical purity," as one enthusiast put it, and the men they re-discovered cooperated with the fantasy—at least to the extent of appearing as old as the music was supposed to be. Most of the musicians welcomed the attention and performed with dignity, and at its best those comebacks succeeded in broaden-ing white musical horizons, drawing new listeners to the blues who might not have taken an interest before.

At its worst, though, the blues revival took on the aura of a circus sideshow. Most of the resurrected heroes were well past their prime—Son House, in particular, was in an ad-vanced stage of alcoholic deterioration—and none of them were prepared for this explosion of white interest in a music that African Americans had moved on from long ago. Uneasy with the role they were allocated, they rarely played it as sin-cerely as their new audience imagined. Skip James, an im-mensely troubled man, made little effort to conceal his contempt for his new public. Contempt seemed the logical response for an audience that responded reverentially to third-rate performances, that seemed to be applauding not so much his talent but the spectacle of him making it through the song at all.

Skip James died in 1969; Son House, in failing health, re-
tired a few years later, and with their disappearance the blues
revival moved back to the disused recordings that first gave it
life. By the late 1960s, LP anthologies of blues reissues were
being released by major industry players like Columbia and
small labels like Yazoo, Roots, and Arhoolie. No longer did
searching for country blues mean relying on trading networks
or scavenging in secondhand stores. Yet unlike the early 1950s,
when reissues of New Orleans jazz rarities had sent the prices
of 78s into a nosedive, in the 1960s when the Delta blues
recordings were reissued, the prices of 78s began to rise. As
early as 1963, James McKune was being forced to exceed his
three-dollar limit and bid upward of fifteen dollars per record.
By the end of the decade, a rare Charley Patton could fetch
seventy dollars, and after that into the hundreds and thousands, unimaginably beyond what the likes of McKune could
afford.

In a way, it was McKune's own doing, for his approach to
collecting had always diverged from that of the *Jazzmen* set.
Collecting race records in an era when 78s were still manufactured, Ramsey and Russell had searched for artists, not objects, and if necessary they were content with reissues: their
interest lay, by and large, with the music, and they were relatively unconcerned with the medium by which it was conveyed. In contrast, McKune and his acolytes (as one collector
put it) "cherished the physical symbols," the sheer materiality
of the original 78s. Already on the wane in the late 1940s, the
78 format vanished altogether by the early 1950s, and for the
Blues Mafia that obsolescence was part of the lure. They
prized the visible, palpable oddity of what Whelan described

as "the rarest labels in the record collecting fraternity: Autograph (red or light blues with nautical checked border), Black Patti (purple with golden peacock that has a monstrous tail), Electrobeam Gennett (black with Old English lettering), Merrit (purple or black with agonized Greek death masks), Paramount (black, purple, blue; 'gold eagle holds the world in its talons')." That, he observed, was "what record collecting intrigue is all about—the music has to be good; beyond that, it is the label and how it LOOKS: the naïve 1920s Cheltenham, Broadway, or Gaudy typefaces and 30-year-old colors that would be too expensive to color-match and print today."

Along with that romance with obsolescence went a sense of the disk as a unique, handcrafted work of art. As the Blues Mafia practiced it, Whelan once observed, "record collecting was not like collecting stamps. It was more like collecting paintings." The disks that McKune hoarded were, in a real sense, rarities: since both jazz collectors and African American buyers had rejected them, they were never in wide circulation, and had been pressed in small quantities to start with. And though they had been mechanically recorded, they retained something of the handmade about them. Used 78s were dusty, battered, and scratchy—they had been heavily handled, if not made by hand—and had been recorded on primitive equipment under poor conditions. (Robert Johnson, for example, made his recordings in makeshift studios in a Dallas warehouse and a San Antonio hotel room.)

Indeed, part of the appeal of McKune's "great country blues singers" may have been the very murkiness of the sound quality. Far from destroying the mystery of black singing, in other words, recording technology conferred it, creating disks whose voices sounded peculiar and striking, muffled and contorted by the machine. It was perhaps no accident that he re-served his highest praise for Charley Patton, whose record-ings are virtually unintelligible, owing in part to Patton's slurred delivery but largely to the "scratches, pops, clicks and hiss" that abound on his surviving 78s. Those layers of surface noise only intensified Patton's aura of mystery, the magic McKune found in those blank, black platters whose spiral grooves, once set in motion, released haunting echoes from another world.

IN THE DECADES SINCE THE BLUES REVIVAL, BLUES CHRONI-clers have fleshed out the narrative the Blues Mafia first sketched, disentangling the blues from politics, sex, the lore of the city, and all suggestions of modernity. Not everyone has approved of the result. "There is an honest and laudable interest in alleviating Negro suffering or at least mak[ing] it known to the world in every blues book," the ethnomusicolo-gist Charles Keil remarked in 1966. "Yet I can almost imag-ine some of these writers helping to set up a 'reservation' or Bantustan for old bluesmen; it is often that sort of liberal-ism." Revivalists privileged an obsolete form of rural black culture in an era when most African Americans lived in cities, and toward contemporary black music they displayed at best ambivalence, more often hostility. That kind of purism has led some black musicians to a blunt conclusion: whites are prepared to laud black creativity only when it is old and decrepit. As blues singer and guitarist Lonnie John-son put it when Keil approached him for an interview in the mid-1960s: "Are you another one of those guys who wants to put crutches under my ass?"

Yet such skepticism has proven remarkably muted, out-weighed by the power of the Delta blues story, a narrative summed up by those hard-bitten black faces adorning album covers and book jackets, those unflinching black loners posed before ramshackle cabins or arid fields or empty highways stretching off into nowhere. In the end, that story even won over Alan Lomax. By the time he wrote his magnum opus on African American music, *The Land Where the Blues Began,* in 1993, he had almost wholly discarded the focus on social conflict and change that had once led him to Jelly Roll Morton. If in 1938 Morton's blues had provided "a rich evocation of underground America," in 1993 they were commercial, superficial, and as such not genuine: "the blues of the professional jazzman are never quite the real thing." The real thing was the blues of the Delta, a personal music of torment and pain, a sorrow song that had gained a wide resonance as the bluesman's "anomie and alienation, orphaning and rootlessness" became key themes of late-twentieth-century life.

The power of that story lies in large part in the ambiguities that suffuse it. If blues revivalists' accounts stressed alienation and anguish, they were not wholly untouched by the erotic. In their celebration of blues poetry's profoundly personal character, its expression of intense inner feeling, enthusiasts infused their romance with the unfettered self with a highly charged sense of the supreme realness of rural black men. A defiant drifter, scorning convention, breaking free from domestic ties, the bluesman embodied the tensions about modern masculinity that from its earliest stirrings in the 1950s simmered beneath the surface of the blues revival. It is surely no accident that so many of the early blues performers that revivalists scorned as inauthentic were women; to them, authenticity had a male voice. In an era of organization manhood and gray-flannel suits, of backyard barbecues and tract homes in the suburbs, bluesmen were nonconformists par excellence: "self-made outcasts," as Frederic Ramsey put it in *Been Here and Gone,* "who prefer this life of impermanence. . . , [who] found that the road, which offered adventure, was better than their homes, which offered nothing." Their authenticity took its power from their stark contrast with the likes of Pat Boone and Bobby Darin, who dominated the era's white-bread mass-market pop, and with the images of domestic contentment and sober white-collar respectability that pervaded America in the Cold War era.

In that sense, the blues revival stands alongside the Beat movement as an opening salvo of what Barbara Ehrenreich has termed the male "flight from commitment" that percolated through postwar American culture. What united both movements was their almost exclusively male constituency and their romance with outsider manhood, with defiant black men who seemed to scorn the suburban breadwinner's stifling, soul-destroying routine. For revivalists, that model was the country bluesman, at heart a "beggar, outcast, near criminal"; for Beats, it was the black urban jazzman, "a frontiersman in the Wild West of American night life," as Norman Mailer described him in his notorious essay on the "white Negro," who had taken the only possible route to authenticity in a conformist world: "to divorce oneself from society, to exist without roots, to set out on that uncharted journey into the rebellious imperatives of the self."

More than any other commentator, Mailer captured (and indeed succumbed to) the intensely wrought fantasies that fueled the Beat romance with black style. For the Beats, the black man was a deeply sexual existential outlaw, a renegade who lived for sex alone.

> Knowing in the cells of his existence that life was war, nothing but war, the Negro (all exceptions admitted) could rarely afford the sophisticated inhibitions of civilization, and so he kept for his survival the art of the primitive, he lived in the enormous present, he subsisted for his Saturday night kicks, relinquishing the pleasures of the mind for the more obligatory pleasures of the body, and in his music he gave voice to the character and quality of his existence, to his rage, and the infinite variations of joy, lust, languor, growl, cramp, pinch, scream and despair of his orgasm.

The blues revivalist romance was kinder, gentler, but it was none the less enthralled by the primitive. Revivalists eschewed Mailer's urban underworld for a setting altogether closer to nature. And although they had little taste for music that gave voice to the cramp, pinch, and scream of the orgasm, there is no denying the erotic charge of the bluesmen whose portraits dominate blues literature. Look, for example, at the tough, callused black hands minutely detailed in Frederic Ramsey's photographs. Or consider this passage from *The Land Where the Blues Began*, in which Alan Lomax recalls a 1941 session with Son House:

> His voice, guttural and hoarse with passion, ripped apart the surface of the music like his tractor-driven deep plow ripped apart the wet black earth in the springtime, making the sap of the earth song run, while his powerful, work-hard hands

snatched strange chords out of the steel strings the way they had snatched so many tons of cotton out of brown thorny cotton bolls in the fall. And with him the sorrow of the blues was not tentative, or retiring, or ironic. Son's whole body wept, as with his eyes closed, the tendons in his powerful neck standing out with the violence of his feeling and his brown face flushing, he sang in an awesome voice the "Death Letter Blues."

But while that romance can be labeled primitivist, it should not be dismissed as mere macho posing. As revivalists drew him, the bluesman could swagger, but he could also be vulnerable, and it was his vulnerability—Son House's weeping body—that drew them most profoundly into his music. Embedded in their search for the authentic was a sensitivity to emotion, a desire to be deeply moved by manifestations of inner feeling. In their hands, the search for authentic black voices was a spiritual quest infused with what for men were forbidden desires: to dissolve boundaries, renounce autonomy, merge with the wellsprings of life. Revivalists channeled that search for life sources into the blues and in the process remade the tradition. At their most positive, they enriched understanding and broadened white horizons. At their worst, they fed on a faintly colonialist romance with black suffering, an eroticization of African American despair.

———

TODAY THE BUILDING THAT ONCE HOUSED THE WILLIAMS-burg YMCA stands in a state of neglect and decay. On the day I visited, I almost did not find it. The Marcy Avenue BMT stop was closed for repairs, so I got off one stop down the line at

Hewes Street and walked back in the opposite direction, past a synagogue, a Muslim community center, a bakery specializing in matzos, and signs for cheap health care in English and Spanish. On Marcy Avenue I found a sea of unfamiliar street numbers, 179 nowhere among them, so I sought help in a corner grocery, where the cashier told me that the street had been renumbered and pointed me in the right direction.

That the building was once a YMCA is discernible only by the crest over the door—the organization moved out long ago, apparently sometime in the 1980s. What had once been the front entrance is boarded up; through a side door visitors have access to the City of New York Human Resources Administration, the North Brooklyn Food Stamp Center, and a branch of the Church of Jesus Christ of Latter-Day Saints. I wandered into the lobby, but it was empty and soulless, so I went back outside and crossed the road and stood on the corner opposite, looking up at the top-floor windows and trying to imagine my way inside.

As much as Son House or Charley Patton, as much as even Robert Johnson, James McKune, in the end, is the enigma at the heart of the Delta blues, enigmatic not least because he so abruptly falls out of its story. Though his protégés succeeded brilliantly at pushing his aesthetic into the spotlight, apart from the columns in *VJM Palaver*, McKune himself played no direct part in the process. He wrote no liner notes, managed no artists, set up no record labels, opened no blues clubs. Instead, he seems to have stopped listening to music altogether. His *VJM* columns, always sporadic, ceased altogether in 1965, and sometime that year he moved out of the Williamsburg YMCA for a room in a Manhattan hostel near 34th Street. Eventually he drifted to the Lower East Side and found a room at the Broadway Central Hotel, a once-elegant watering hole gone to seed. Though the lower floors retained a kind of lowlife glamour—home to the Mercer Arts Center, a gathering place for New York's nascent punk underground, where by 1973 the New York Dolls would be in residence—McKune settled on the floors above, given over to single rooms inhabited by junkies, hookers, and derelicts, into whose ranks he quietly slid. Reports of acquaintances who occasionally spotted him suggest that he used his room only infrequently; mostly, he lived on the streets. When police found his body in September 1971, the only clue to his earlier life lay in a letter in the room from Bernie Klatzko, one of the stalwarts of the Blues Mafia. There was no trace of a record collection: McKune had either sold it or given it away.

Perhaps McKune's abandonment of the blues was inevitable. He had always had a fervent sense of his own importance, an unswerving belief in his aesthetic judgments, and a taste for enveloping himself in mystery. Making himself elusive was a way of emphasizing his maverick status, the cutting-edge character of his musical tastes. He was a preacher who feared converts; he proselytized passionately for his salvaged recordings but lost interest once others caught on. The pleasures of collecting lie in creating a personal system, an alternative universe of aesthetics and taste. Lose control of that universe and the collector's pride and bravado become envy and frustration; his excitement and euphoria become depression and despair. McKune's story might illuminate the dark side of collecting, the devastation of the connoisseur who finds that his private passion is private no longer, that his role as a tastemaker has been usurped.

Most likely we will never know what propelled McKune into his fascination with the blues, but it is hard not to speculate about how his aesthetic resonated with his inner needs. McKune dedicated his life to finding a blues voice that was intense, raw, and defiantly marginal, and he ended his days as a homeless, friendless wanderer, dying in circumstances as violent, mysterious, and sexually charged as Robert Johnson himself. It is perhaps too pat, too easy, but not wholly unjustified, to let that image sum up his story: the record collector down and out on Skid Row, clinging fiercely to his blues vision— living the life of the alienated drifter, scorning the pull of the marketplace, uncorrupted to the very end.

☞ ACKNOWLEDGMENTS ☜

T HIS BOOK BEGAN IN MY IMAGINATION AS A BIOGRAPHY of Little Richard. That it became something very different owes a lot to my agent David Godwin, whose readings of my earliest drafts encouraged me to push my ideas to the foreground and follow them where they wanted to lead. My editor at Jonathan Cape, Dan Franklin, believed in this book early on, was patient while I reworked it, and made incisive comments in the concluding stages. At Basic Books, Lara Heimert's enthusiasm cheered me through the final revisions.

I was helped in my research by financial assistance from the British Academy, the Leverhulme Trust, and Birkbeck College, and by the knowledge and expertise of the staff of several archives: the Archive of Folk Culture, Library of Congress; the Southern Historical Collection, University of North Carolina at Chapel Hill; the Center for American History, University of Texas at Austin; the Special Collections Library at Baylor University; the Blues Archive, University of Mississippi; the Moorland-Spingarn Research Center, Howard University; the Special Collections Library, Fisk University; the Ralph Rinzler Folklife Archives and Collections at the Smithsonian Center for Folklife and Cultural Heritage; the Beinecke Library, Yale University; the Institute of Jazz Studies, Rutgers University; and the Alan Lomax Archive at Hunter College (much of which is now held at the Library of Congress). Ruth Beecher's research assistance brought me fresh material on Alan Lomax. Mary Frances Odum Schinhan, Anna Lomax Wood, and Alida Ramsey Porter and Martha Ramsey kindly shared their memories of their fathers and allowed me to see unpublished papers. Pete Whelan, Dick Spottswood, and Henry Renard gave me wonderful material about blues record collecting and shared their recollections of James McKune.

Alison Light deserves thanks beyond measure for reading every word of this manuscript in its many incarnations. Her imagination, insight, and daring shaped it throughout. Hera Cook helped the book to get off the ground and stepped in again in the final stages, and I benefited greatly from her smart, critical readings. At a crucial moment, Barbara Taylor offered to read the whole manuscript; without her help I would probably still be working on it. For debate, suggestions, encouragement, and enthusiasm, a thousand thanks too to Paul Anderson, Robert Cantwell, John Carson, Tim Dee, David Feldman, Eric Hobsbawm, Rebecca Lemov, W. T. Lhamon, Peter Mandler, Greil Marcus, Daniel Rodgers, Luc Sante, Matt Seaton, Christine Stansell, and Sean Wilentz.

Ken Arnold read endless drafts, wrote up voluminous comments, talked, argued, and listened to more Delta blues than he ever wanted to hear. Jackson Arnold and Lukas Hamilton made the book worth writing, and certainly worth finishing. This is for them, with love.

⁓ NOTES ⁓

One: The Delta Revisited

1   **the opening years of the blues revival:** Although the cultural roots of the blues revival have received little attention from historians, some useful studies of the revival itself have begun to appear. See Jeff Todd Titon, "Reconstructing the Blues: Reflections on the 1960s Blues Revival," in Neil V. Rosenberg, ed., *Transforming Tradition: Folk Music Revivals Examined* (Urbana: University of Illinois Press, 1993), 220–240; Jim O'Neal, "I Once Was Lost, But Now I'm Found: The Blues Revival of the 1960s," in Lawrence Cohn, ed., *Nothing but the Blues: The Music and the Musicians* (New York: Abbeville Press, 1993), 347–387; Stephen Calt, *I'd Rather Be the Devil: Skip James and the Blues* (New York: Da Capo Press, 1994); and Elijah Wald, *Escaping the Delta: Robert Johnson and the Invention of the Delta Blues* (New York: Amistad Press, 2004).

2   **90 percent of the Delta was covered in swamps:** James C. Cobb, *The Most Southern Place on Earth: The Mississippi Delta and the Roots of Regional Identity* (New York: Oxford University Press, 1992), viii.

2   **"Nowhere in Mississippi have antebellum conditions of landholding":** Quoted in Cobb, *Most Southern Place on Earth*, 98.

2   **northern anthropologists flocked to the region:** John Dollard, *Caste and Class in a Southern Town* (New Haven, CT: Yale University Press, 1937); Hortense Powdermaker, *After Freedom: A Cultural Study in the Deep South* (New York: Atheneum, 1969; originally published 1939); Allison Davis, Burleigh B. Gardner, and Mary R. Gardner, *Deep South: A Social Anthropological Study of Caste and Class* (Chicago: University of Chicago Press, 1941).

3   **"rough, spontaneous, crude and unfinished":** Pete Welding, "Stringin' the Blues: The Art of Folk Blues Guitar," *Down Beat*, July 1, 1965, 22. See also Samuel Charters, *The Bluesmen* (New York: Oak Publications, 1967), 27–32.

4   **the primeval scene was in fact the product of a very modern process:** On the Delta as a postbellum industrial product, see Cobb, *The Most Southern Place on Earth*.

6   **"the very idea of America":** Greil Marcus, *Mystery Train: Images of America in Rock 'n' Roll Music* (London: Penguin Books, 1991; originally published 1975), 39.

6   **"a world without salvation, redemption, or rest":** Marcus, *Mystery Train*, 21.

6   **"made the terrors of the world . . . more real":** Marcus, *Mystery Train*, 29.

6   **"a two minute image of doom":** Marcus, *Mystery Train*, 33.

7   **OKeh Records released "Crazy Blues" by Mamie Smith:** On the significance of Smith's recording and on the early history of "race records," see Francis Davis, *The History of the Blues* (London: Secker and Warburg, 1995), chap. 2; William Barlow, *Looking Up at Down: The Emergence of Blues Culture* (Philadelphia: Temple University Press, 1989), chap. 5; Lawrence Levine, *Black Culture and Black Consciousness: Afro-American Folk Thought from Slavery to Freedom* (New York: Oxford University Press, 1977), 225–227.

10   **"more vividly and more intensely than any mere poet":** Leon Litwack, *Trouble in Mind: Black Southerners in the Age of Jim Crow* (New York: Knopf, 1998), 457.

10   **"How much history can be transmitted by pressure on a guitar string?":** Robert Palmer, *Deep Blues: A Musical and Cultural History of the Mississippi Delta* (New York: Penguin Books, 1981), quoted in Litwack, *Trouble in Mind*, xvii.

11   **Charley Patton's recordings sold only moderately:** Palmer, *Deep Blues*, 123–124.

11   **A Fisk University sociologist:** "List of Records on Machines in Clarksdale Amusement Places," Folder 7 (Lists), Fisk University Mississippi Delta Collection, Archive of Folk Culture, Library of Congress, Washington, DC. The list, compiled by sociologist Lewis Jones, dates from 1941 or 1942.

13   **"You couldn't get anything on Paramount":** Stephen Calt and Gayle Dean Wardlow, "The Buying and Selling of Paramount—Part 3," *78 Quarterly* 1, no. 5 (1990), 8.

14   **when the Edison Corporation set out to market:** Emily Thompson, "Machines, Music, and the Quest for Fidelity: Marketing the Edison Phonograph in America, 1877–1925," *Musical Quarterly* 79 (1995), 131–171.

14   **"the mechanical, nickel phonograph":** Quoted in Levine, *Black Culture and Black Consciousness*, 231.

14   **"No, ma'am, they don't make up many songs":** Zora Neale Hurston, "Turpentine," in Pamela Bordelon, ed., *Go Gator and Muddy the Water: Writings by Zora Neale Hurston from the Federal Writers' Project* (New York: W. W. Norton, 1999), 129.

15   **"Enclosed find all of the material that I have transcribed into ink":** Zora Neale Hurston to Franz Boas, March 29, 1927, reprinted in Carla Kaplan, ed., *Zora Neale Hurston: A Life in Letters* (New York: Doubleday, 2002), 96–97.

15   **"The bulk of the population spends its leisure":** Quoted in Robert Hemenway, *Zora Neale Hurston: A Literary Biography* (Urbana: University of Illinois Press, 1977), 92.

15   **"There was a valley . . . with smoke-wreaths during the day and mist at night":** Jean Toomer, "Autobiographical Selection," in Toomer, *Cane: An Authoritative Text, Backgrounds, Criticism,* ed. Darwin T. Turner (New York: W. W. Norton, 1988), 141–142.

16   **"The supreme fact of mechanical civilization":** Jean Toomer to Waldo Frank, late 1922/early 1923, in Toomer, *Cane: An Authoritative Text,* 151.

16   **"lush glades of primitive imagination":** Zora Neale Hurston, "Go Gator and Muddy the Water," in Bordelon, *Go Gator and Muddy the Water,* 69.

17   **"There is an enemy at the doors of folk-music":** Hubert Parry, "Inaugural Address to the Folk Song Society," *Journal of the Folk Song Society* 1 (1899), 2–3, quoted in Richard Middleton, *Studying Popular Music* (Milton Keynes, UK: Open University Press, 1990), 131.

17   **"Rude and apparently incoherent":** Frederick Douglass, *Narrative of the Life of Frederick Douglass, An American Slave, Written by Himself* (New York: Signet Books, 1968; originally published 1845), 31–32.

18   **"that life was joyous to the black slave, careless and happy":** W. E. B. Du Bois, *The Souls of Black Folk* (1903), in John Hope Franklin, ed., *Three Negro Classics* (New York: Avon Books, 1965), 380.

18   **"death and suffering and unvoiced longing toward a truer world":** Du Bois, *Souls of Black Folk,* 380.

18   **"men will judge men by their souls and not by their skins":** Du Bois, *Souls of Black Folk,* 386.

18   **"There is no true American music":** Du Bois, *Souls of Black Folk,* 220.

18   **"All in all, we black men seem the sole oasis of simple faith":** Du Bois, *Souls of Black Folk,* 220.

19   **"a new analytical way of listening to music":** Ralph Ellison, *Invisible Man* (New York: Vintage Books, 1972; originally published 1952), 8.

19   **"long, lonely sing-song of the fields":** Charles Peabody, "Notes on Negro Music," *Journal of American Folklore* 16 (1903), 152. On the cult of the spirituals, see Jon Cruz, *Culture on the Margins: The Black Spiritual and the Rise of American Cultural Interpretation* (Princeton, NJ: Princeton University Press, 1999); and Ronald Radano, "Denoting Difference: The Writing of Slave Spirituals," *Critical Inquiry* 22 (1996), 506–554.

20   **"It is difficult to express the entire character":** Lucy McKim, "Songs of the Port Royal Contrabands," *Dwight's Journal of Music* 21, November 8, 1862, reprinted in Bruce Jackson,

ed., *The Negro and His Folklore in Nineteenth-Century Periodicals* (Austin: University of Texas Press, 1967), 62.

20 **"The best we can do . . . with paper and types, or even with voices":** William Francis Allen, Charles Pickard Ware, and Lucy McKim Garrison, eds., *Slave Songs of the United States* (New York: A. Simpson and Company, 1867), iv–v.

20 **"Never, it seems to me, since man first lived and suffered":** Thomas Wentworth Higginson, "Negro Spirituals," *Atlantic Monthly* 19 (June 1867), reprinted in Jackson, ed., *The Negro and His Folklore,* 92.

21 **white listeners could absorb it and experience something of the sublime:** Radano, "Denoting Difference," 518–519.

21 **"the whites of the South to keep *one* bunch of negroes":** Quoted in Deborah Kodish, *Good Friends and Bad Enemies: Robert Winslow Gordon and the Study of American Folksong* (Urbana: University of Illinois Press, 1986), 140.

21 **"When black takes on the prowlings and pratings of the white race":** Review of Howard Odum and Guy Johnson, *The Negro and His Songs,* in *Memphis Commercial Appeal,* undated clipping in file labeled "*Negro and His Songs* (1925): Clippings," in Box 22, Howard Washington Odum Papers (hereinafter HWOP), Southern Historical Collection, Wilson Library, University of North Carolina at Chapel Hill.

Two: Impartial Testimony

27 **"one night in Tutwiler":** W. C. Handy, *Father of the Blues* (New York: Macmillan, 1941), 78.

28 **"Suffering and hard luck were the midwives":** Handy, *Father of the Blues,* 76.

29 **a bespectacled twenty-three-year-old, Howard Odum:** My account of Howard Odum's early life draws on Daniel Joseph Singal, *The War Within: From Victorian to Modernist Thought in the South, 1919–1945* (Chapel Hill: University of North Carolina Press, 1982), 115–152; and Wayne Brazil, *Howard W. Odum: The Building Years* (New York: Taylor and Francis, 1988).

32 **"in and out across swollen streams and backwoods and pinehills"; "I myself have known Yoknapatawpha":** Howard Odum, "On Southern Literature and Southern Culture," in Louis D. Rubin, Jr., and Robert D. Jacobs, *Southern Renascence: The Literature of the Modern South* (Baltimore: Johns Hopkins Press, 1953), 97.

32 **Comprising 45 percent of the county's population:** On Lafayette County, see Joel Williamson, *William Faulkner and Southern History* (New York: Oxford University Press, 1993), 153. On Reconstruction, see Eric Foner, *Reconstruction: America's Unfinished Revolution, 1863–1877* (New York: Harper and Row, 1988).

33 **"If necessary every Negro in the state will be lynched":** Quoted in Neil McMillen, *Dark Journey: Black Mississippians in the Age of Jim Crow* (Urbana: University of Illinois Press, 1989), 6–7. For life under Jim Crow more generally, see Leon Litwack, *Trouble in Mind: Black Southerners in the Age of Jim Crow* (New York: Knopf, 1999); Joel Williamson, *The Crucible of Race: Black/White Relations in the American South since Emancipation* (New York: Oxford University Press, 1984); C. Van Woodward, *The Strange Career of Jim Crow* (New York: Oxford University Press, 1957).

33 **"slipped off and went home":** Howard Odum, *An American Epoch: Southern Portraiture in the National Picture* (New York: Henry Holt, 1930), 88.

34 **"his broad forehead moist with perspiration":** Odum, *An American Epoch,* 88.

35 **"what I designated as A. I. U. P.":** Howard Odum, untitled address circa 1954, held in "Odum Manuscripts" file, Box 73, Howard Washington Odum Papers (hereinafter HWOP), Southern Historical Collection, Wilson Library, University of North Carolina at Chapel Hill.

35 **"Science, and science alone, star-eyed science":** Thomas Pearce Bailey, *Race Orthodoxy in the South and Other Aspects of the Negro Question* (New York: Neale Publishing, 1914), 58.

36 **"Does the Negro show potentialities as a race?":** Bailey, *Race Orthodoxy,* 380.

36 **"the physical stock of the higher racial types":** Bailey, *Race Orthodoxy,* 94.

36 **"Is the Negro really adaptable, or is he parasitic?":** Bailey, *Race Orthodoxy*, 380–381.

37 **"The Negro has a life and an environment of his own":** Howard W. Odum, *Social and Mental Traits of the Negro* (New York: Columbia University Press, 1910), 13.

37 **"what he *is* rather than what he appears to be":** Howard Odum, "Religious Folk Songs of the Southern Negroes," *American Journal of Religious Psychology and Education* 3 (July 1909), reprinted in Katharine Jocher et al., *Folk, Region and Society: Selected Papers of Howard Odum* (Chapel Hill: University of North Carolina Press, 1964), 8.

37 **sociologist William Graham Sumner's 1907 book *Folkways*:** For a discussion of the influence of the concept of "folkways" on Odum's thought, see Daniel T. Rodgers, "Regionalism and the Burdens of Progress," in J. Morgan Kousser and James M. McPherson, eds., *Region, Race, and Reconstruction* (New York: Oxford University Press, 1982), 3–26.

37 **"impartial testimony":** Odum, "Religious Folk Songs," 8.

37 **Odum had read the rapturous accounts of the spirituals:** Odum discusses the northern accounts of the spirituals in "Religious Folk Songs," 6–8. He quotes from the final chapter of *The Souls of Black Folk* in an extraordinary passage in *Social and Mental Traits of the Negro* in which he indicts Negro song for obscenity: "With the gifted music physicians, musicianers, and songsters, a vast throng 'swelling with song—instinct with life, tremulous treble and darkening bass,' with the 'gift of story and song,' comes also the inexpressible wilderness of vulgarity and indecency" (166). At no point does he identify the text or the author he is quoting here; clearly, Du Bois's book was too threatening to acknowledge by name.

38 **"faith in the ultimate justice of things":** W. E. B. Du Bois, *The Souls of Black Folk* (1903), in John Hope Franklin, ed., *Three Negro Classics* (New York: Avon Books, 1965).

38 **"at all manner of occasions, from funerals to yachting parties":** William E. Barton, *Old Plantation Hymns* (New York: AMS Press, 1972; originally published 1899), 3.

38 **"the truest representation of the negro's real self":** Odum, "Religious Folk Songs," 7.

38   **"have commonly been accepted as the characteristic mu-sic of the race"**: Odum, "Religious Folk Songs," 7.

39   **"We will be able to preserve and hear again"**: Thomas Edison, "The Phonograph and Its Future," *North American Review* 126 (May–June 1878), 530–536.

39   **"I don't want the phonograph sold for amusement purposes, it is not a toy"**: Quoted in Oliver Read and Walter L. Welch, *From Tin Foil to Stereo: Evolution of the Phonograph* (Indianapolis: Bobbs-Merrill, 1976), 55.

40   **the new scholarly discipline of social science:** On the use of the phonograph as an ethnographic tool, see Erika Brady, *A Spiral Way: How the Phonograph Changed Ethnography* (Jackson: University of Mississippi Press, 1999).

40   **"The apparatus proves to be a means by which the actual sound itself"**: Quoted in Brady, *Spiral Way*, 81.

41   **"notes between the notes"**: Michael Chanan, *Repeated Takes: A Short History of Recording and Its Effects on Music* (London: Verso, 1995), 10.

41   **the intellectual revolution that anthropologist Franz Boas produced:** For a clear, concise summary of this topic, see George W. Stocking, "Introduction," in Stocking, ed., *The Shaping of American Anthropology: A Franz Boas Reader* (New York: Basic Books, 1974), 1–20.

42   **The purpose of fieldwork, as Boas conceived it:** Brady, *A Spiral Way*, 52–88; George W. Stocking, *The Ethnographer's Magic and Other Essays in the History of Anthropology* (Madison: University of Wisconsin Press, 1992); Richard Handler, "Boasian Anthropology and the Critique of American Culture," *American Quarterly* 42 (June 1990), 252–273.

42   **black Americans did not have cultural patterns:** For reflections on this point, see Sidney Mintz, "Foreword," in Norman E. Whitten, Jr., and John F. Szwed, eds., *Afro-American Anthropology: Contemporary Perspectives* (New York: Free Press, 1970), 1–16.

43   **Howard Odum, it seems, was the first:** John H. Cowley, "Don't Leave Me Here: Non-commercial Blues: The Field Trips, 1924–60," in Lawrence Cohn, ed., *Nothing but the Blues: The Music and the Musicians* (New York: Abbeville Press, 1993),

265–311. Certainty on this point is impossible, since few folklorists or ethnographers left written accounts of their collection process, and (at least before the 1920s) they were far less concerned than one might have expected with preserving the recordings they made. Cylinder recordings were valued primarily as aids to transcription, as tools for constructing a model of how song, story, or narrative forms operated in particular cultures, and once transcription was completed, the cylinder's wax surface was often scraped smooth for reuse—no more valuable, writes Erika Brady, than steno pads after a letter has been sent. See Brady, *A Spiral Way*, 62.

43 **"music physicianers," "musicianers," and "songsters"**: Howard Odum, "Folk-Song and Folk-Poetry as Found in the Secular Songs of the Southern Negroes," *Journal of American Folklore* 24 (July–September 1911), 259.

43 **"I'm po' boy long way from home"**: Odum, "Folk-Song and Folk-Poetry," 270.

44 **"coon songs," "rag times," "knife songs," "devil songs," "breakdowns"**: Odum, "Folk-Song and Folk-Poetry," 260.

44 **LINES AND TITLES OF SONGS COLLECTED TWENTY YEARS AGO:** Howard W. Odum and Guy B. Johnson, *Negro Workaday Songs* (Chapel Hill: University of North Carolina Press, 1926), 24–25.

45 **"mind's eye"**: Mary Frances Odum Schinhan, letter to the author, June 15, 2001.

45 **"We should all try to discharge our duty"**: Calendar entry for January 3, 1907, found in folder 842, HWOP.

46 **"an independent ethics of vagrancy"**: Odum, *Social and Mental Traits*, 220.

46 **"The Negro has little home conscience or love of home"**: Odum, *Social and Mental Traits*, 343.

46 **"Filth and uncleanness is everywhere predominant"**: Odum, *Social and Mental Traits*, 160.

46 **"openly descriptive of the grossest immorality," "vicious and obscene," "rotten with filth"**: Odum, *Social and Mental Traits*, 166.

46 **"The student finds difficulty"**: Odum, *Social and Mental Traits*, 19.

47   **"a serious attempt to delve into a mine of rich and varied ore":** Countee Cullen, *Survey Graphic* (September 1925).

47   **"his face with blood vessels standing out":** Howard W. Odum to Cecile Phillips, December 5, 1927, HWOP.

48   **John Wesley Gordon, alias "Left Wing":** Howard W. Odum to H. L. Mencken, June 19, 1925, HWOP. In *Negro Workaday Songs* (1926), which included a brief portrait of Gordon, Odum described him as "very real," but in time he began to equivocate. After the publication of *Rainbow,* he claimed that Gordon was a composite portrait of several real-life laborers. Nearer the end of his life, when asked if Gordon had genuinely existed, he replied, "What difference does it make?" Guy Benton Johnson and Guion Griffis Johnson, *Research in Service to Society: The First Fifty Years of the Institute for Research in Social Science at the University of North Carolina* (Chapel Hill: University of North Carolina Press, 1980), 137.

48   **"the Negro's own story, the autobiography of the Negro supertramp":** D. L. Chambers to Howard W. Odum, January 7, 1928, HWOP.

48   **"exactly as given," "all pictures, all concreteness," an "untouched phototype":** Howard W. Odum to D. L. Chambers, January 6, 1927, and January 4, 1928, HWOP.

48   **Dictating in his office for hours at a stretch:** Odum's stream-of-consciousness method of composition is described in Brazil, *The Building Years,* 591.

49   **"folk blues":** Odum and Johnson, *Negro Workaday Songs,* 17–34.

49   **"Good Lawd, I can't be satisfied":** Howard W. Odum, *Rainbow Round My Shoulder: The Blue Trail of Black Ulysses* (Cincinnati: Bobbs-Merrill, 1928), 319–320.

50   **"so strange and varied as to reveal a sort of superhuman evidence of the folk soul":** Odum, *Rainbow,* 254.

50   **"There will be the folk blues":** Odum and Johnson, *Negro Workaday Songs,* 34.

50   **"All manner of 'ragtimes,' 'coon-songs,' and the latest 'hits'":** Odum, "Folk-Song and Folk-Poetry," 259.

51   **"the young negro who wished to call out his name":** Odum, "Folk-Song and Folk-Poetry," 262.

51   **"soft, stirring melodies of a folklife"**: Odum, *Social and Mental Traits*, 167.

Three: On the Trail
of Negro Folk Songs

53   **Often in the years that followed:** Dorothy Scarborough interviewed John Wyeth in 1921 on a Sunday evening in late April or early May. She did not leave a detailed account of her visit (though she noted Wyeth's cane and his broken hip), so in this first section my account of the interview is drawn from her scattered remarks in *On the Trail*, Wyeth's autobiography *With Sabre and Scalpel*, and a letter Scarborough wrote days later to Thomas Nelson Page (one of the only letters from her to be found in her papers at Baylor University). The décor of Wyeth's home and his manner in beginning their interview are my invention, drawing on biographical details and photographs included in his autobiography. I do not know whether Scarborough ever heard "Crazy Blues," either from her roof garden or elsewhere, though she notes the noise of her New York neighbors' victrolas when mentioning her roof garden in *From a Southern Porch*. In both the letter to Page and *On the Trail*, she describes Wyeth tossing aside his cane and performing a double shuffle and a plantation breakdown. My description of the steps themselves comes from a nineteenth-century manual of plantation dances available online and held at the Library of Congress. In devising this opening section, which blends verifiable fact with supposition and invention, I have been inspired by Rachel Cohen's luminous study of American cultural history, *A Chance Meeting: Intertwined Lives of American Writers and Artists* (New York: Random House, 2004).

54   **she had an intimate knowledge of Southern patriarchs:** For biographical information on Dorothy Scarborough, see Sylvia Ann Grider, "Introduction," in Dorothy Scarborough, *The Wind* (Austin: University of Texas Press, 1986; originally published 1925); Grider, "Scarborough, Emily Dorothy," *Handbook of Texas Online*, http://www.tsha.utexas.edu/handbook/online/articles/SS/fsc1.html.

56   **"I can see a black woman going by on the road":** Dorothy
      Scarborough, *From a Southern Porch* (New York: G. P. Putnam's
      Sons, 1919), 7–8.

56   **"the hurdy-gurdy of the street beyond":** Scarborough, *From
      a Southern Porch*, 31.

57   **"I am trying to make as complete a collection of these as
      possible":** Dorothy Scarborough, letter ca. January 1921,
      Dorothy Scarborough Papers (hereinafter DSP), Texas Collec-
      tion, Baylor University Library, Baylor University, Waco, Texas.

58   **"so many of the best people in the South":** John Allan
      Wyeth, *With Sabre and Scalpel: The Autobiography of a Soldier
      and Surgeon* (New York: Harper and Brothers, 1914), 54.
      Wyeth's memoir can be found online at http://docsouth.unc.edu/
      wyeth/wyeth.html.

58   **"of fine character":** Wyeth, *With Sabre and Scalpel*, 53.

58   **"When the boy became more proficient than the old
      man":** Dorothy Scarborough, *On the Trail of Negro Folk-Songs*
      (Cambridge, MA: Harvard University Press, 1925), 23.

59   **"low order of development":** Scarborough, *On the Trail of
      Negro Folk-Songs*, 99.

59   **"He evoked melodies of wistful gaiety":** Scarborough, *On
      the Trail of Negro Folk-Songs*, 100.

59   **"This is astounding to anybody who has seen him in the
      operating room":** Dorothy Scarborough to Thomas Nelson
      Page, May 5, 1921, DSP.

60   **"I felt transported":** Scarborough, *On the Trail of Negro Folk-
      Songs*, 100.

60   **by 1920 there were one million of her records in circula-
      tion:** Lawrence Levine, *Black Culture and Black Consciousness:
      Afro-American Folk Thought from Slavery to Freedom* (New
      York: Oxford University Press, 1977), 225.

60   **"Hundreds of 'race' singers have flooded the market":**
      Stephen Calt, "The Anatomy of a 'Race' Label, Part II," *78
      Quarterly* 1, no. 4 (1989), 11.

61   **"the problem of the color line":** W. E. B. Du Bois, *The Souls
      of Black Folk* (1903), in John Hope Franklin, ed., *Three Negro
      Classics* (New York: Avon Books, 1965), 221.

61   **"the lighter, happier side of slavery":** Scarborough, *On the
      Trail of Negro Folk-Songs*, 128.

61 **irrational, illogical "colored mind":** Scarborough, *On the Trail of Negro Folk-Songs,* 272.

63 **"the fairy tale of a happy slave civilization":** Quoted in Grace Elizabeth Hale, *Making Whiteness: The Culture of Segregation in the South, 1890–1940* (New York: Pantheon Books, 1998), 51.

63 **"Sometimes I wonder iffen de white folks didn't make dat song up":** Quoted in Eugene Genovese, *Roll, Jordan, Roll: The World the Slaves Made* (New York: Vintage Books, 1972), 618.

64 **the minstrel show's legacy of ambivalent racial emotions:** W. T. Lhamon, *Raising Cain: Blackface Performance from Jim Crow to Hip Hop* (Cambridge, MA: Harvard University Press, 2000); Eric Lott, *Love and Theft: Blackface Minstrelsy and the American Working Class* (New York: Oxford University Press, 1993).

64 **self-styled "darky dialecticians":** For an insightful analysis of late-nineteenth-century dialect fiction, see Gavin Jones, *Strange Talk: The Politics of Dialect Literature in Gilded Age America* (Berkeley: University of California Press, 1999).

64 **the protean nature of "authenticity" itself:** On the concept of authenticity, see Miles Orvell, *The Real Thing: Imitation and Authenticity in American Culture, 1880–1940* (Chapel Hill: University of North Carolina Press, 1989); Regina Bendix, *In Search of Authenticity: The Formation of Folklore Studies* (Madison: University of Wisconsin Press, 1997); Benjamin Filene, *Romancing the Folk: Public Memory and American Roots Music* (Chapel Hill: University of North Carolina Press, 2000).

65 **"a region of uncontaminated beauty and pastoral dreams":** R. Emmet Kennedy, *Mellows: A Chronicle of Unknown Singers* (New York: A. and C. Boni, 1925), 144.

65 **most seem to have heard in slave song simply savage wails**: Jon Cruz, *Culture on the Margins: The Black Spiritual and the Rise of American Cultural Interpretation* (Princeton, NJ: Princeton University Press, 1999), 19–66.

66 **"the fast-vanishing remains of folklore in America":** William Wells Newell, "On the Field and Work of a Journal of American Folklore," *Journal of American Folklore* 1 (1888), 3.

66 **"Many a dear little Southern lady":** Quoted in Deborah Kodish, *Good Friends and Bad Enemies: Robert Winslow*

Gordon and the Study of American Folksong (Urbana: University of Illinois Press, 1986), 186.

67 **"a queer combination of bookworm and tomboy":** Quoted in "Scarborough, Dorothy," *Biographical Cyclopedia of U.S. Women: Ancestry.com,* December 9, 2004, http://search.ancestry.com/db-bcaw/P291.aspx.

67 **she had attended a religious revival:** This episode is described in the first chapter of Scarborough's autobiographical novel *The Unfair Sex,* which was serialized in 1925. The manuscript can be found in the Dorothy Scarborough Papers at Waco University.

67 **"readers found them more interesting":** Scarborough, *On the Trail of Negro Folk-Songs,* 11.

68 **"How many memories of my childhood and youth":** Scarborough, *On the Trail of Negro Folk-Songs,* 6, 9–10.

69 **"highest gift, his spontaneity":** Robert Littell, Review of Howard Odum and Guy Johnson, *The Negro and His Songs,* in the *New Republic,* September 9, 1926, 74.

69 **"The plantation Master and the plantation Negro stand today":** DuBose Heyward, "The Negro in the Low Country," in Augustine T. Smythe et al., eds., *The Carolina Low Country* (New York: Macmillan, 1932), 185–186.

70 **"I sat in the kitchen and learned songs":** Typescript in folder 209, box 2C114, DSP.

70 **"Once the trusted servant and almost constant companion":** J. E. Morrow, "Negro Folk Songs," unpublished, undated ms in DSP, 1.

71 **"The Negro is by nature a mimetic creature":** Scarborough, *On the Trail of Negro Folk-Songs,* 65.

72 **"I was ploughing when I got the word":** Scarborough, *On the Trail of Negro Folk-Songs,* 17.

73 **"A Negro man came up to him after supper":** Scarborough, *On the Trail of Negro Folk-Songs,* 31.

74 **"our demure, delicate, poised, other-minded Dot":** Quoted in Grider, "Introduction," xiv.

74 **"I have wandered through the colored quarters":** Dorothy Scarborough, unpaginated introduction to manuscript of *On the Trail of Negro Folk-Songs,* box 2C112, DSP.

75   **"with each immersion the excitement grew":** Scarborough, *On the Trail of Negro Folk-Songs,* 15–16.

76   **Scarborough began hunting for the machines early on in her research:** Scarborough's request for a cylinder phonograph is referred to in a letter from John A. Sherman of Thomas A. Edison, Inc., to Dorothy Scarborough, April 28, 1921, DSP.

77   **"I lack entire faith in the [making] of wax records":** Natalie Curtis Burlin, *Negro Folk-Songs: Hampton Series* (New York: G. Schirmer, 1919), 3.

79   **"crooning sweetness"; "a racial mother-heart which can take in not only its own babies, but those of another, dominant, race as well"; "What other nation of mothers":** Scarborough, *On the Trail of Negro Folk-Songs,* 159–160.

79   **"We wear the mask":** Paul Laurence Dunbar, "We Wear the Mask," in Joanne M. Braxton, ed., *The Collected Poetry of Paul Laurence Dunbar* (Charlottesville: University Press of Virginia, 1993), 71.

80   **"She told him how on Saturday afternoons":** Dorothy Scarborough, *The Stretch-berry Smile* (Indianapolis: Bobbs-Merrill, 1932), 312–313.

80   **"greatest Negro city in the world":** Dorothy Scarborough, "The New Negro and the Old," review of R. Emmet Kennedy, *Mellows,* and Alain Locke, ed., *The New Negro,* uncited clipping, 1925, DSP.

81   **"White critics, whom 'everybody' knows":** "A Negro Renaissance," originally published in *New York Herald Tribune,* reprinted in *Opportunity* (June 1925), 187. On the Harlem Renaissance, see George Hutchinson, *The Harlem Renaissance in Black and White* (Cambridge, MA: Harvard University Press, 1995); David Levering Lewis, *When Harlem Was in Vogue* (New York: Knopf, 1981); Nathan I. Huggins, *Harlem Renaissance* (London: Oxford University Press, 1973); Paul Allen Anderson, *Deep River: Music and Memory in Harlem Renaissance Thought* (Durham, NC: Duke University Press, 2001).

81   **"The day of 'aunties,' 'uncles' and 'mammy' is gone":** Alain Locke, "Enter the New Negro," *Survey Graphic* (March 1925), 631.

81   **"more of a myth than a man":** Locke, "Enter the New Negro," 631.

82   **"the energy and awakening of the Negro scholar and folklorist":** Eric Walrond, "Negro Folk-Song," *Saturday Review of Literature* (July 11, 1925), 891.

82   **"I am now struggling with Kennedy's *Mellows*":** Alain Locke to Dorothy Scarborough, January 19, 1926, DSP.

82   **"I am considered something of an authority":** Dorothy Scarborough to C. A. Hibbard, August 8, 1925, DSP.

83   **"For the last several years"; "like a cripple dancing because of some irresistible impulse"; "like the whip-crack surprise at the end of an O. Henry story"; "to have little relation to authentic folk-music of the Negroes"; "to trace it back to its origin":** Scarborough, *On the Trail of Negro Folk-Songs*, 264.

84   **"taken up by many singers":** Scarborough, *On the Trail of Negro Folk-Songs*, 265.

84   **"essentially of our race":** Scarborough, *On the Trail of Negro Folk-Songs*, 270.

84   **"Each one of my blues is based on some old Negro song":** Scarborough, *On the Trail of Negro Folk-Songs*, 265.

85   **"wild shouting voice":** Scarborough, *The Wind*, 3.

85   **"seemed to me necessary to make the life of the section adequately real":** Dorothy Scarborough, *A Song Catcher in Southern Mountains: American Folk Songs of British Ancestry* (New York: Columbia University Press, 1937), ix.

86   **"incredibly arid and difficult"; "No beauty of Greek columns here":** Scarborough, *Song Catcher*, 6.

86   **"remote from the centers of commerce":** Scarborough, *Song Catcher*, 3.

87   **"On my trips to collect material"; "The Dictaphone records, being of wax":** Scarborough, *Song Catcher*, ix–x.

88   **"I was a Southerner born and bred":** Scarborough, *On the Trail of Negro Folk-Songs*, 30.

88   **"There isn't a radio in the district":** Undated, unpaginated manuscript for *A Song Catcher in Southern Mountains* in DSP.

89   **"floating on the breezes":** Untitled manuscript in folder 209, box 2C114, DSP.

89   **"songs I knew but did not know that I knew"**: "Radio Talks," folder 297, DSP.

89   **"Why not say that it was typical of all publication offices"**: Draft of *On the Trail* in file 232, DSP.

Four: Sound Photographs
of Negro Songs

91   **Louisiana Highway 66 is one of those meandering southern roads**: John and Alan Lomax described their initial meeting with Leadbelly many times, most enduringly in their 1936 book *Negro Folk Songs as Sung by Leadbelly* (New York: Macmillan, 1936). For fresh perspectives on the encounter, as well as on John Lomax himself, I am indebted to Nolan Porterfield, *Last Cavalier: The Life and Times of John Lomax, 1867–1948* (Urbana: University of Illinois Press, 1996); Benjamin Filene, *Romancing the Folk: Public Memory and American Roots Music* (Chapel Hill: University of North Carolina Press, 2000); Charles Wolfe and Kip Lornell, *The Life and Legend of Leadbelly* (New York: HarperCollins, 1992); and Jerrold Hirsch, "Modernity, Nostalgia, and Southern Folklore Studies: The Case of John Lomax," *Journal of American Folklore* 105 (Spring 1992), 183–207. For a meticulous chronology of the encounter between Huddie Ledbetter and the Lomaxes, see the Alan Lomax Archive website, http://www.alan-lomax.com/links_leadbelly.html.

93   **"on the upper crust of the po' white trash"**: John Lomax, *Adventures of a Ballad Hunter* (New York: Macmillan, 1947), 1.

94   **That conviction placed Lomax at odds with a generation of scholars:** Hirsch, "Modernity, Nostalgia, and Southern Folklore Studies," 189; Filene, *Romancing the Folk,* chap. 1.

95   **"down-and-out classes":** John Lomax, "Some Types of American Folk-Song," *Journal of American Folklore* 28 (1915), 3.

95   **the archive was the brainchild of Robert Winslow Gordon**: See Debora Kodish's insightful study, *Good Friends and Bad Enemies: Robert Winslow Gordon and the Study of American Folksong* (Urbana: University of Illinois Press, 1986).

98   **"heard for the first time the wail of the Negro woodsman":** John Lomax to Ruby Terrill, July 11, 1933, Box 3D149,

Lomax Family Papers (hereinafter LFP), Barker Center for American History, University of Texas at Austin.

98   **"the words of enough folk songs":** John Lomax to Ruby Terrill, July 7, 1933, Box 3D149, LFP.

98   **"for his wife objected to his singing":** John Lomax to Ruby Terrill, July 21, 1933, Box 3D149, LFP.

98   **"how Christ took his persecution":** John Lomax to Ruby Terrill, July 21, 1933, Box 3D149, LFP.

100   **"Everybody knows the story of how Leadbelly sang his way to freedom":** Francis Davis, *The History of the Blues* (London: Secker and Warburg, 1995), 165.

102   **"Through the Music Division in the Library of Congress":** John Lomax, "'Sinful Songs' of the Southern Negro," *Musical Quarterly* 20 (1934), 181.

103   **"The songs would make a sensation in cultured centers":** Undated letter written in Parchman, Mississippi, in file marked "General Correspondence, 1933–1939," John Lomax Papers, Archive of Folk Culture, Library of Congress.

103   **"Folk songs flourish, grow":** John A. Lomax, "Report of the Honorary Consultant and Curator," from *Report of the Librarian of Congress for the Fiscal Year Ending June 30, 1934*, reprinted in *Archive of American Folk Song: A History, 1928–1939*, compiled from the Annual Reports of the Librarian of Congress, Washington, DC, 1940, 27.

104   **"contented and carefree as a group of children":** Lomax, *Negro Folk Songs as Sung by Lead Belly*, 38.

104   **"Negro songs in their primitive purity":** John A. Lomax, "Report of the Honorary Consultant and Curator," from *Report of the Librarian of Congress for the Fiscal Year Ending June 30, 1933*, reprinted in *Archive of American Folk Song: A History*, 24.

104   **"dish 'ere w'at dey calls de fonygraf":** Joel Chandler Harris, "The Phonograph," in Harris, *Uncle Remus: His Songs and His Sayings* (New York: Appleton, 1881), accessible online at http://www.uncleremus.com/phonograph.html.

105   **Title: "Angola, Louisiana":** Gebhard's transcription is printed in Charles Wolfe and Kip Lornell, *The Life and Legend of Leadbelly* (New York: HarperCollins, 1992), 164–166.

110   **"Dear Sir Just a few lines to let you no iom out"**: Huddie
       Ledbetter to John Lomax, undated (but ca. September 6, 1934),
       Box 3D157, LFP.

110   **"Dear Mr. Lomax"**: Zora Neale Hurston to John Lomax, Janu-
       ary 5, 1935, Box 3D160, LFP.

111   **"impossible to transport Negro folk-singers from the
       South"**: Lomax, "Sinful Songs," 182.

111   **"Contact with whites soon brings about cheap imitations"**:
       Undated letter written in Parchman, Mississippi, in file marked
       "General Correspondence, 1933–1939," John Lomax Papers,
       Archive of Folk Culture, Library of Congress.

112   **"I do not think there is a boy in the institution"**: Grube B.
       Cornish to John Lomax, January 15, 1935, Box 3D171, LFP.

112   **"After a thorough investigation"**: Robert J. Booth to John
       Lomax, January 17, 1935, Box 3D171, LFP.

112   **"blinding themselves to the power and beauty"**: John Lo-
       max to Ruby Terrill, August 1, 1933, Box 3D149, LFP.

113   **"amid a people we really know little about"**: John Lomax to
       Ruby Terrill, August 1, 1933, Box 3D149, LFP.

113   **"Other singers hearing him became ambitious"**: Lomax,
       Negro Folk Songs as Sung by Lead Belly, 37.

113   **"the reels or so-called 'jump-up,' 'made-up,' or 'sinful
       songs' of the blacks"**: Lomax, "Sinful Songs," 181.

113   **"Negro spirituals abound in idioms and phrases"**: Lomax,
       "Sinful Songs," 183.

114   **"We sat at a point in the run-around"**: Lomax, *Negro Folk
       Songs as Sung by Lead Belly*, 37.

114   **well over two hundred disk recordings:** John A. Lomax,
       "Report of the Honorary Consultant and Curator," from *Report
       of the Librarian of Congress for the Fiscal Year Ending June
       30, 1935*, reprinted in *Archive of American Folk Song: A
       History*, 32.

115   **"to 'show off' among his own color"**: Lomax, *Negro Folk
       Songs as Sung by Lead Belly*, 38.

115   **"Before we reached the farm"**: Lomax, *Negro Folk Songs as
       Sung by Lead Belly*, 36–37.

115   **"I'm tired of lookin' at niggers in the penitentshuh"**: Lo-
       max, *Negro Folk Songs as Sung by Lead Belly*, 39.

116   **"smacked of sensationalism"**: Lomax, *Negro Folk Songs as Sung by Lead Belly*, 45.

117   **"Lomax Arrives with Leadbelly, Negro Minstrel"**: *New York Herald Tribune*, January 3, 1935.

117   **"absolute sincerity"**: *New York Herald Tribune*, January 5, 1935.

117   **"My chauffeur, while Alan is sick"**: Uncited clipping ca. 1934 in Box 2.325/V62, folder 5, LFP.

119   **"Boss, I'se nothin' but a nigger"**: Lomax, *Negro Folk Songs as Sung by Lead Belly*, 41.

119   **"Already the pure nigger in him"**: *Brooklyn Daily Eagle*, January 17, 1935.

119   **"We (Alan and I) are disturbed and distressed"**: Lomax to Ruby Terrill, January 14, 1935, Box 3D150, LFP.

120   **"We saw no printed page of music either in his prison cell or in his home"**: Lomax, *Negro Folk Songs as Sung by Lead Belly*, xiii.

120   **"I learned by listening to other singers once in a while off phonograph records"**: Quoted in Filene, *Romancing the Folk*, 15.

120   **"the most famous nigger in the world"**: Lomax to Ruby Terrill, ca. January 7, 1935, Box 3D150, LFP.

121   **"natural and sincere as he was while in prison"**: Lomax to Ruby Terrill, January 14, 1935, Box 3D150, LFP.

121   **"a low, dirty back room"**: Lomax, *Negro Folk Songs as Sung by Lead Belly*, 59.

121   **"I ain't goin' to sing no more for you"**: Lomax, *Negro Folk Songs as Sung by Lead Belly*, 59.

122   **"I wants my money"**: Lomax, *Negro Folk Songs as Sung by Lead Belly*, 60.

122   **"The experience has shattered my nerves"**: Lomax to Ruby Terrill, March 11, 1935, Box 3D150, LFP.

122   **"I think the main reason I feel about Huddie as I do"**: Lomax to Ruby Terrill, March 17, 1935, Box 3D150, LFP.

122   **"The little drama was played out"**: Lomax, *Negro Folk Songs as Sung by Lead Belly*, 63–64.

123   **"Among his own kind"**: John Lomax to Ruby Terrill, April 16, 1936, Box 3D151, LFP.

123 **"Tell Alan that I drove":** John Lomax to Ruby Terrill, May 26, 1936, Box 3D151, LFP.

123 **"If I stay up here very long":** John Lomax to Ruby Terrill, May 22, 1936, Box 3D151, LFP.

124 **"She expressed no interest in Iron Head":** John Lomax to Ruby Terrill, May 29, 1936, Box 3D151, LFP.

125 **"Because Alan will drive recklessly":** John Lomax to Ruby Terrill, June 29, 1933, Box 3D149, LFP.

125 **"I have no means of knowing":** John Lomax to Ruby Terrill, July 3, 1933, Box 3D149, LFP.

125 **"music and mystery and wistful sadness":** John Lomax to Ruby Terrill, July 11, 1933, Box 3D149, LFP.

125 **"the simple directness and power of this primitive music":** John Lomax to Ruby Terrill, August 10, 1933, Box 3D149, LFP.

125 **"As I think back, and in my dreams":** John Lomax to Ruby Terrill, August 17, 1933, Box 3D149, LFP.

126 **"of hopeless longing, of remoteness":** Undated memo in "General Correspondence 1933–38" folder, John Lomax Papers, Archive of Folk Culture, Library of Congress.

126 **"The truest, the most intimate folk music":** John Lomax and Alan Lomax, *American Ballads and Folk Songs* (New York: Macmillan, 1934), xxxv.

126 **the southern novelist Samuel Derieux:** Scarborough, *On the Trail of Negro Folk-Songs,* 209.

126 **"chain gang songs and jail house blues":** Odum, *Rainbow Round My Shoulder,* 283.

127 **"drove steadily and silently, his black, black face shining"; "I can find no little feeling for beauty in him":** John Lomax to Ruby Terrill, October 26, 1934, Box 3D150, LFP.

127 **"Penitentiary wardens all tell me that I set no value on my life":** Uncited clipping ca. 1934 in Box 2.325/V62, folder 5, LFP.

127 **Those questions had become national ones by March 1931:** For a brilliant account of the Scottsboro case, see James Goodman, *Stories of Scottsboro* (New York: Vintage Books, 1995; originally published 1994).

128 **John Spivak investigated prison conditions in Georgia:** John L. Spivak, *Georgia Nigger* (New York: Brewer, Warren,

and Putnam 1932); see also Spivak's essay, "Flashes from Georgia Chain Gangs," in Nancy Cunard, ed., *Negro Anthology* (London: Wishart, 1934).

128 **"The trouble we have had in Georgia":** John Lomax to Ruby Terrill, December 18, 1934, Box 3D150, LFP.

128 **"terrible story of the fear of a negro":** John Lomax to Ruby Terrill, August 10, 1933, Box 3D149, LFP.

129 **"when convicts were leased by the State":** John Lomax, "Sinful Songs," 180.

129 **"Negroes who have been convicted on Negro evidence only":** John Lomax to Honorable Governor James L. Allred, October 29, 1936, Box 3D171, LFP.

129 **"the Negro's desire, as one said, 'to git away f'om here' ":** Lomax, *American Ballads,* xxxii.

129 **"the injustice of the white man":** Lomax, *Negro Folk Songs as Sung by Lead Belly,* ix.

129 **The comeback began inauspiciously:** My account of Leadbelly's return to New York draws on Wolfe and Lornell, *Life and Legend of Leadbelly,* 178–210.

130 **"stayed away in droves":** Wolfe and Lornell, *Life and Legend of Leadbelly,* 188.

130 **"The advance publicity stated that this man":** Quoted in Wolfe and Lornell, *Life and Legend of Leadbelly,* 189.

130 **he turned to Mary Elizabeth Barnicle:** On Mary Elizabeth Barnicle, see Wolfe and Lornell, *Life and Legend of Leadbelly,* 189–190; "Biographical Note," http://cass.etsu.edu/ARCHIVES/afindaid/a347.html#bio%20note.

131 **"to collect, study, and popularize American folk music and its traditions":** Quoted in Wolfe and Lornell, *Life and Legend of Leadbelly,* 192. For more on left folk song in the Popular Front era, see Filene, *Romancing the Folk,* 47–75; Steven Garabedian, "Lawrence Gellert, 'Negro Songs of Protest,' and the Left-Wing Folk-Song Revival of the 1930s and 1940s," *American Quarterly* 57 (2005), 179–206; Robbie Lieberman, *"My Song Is My Weapon": People's Songs, American Communism, and the Politics of Culture, 1930–1950* (Urbana: University of Illinois Press, 1989).

131 **"Huddie Ledbetter, Famous Negro Folk Artist":** *Daily Worker,* August 12, 1937, 7.

133 **"The camp was in an uproar"**: Quoted in Filene, *Romancing the Folk*, 72.

133 **Lawrence Gellert, an activist and folk song hunter**: On Lawrence Gellert, see Wolfe and Lornell, *Life and Legend of Leadbelly,*194; Garabedian, "Lawrence Gellert, 'Negro Songs of Protest.'"

134 **"propaganda," music "as a weapon"**: Quoted in Garabedian, "Lawrence Gellert, 'Negro Songs of Protest,'" 182.

134 **"the nonsensical jingles served up for the white man's amusement"**: *New Masses*, November 20, 1934, 19.

134 **"Getting 'our niggers' out of difficulties with the Law"**: *New Masses*, December 11, 1934, 22.

135 **"Imagine Ben Davis Jr., editor of the *Negro Liberator*"**: *New Masses*, December 11, 1934, 22.

136 **the presence of Clarence Norris and Heywood Patterson**: Patterson and Norris were transferred from the Jefferson County Jail in Birmingham to Kilby Prison on February 4, 1934, and remained there for the rest of the year. See Goodman, *Stories of Scottsboro*, 233–253.

136 **"I am going to Be the Blues King"**: Goodman, *Stories of Scottsboro*, 270–271.

136 **"embodies the master-slave relationship intact"**: *New Masses*, December 11, 1934, 22.

137 **"On southern chain gang and jail"**: *New Masses*, November 20, 1934, 19.

137 **"Some time ago when I was recording"**: John Lomax, undated memo to Henry J. Alsberg, Box 3D171, LFP.

138 **He swaggers through the pages of recent accounts of the blues**: See, for example, Filene, *Romancing the Folk*, 47–75; Hazel Carby, *Race Men* (Cambridge, MA: Harvard University Press, 1998), 101–109, 115.

139 **"Now Mr. Lomax, my god he hated old Roosevelt"**: James McNutt, "John Henry Faulk: An Interview," *Folklore Annual* (1987), 113, in Alan Lomax Collection (hereinafter ALC), Archive of Folk Culture, Library of Congress. See also Porterfield, *Last Cavalier*, 431–432.

139 **"Because Lomax was unquestionably a genius"**: Porterfield, *Last Cavalier*, 434.

139 **"all I had to do was turn over the records":** Porterfield, *Last Cavalier*, 393.

140 **"a hundred negroes resting in their quarters":** Lomax to Honorable Burnet R. Maybank, June 30, 1941, Box 3D171, LFP.

140 **"never questioned the system":** Porterfield, *Last Cavalier*, 434.

140 **"the forgotten ones who have no influential friends":** John Lomax to Honorable Governor James L. Allred, October 29, 1936, Box 3D171, LFP.

141 **"I heard a washerwoman striding along the road":** Lawrence Gellert, "Negro Songs of Protest," *New Masses* (November 1930 and January 1931).

141 **"For more than a dozen years":** Lawrence Gellert, *Negro Songs of Protest* (New York: American Music League, 1936), 6–7.

142 **The historian William Stott has written:** William Stott, *Documentary Expression and Thirties America* (New York: Oxford University Press, 1973).

142 **"a portion of unimagined existence":** James Agee, "Preface," in Agee and Walker Evans, *Let Us Now Praise Famous Men* (Boston: Houghton Mifflin, 1988; originally published 1941), xlvi.

142 **left-liberal folklorists like Herbert Halpert and Benjamin Botkin:** On the work of left folklorists, see Jerrold Hirsch, *Portrait of America: A Cultural History of the Federal Writers Project* (Chapel Hill: University of North Carolina Press, 2003); Jerrold Hirsch, "Folklore in the Making: B. A. Botkin," *Journal of American Folklore* 100 (1987), 3–38.

143 **"cut up," torn, and deeply upset:** John Lomax to Ruby Terrill, March 12, 1935, Box 3D150, LFP.

144 **"bare-throated, bearded, rough, but clean inside and out":** Porterfield, *Last Cavalier*, 339.

145 **"intensely American and flagrantly and vagrantly modern":** Porterfield, *Last Cavalier*, 339.

145 **"We did well for so short a stay":** John Lomax to Ruby Terrill, July 3, 1933, Box 3D149, LFP.

145 **"It distressed my father very, very much":** My account of the Harvard incident draws on material held in Alan Lomax's

FBI file, which came to light in April 2006 when the music historian Ted Gioia publicized the findings of his Freedom of Information Act request. The FBI's surveillance of Alan Lomax seems to have begun in the early 1940s, and in a sense it was a consequence of the family tensions I discuss here. Sometime in the late 1930s, John Lomax attended a wedding reception and told a few guests of his worries about his son's political leanings. (Alan had allegedly told him: "I am just as much a Communist as I ever was—if not a stronger one, but don't say anything about it for you will only get me in trouble.") Those remarks were reported to the FBI's St. Louis bureau, and in response the bureau launched an investigation of Alan Lomax that lasted until 1980. Alan Lomax's remarks here were made in 1942, when he was questioned about the demonstration by federal agents. He denied charges that he had distributed communist literature or made speeches in support of the party. See Ted Gioia, "The Red-Rumor Blues," *Los Angeles Times,* April 23, 2006.

145   **"communistic activities"**: Filene, *Romancing the Folk,* 48.

145   **"He needs to build himself up physically"**: John Lomax to Ruby Terrill, August 17, 1933, Box 3D149, LFP.

146   **"a ballad in himself"**: John Lomax to Ruby Terrill, March 22, 1935, Box 3D150, LFP.

146   **"generosity to me and mine"**: John Lomax to Ruby Terrill, March 18, 1935, Box 3D150, LFP.

146   **"I am quite satisfied to have Alan under her influence"**: John Lomax to Ruby Terrill, March 16, 1935, Box 3D150, LFP.

146   **"the most exciting field trip I have made"**: Alan Lomax to Oliver Strunk, August 3, 1935, ALC.

147   **My dear Mr. Lomax:** Zora Neale Hurston to John Lomax, September 16, 1935, Box 3D160, LFP.

149   **At the core of Hurston's long, furious letter was an accusation:** Just how seriously one should take Hurston's account of the events in Georgia and Florida is an open question. Hurston herself was hardly a disinterested party: intensely hostile to the radical left (whose ranks, by 1935, included many of her one-time kindred spirits in the New Negro intelligentsia); prone to dramatic, acrimonious splits with close friends (like, for example, Langston Hughes); and sometimes inclined to embroider

her facts. She had been much enamored of Barnicle when she met her the previous spring. "Will you invite Miss Barnicle to the tea?" she wrote to her friend Annie Nathan Meyer in March. "She teaches the ballad at NYU. Oh, she is grand!" In later years she would claim that she left the expedition when Barnicle demanded that she take a photograph of a black child eating a watermelon. See Valerie Boyd, *Wrapped in Rainbows: The Life of Zora Neale Hurston* (New York: Scribner's, 2003), 275–277. Hurston's letters are reprinted in Carla Kaplan, ed., *Zora Neale Hurston: A Life in Letters* (New York: Doubleday, 2002).

149 **Just how Lomax responded to Hurston's letter is hard to gauge:** The closest thing to a direct comment from Lomax came in a note that he scribbled on the bottom of a letter Hurston sent him on August 30, 1935: "This is the Negro woman novelist who was with Miss B and Alan a part of the summer. The two females 'fell out.'" Box 3D160, LFP.

149 **Barnicle was still writing him warm and effusive letters:** On October 1, 1935, Barnicle wrote: "It is I who am owing Alan—my regret and shame is that I haven't anything to offer him. In every way I am wholly his debtor—all summer long he shared everything he had with me and gave me open and free and beautiful the treasure of himself. . . . I am glad that your pain has let up—I hope permanently—and dreadfully sorry that you had such a physically miserable summer. . . . When are you coming to NY? Is the Leadbelly book coming out soon? What are you working on now? Good luck to you in everything you do and my love to you and Miss Terrill." Box 3D160, LFP.

149 **in the ensuing years he filled the archive's shelves:** On Alan Lomax's activities in the late 1930s, see Ed Kahn, "1934–1950: The Early Collecting Years," in Ronald D. Cohen, ed., *Alan Lomax: Selected Writings, 1934–1997* (New York: Routledge, 2003), 1–8.

149 **He even pushed for the accession of commercial recordings:** Alan first broached the possibility of the race and hillbilly records survey in 1935, when he included it as part of his father's proposal for funding to the Carnegie Corporation. See the memo (in Alan's handwriting) in the file of materials related to

Lomax's Carnegie Corporation grants, 1933–1935, Box 3D170, LFP.

150   **"The commercial recording companies have done a broader and more interesting job":** Alan Lomax to Harold Spivacke, April 8, 1939, ALC. The list (first made available in 1940) can be found in the Alan Lomax Collection.

150   **what his friend Benjamin Botkin termed "living lore":** B. A. Botkin, "Folklore as a Neglected Source of Social History," in Caroline F. Ware, *The Cultural Approach to History* (New York: Columbia University Press, 1940), 311–312.

150   **"folklore in the making":** B. A. Botkin, "WPA and Folklore Research: 'Bread and Song,'" in Burt Feintuch, ed., *The Conservation of Culture: Folklorists and the Public Sector* (Lexington: University of Kentucky Press, 1988), 259.

151   **"the blues and reels and the work songs":** Botkin, "Folklore as a Neglected Source of Social History," 312.

151   **a two-year survey of black music in Coahoma County, Mississippi:** The genesis of the expedition and Lomax's treatment of his African American colleagues have become the subject of much controversy. See Robert Gordon and Bruce Nemerov, eds., *Lost Delta Found: Rediscovering the Fisk University-Library of Congress Coahoma County Study, 1941–1942* (Nashville: Vanderbilt University Press, 2005); Alan Lomax, *The Land Where the Blues Began* (New York: Pantheon, 1993); and the responses gathered on Lomax's behalf at http://www.alan-lomax.com/media_books_LostDeltaFound.html.

151   **"to explore objectively and exhaustively":** Alan Lomax, memo to Library of Congress, September 18, 1941, ALC.

151   **"It is a folklorist's illusion":** Alan Lomax, field notebook, dated July 1942, ALC.

152   **"to record what you find, regardless of its import":** John Lomax to Alan Lomax, October 9, 1941, cited in Porterfield, *Last Cavalier*, 435.

152   **"hopelessly involved in the slimy toils of Communism":** John Lomax to John Lomax, Jr., February 28, 1940, cited in Porterfield, *Last Cavalier*, 427.

152   **more often than not he left them unanswered:** Porterfield, *Last Cavalier*, 427–428.

152   **"a bourgeois southerner":** John Lomax to Alan Lomax, October 9, 1941, cited in Porterfield, *Last Cavalier*, 435.

152   **he brought Leadbelly along with him:** On Alan's continuing work with Leadbelly, see Wolfe and Lornell, *Life and Legend of Leadbelly*, 186–239.

153   **"an absolute zero on any program at any time":** John Lomax to Alan Lomax, April 25, 1940, cited in Porterfield, *Last Cavalier*, 421.

153   **a bruising encounter with Mary Elizabeth Barnicle:** John Lomax to Alan Lomax, July 23, 1940, cited in Porterfield, *Last Cavalier*, 370.

153   **"Save for being a triple murderer":** John Lomax to "Kathy" [no surname supplied], February 20, 1944, Box 3D157, LFP.

154   **when his father carried him outdoors on hot Texas nights:** Alan described this to Zora Neale Hurston while they were collecting folk songs in Georgia. See her letter to John Lomax, August 30, 1935, Box 3D160, LFP.

154   **he watched Alan fiddle with the controls on the disk recorder:** Lomax, *Adventures of a Ballad Hunter*, 114.

154   **"the core and center of my being":** John Lomax to Alan Lomax, August 2, 1940, cited in Porterfield, *Last Cavalier*, 428.

154   **"an outrageous slander on the Southern white man":** John Lomax to Alan Lomax, October 10, 1941, quoted in Porterfield, *Last Cavalier*, 434.

155   **His publisher, however, thought its inclusion "unwise":** My account of this episode draws on Porterfield, *Last Cavalier*, 478–479.

155   **"From Nat I learned my sense of rhythm":** Lomax, *Adventures of a Ballad Hunter*, 9–12.

Five: Been Here and Gone

157   **When they looked back to the beginning:** I don't know when, or indeed if, William Russell, Charles Edward Smith, and Frederic Ramsey went together to the Jungle Inn to see and hear Jelly Roll Morton. To imagine this encounter, I have drawn on each man's accounts of his meetings with Morton: Charles Edward Smith, "Oh, Mister Jelly!" *Jazz Record* (February 1944),

8–10, accessed online at http://www.doctorjazz.freeserve.co.uk/ posth.html#cesmith; Frederic Ramsey, Jr., reminiscence included in William Russell, ed., *"Oh, Mister Jelly": A Jelly Roll Morton Scrapbook* (Copenhagen: Jazz Media ApS, 1999), 495–505; William Russell, "Charles Edward Smith, 1904–1970," in Russell, *"Oh, Mister Jelly,"* 474–485. For information on the interior of the Jungle Inn, I drew as well on Roy Carew, "1211 U Street, Northwest," in Albert J. McCarthy, ed., *Jazzbook 1955*, 109–116, accessed online at http://www.doctorjazz.freeserve .co.uk/page28.html.

158 **it was William Russell who had heard him first:** For information on Russell's experience hearing and collecting race records, I drew on Bruce Boyd Raeburn, "The Musical Worlds of William Russell," *Southern Quarterly* 36 (Winter 1998), 12–13; William Frederick Wagner, "A Brother Remembers William Russell," *Southern Quarterly* 36 (Winter 1998), 20; and Russell's letters to Frederic Ramsey, which form part of Ramsey's collected papers and manuscripts (the Frederic Ramsey Papers, hereinafter FRP). At the time of my research Ramsey's papers were still in the family's possession, and I am indebted to his daughters Alida Ramsey Porter and Martha Ramsey for allowing me to see them. The Ramsey papers have since been acquired by the Historic New Orleans Collection, New Orleans, Louisiana, where William Russell's papers are also housed.

158 **The sheer complexity of the music was what was most immediately striking:** William Russell and Stephen W. Smith, "New Orleans Music," in Frederic Ramsey and Charles Edward Smith, eds., *Jazzmen* (New York: Harcourt, 1939), 10.

158 **you could buy the records in bulk for as little as thirty-five cents a box:** William Russell to Frederic Ramsey, October 14, 1939, FRP.

160 **"To many who have wondered what has become of 'Jelly Roll' Morton":** Andy Andrusia, "'Jelly Roll' Gives Out for Capitol Cats," *Down Beat*, May 1937, 11, accessed online at http://www.doctorjazz.freeserve.co.uk/page10.html.

160 **a coterie gathered around him:** Smith, "Oh, Mister Jelly!" 8–10.

161   **"Dear Mr. Ripley":** Morton's letter, dated March 31, 1938, can be found online at http://www.doctorjazz.freeserve.co.uk/page10 bc.html#washdc.

162   **Smith recommended him to Alan Lomax:** Frederic Ramsey recalls that in his letter to Charles Edward Smith, April 5, 1954, FRP.

162   **Perhaps Lomax even told him of a book he had been reading:** Alan Lomax recalls the influence Odum's book had upon him in his memoir, *The Land Where the Blues Began* (New York: Pantheon Books, 1993), 493.

163   **"[Morton] will trace by piano and narrative":** Harold Phillips, "Jelly Roll Charts Jazz," *Washington Daily News,* March 19, 1938, 6.

163   **once they heard the copies of the recordings that Lomax dubbed for them:** Orrin Keepnews, "Sweet Papa Jelly Roll: Ten Year History of Morton's Library of Congress Recordings," *Record Changer* (February 1948), 6–7, accessed online at http://www.doctorjazz.freeserve.co.uk/page21.html.

163   **Morton would unleash a flood of remembered melody and anecdote:** My account of Morton's reminiscences draws on Alan Lomax, *Mister Jelly Roll: The Fortunes of Jelly Roll Morton, New Orleans Creole and Inventor of Jazz* (London: Virgin Books, 1991; originally published 1950) and on the transcribed version of the Library of Congress session, available online at http://www.doctorjazz.freeserve.co.uk/locspeech1.html. *Jelly Roll Morton: The Complete Library of Congress Recordings* is now available on CD from Rounder Records (CDROUN1888).

166   **so obscene in places that some of the sessions remained buried in the library vaults:** See, for example, "Winin' Boy Blues," described by Morton as "one of my first tunes in the blues line down in New Orleans in the very early days," which includes the line, "I fucked her till her pussy stunk." The track can be found on *Winin' Boy Blues: Jelly Roll Morton: The Library of Congress Recordings,* Vol. 4 (Rounder 1094) and on *Jelly Roll Morton: The Complete Library of Congress Recordings.*

167   **"moldy figs":** See Bernard Gendron, "'Moldy Figs' and Modernists: Jazz at War (1942–46)," in Krin Gabbard, ed., *Jazz*

Among the Discourses (Durham, NC: Duke University Press, 1995), 31–56.

167 **Jazz historians tend to scorn them:** For a discussion of the place of New Orleans revivalists in jazz historiography, see Eric Hobsbawm, "The Caruso of Jazz," in his *Uncommon People: Resistance, Rebellion, and Jazz* (New York: New Press, 1998), 240.

167 **a vibrant circle of jazz aficionados:** The Popular Front jazz subculture is discussed in Michael Denning, *The Cultural Front: The Laboring of American Culture in the Twentieth Century* (London: Verso, 1997), 328–338; David W. Stowe, *Swing Changes: Big-Band Jazz in New Deal America* (Cambridge, MA: Harvard University Press, 1994); and Gendron, "'Moldy Figs' and Modernists."

168 **"There is a world of difference between the blues as collectors know them":** *H.R.S. Rag* 1 (1939), 11, quoted in Paul Lopes, *The Rise of a Jazz Art World* (Cambridge: Cambridge University Press, 2002), 194.

168 **the mass production of popular music generated a vast amount of waste matter:** My thoughts on record collecting have been influenced by Michael Thompson, *Rubbish Theory: The Creation and Destruction of Value* (New York: Oxford University Press, 1979).

169 **"looked much like his pictures in the old Victor Race Catalogues":** Kenneth Hulsizer, "Jelly Roll Morton in Washington," in Kenneth Williamson, ed., *This Is Jazz* (London: Newnes, 1960), 202–216.

170 **replaced by new, larger recording conglomerates:** See Andre Millard, *America on Record: A History of Recorded Sound* (Cambridge: Cambridge University Press, 1995), chap. 8.

170 **Ramsey had grown up in a hothouse of art and ideas:** For biographical information on Frederic Ramsey, I learned a great deal from his daughters Alida Ramsey Porter and Martha Ramsey, as well as from the materials contained in his collected papers.

171 **"I liked your letter for its emphasis upon the good jazz of other years":** Charles Edward Smith to Frederic Ramsey, July 31, 1936, FRP.

172 **"one solid row of junk shops":** Collector George Hoefer, quoted in Lopes, *Rise of a Jazz Art World*, 160.

172   **"Make out a want list":** William Russell to Frederic Ramsey,
        October 17, 1938, FRP.
173   **"a worthy cultural object of study":** "Country's Hot Clubs
        Founded by 'Swing' Devotees at Yale," quoted in William How-
        land Kenney, *Recorded Music in American Life: The Phono-
        graph and Popular Memory, 1890–1945* (New York: Oxford
        University Press, 1999), 16.
173   **"There will always be wayward, instinctive, and primitive
        geniuses":** Gilbert Seldes, "Toujours Jazz," *Dial* 8 (1923), 160,
        quoted in Lopes, *Rise of a Jazz Art World,* 61.
174   **"everyone was talking Bix and Chicago":** Undated, untitled
        memo from Frederic Ramsey, FRP.
174   **Frederic Ramsey was approached by an editor at Har-
        court Brace:** Pete Whelan, "Fred Ramsey Speaks Out!" *78
        Quarterly* 1, no. 4 (1989), 33.
176   **That Ramsey and Russell swallowed his tales has led many
        historians to dismiss them as credulous dupes:** See Peter
        Goldsmith, *Making People's Music: Moe Asch and Folkways
        Records* (Washington, DC: Smithsonian, 2000), 171: "So eager
        were they for the 'truth' about the origins of jazz that the authors
        of *Jazzmen* took Johnson largely at his word. . . .[M]usicologists
        have since been left to sort fact from fiction in his account of the
        turn-of-the-century bands."
177   **"folk history":** On the 1930s fascination with "folk history," see
        James S. Miller, "Inventing the 'Found' Object: Artifactuality,
        Folk History, and the Rise of Capitalist Ethnography in 1930s
        America," *Journal of American Folklore* 117 (2004), 373–393;
        Robert Dorman, *Revolt of the Provinces: The Regionalist Move-
        ment in America, 1920–1945* (Chapel Hill: University of North
        Carolina Press, 1998); Michael Kammen, *Mystic Chords of
        Memory* (New York: Vintage Books, 1991); William Stott, *Docu-
        mentary Expression and Thirties America* (New York: Oxford
        University Press, 1973); Warren Susman, "The Culture of the
        Thirties," in his *Culture as History: The Transformation of
        American Society in the Twentieth Century* (New York: Pan-
        theon, 1984).
177   **"One or another of the authors":** Ramsey and Smith,
        Jazzmen, xiii.

177   **"the most glamorous, as well as the most notorious":** Ramsey and Smith, *Jazzmen,* 31.

178   **"One of the most popular of these combinations":** Herbert Asbury, *The French Quarter: An Informal History of the New Orleans Underworld* (New York: Knopf, 1936), 437–438.

180   **the voyeuristic taste for "slumming":** See David Levering Lewis, *When Harlem Was in Vogue* (New York: Knopf, 1982); Nathan Huggins, *Harlem Renaissance* (New York: Oxford University Press, 1973).

180   **"elemental conjure woman":** Carl Van Vechten, "Negro 'Blues' Singers," *Vanity Fair* (March 1926), 67, 106.

180   **"I said we were trying to avoid the Van Vechtian line":** Charles Edward Smith to Frederic Ramsey, June 21, 1939, FRP.

181   **the "sensation" "King Bolden" created:** E. Belfield Spriggins, "Excavating Local Jazz, Part One," *Louisiana Weekly,* April 22, 1933, reprinted in Lynn Abbott, "Remembering Mr. E. Belfield Spriggins, First Man of Jazzology," *78 Quarterly* 10 (1999), 14–18.

182   **"that the musicians found no appreciative audience in dives":** Charles Edward Smith to Frederic Ramsey, February 15, 1940, FRP.

182   **"jammed every night with river rowdies":** Ramsey and Smith, *Jazzmen,* 34–35.

182   **"Inside the low, smoky room":** Ramsey and Smith, *Jazzmen,* 63.

182   **"hated the long hours, the low pay":** Charles Edward Smith, "Men Who Created Jazz," *Jazz Information,* September 26, 1939.

183   **a ribald, plebeian Garden of Eden:** See the discussion of *Jazzmen* in Scott DeVeaux, "Constructing the Jazz Tradition," in Robert O'Meally, ed., *The Jazz Cadence of American Culture* (New York: Columbia University Press, 1998), 489.

183   **"the ideal successor to the throne of King Bolden":** Ramsey and Smith, *Jazzmen,* 23.

184   **"a transcribed history":** Charles Edward Smith et al., *The Jazz Record Book* (New York: Smith and Durrell, 1942), vii.

184   **"shallow emotionalism":** Charles Edward Smith, "Collecting Hot," *Esquire* (February 1934), 96.

184 **Ramsey and Smith kept hearing rumors of a wax cylinder:** Charles Edward Smith, "The Bolden Cylinder," *Saturday Review of Literature,* March 16, 1957, 34–35. See also Tim Brooks, *Lost Sounds: Blacks and the Birth of the Recording Industry 1890–1919* (Chicago: University of Illinois Press, 2004), 514–515.

185 **"mean and dirty":** Ramsey and Smith, *Jazzmen,* 13.

185 **Even as Smith, Ramsey, and Russell were writing:** For an account of these events, as well as examples of some of Russell's photographs, see Al Rose, *Storyville, New Orleans* (Tuscaloosa: University of Alabama Press, 1974), ix–x, 166–183.

186 **"The barrelhouse was the refuge of the tragically destitute":** Rudi Blesh, "Jazz Begins," in George S. Rosenthal and Frank Zachary, eds. (in collaboration with Frederic Ramsey and Rudi Blesh), *Jazzways* (London: Musicians Press, 1946), 15.

187 **Johnson's recordings were circulating among a small but ardent group of New Orleans enthusiasts:** This phenomenon has been little discussed, though John Hammond's zeal for Johnson has been widely noted (he attempted to book the singer for his "From Spirituals to Swing" concert at Carnegie Hall in December 1938, not knowing that Johnson had been murdered a few months earlier). See, for example, Elijah Wald, *Escaping the Delta: Robert Johnson and the Invention of the Blues* (New York: Amistad Press, 2004), 228–230.

187 **In 1939, Hammond loaned his copies to Alan Lomax:** Lomax, *Land Where the Blues Began,* 13. The titles he listed were "Hellhound on My Trail," "Crossroads Blues," "Terraplane Blues," "The Last Fair Deal Going Down," "Ramblin' on My Mind," "Stones in My Passway," "32–20 Blues," and "Kind-hearted Woman."

187 **"dry on the ear as some wine may be on the tongue":** Rudi Blesh, *Shining Trumpets: A History of Jazz* (New York: Knopf, 1946), 108.

188 **stories of musical origins are always social and political fables:** For reflections on this point, see Eric Lott, *Love and Theft: Blackface Minstrelsy and the American Working Class* (New York: Oxford University Press, 1993), 55.

188 **"New Orleans became a multiple myth and symbol":** Hobsbawm, *Uncommon People*, 242.

189 **in 1942 he spent a fruitless afternoon trying to coax stories:** Lomax's interview with Jaybird Jones can be heard on *Field Recordings*, vol. 3: *Mississippi (1936–1942)* (Document DOCD–5577).

189 **"were on the whole ignorant of the songs we wanted":** Alan Lomax, "'Sinful' Songs of the Southern Negro: Experiences Collecting Secular Folk-Music," *Southwest Review* 19 (1933–1934), 120.

189 **"of protest and of pride":** Lomax, *Mister Jelly Roll*, xv.

189 **"streets thronging with pimps, chippies, rotten police, and Babbitts on a binge":** Lomax, *Mister Jelly Roll*, 100.

190 **"a marvel that has spawned a monster":** Lomax, *Mister Jelly Roll*, xiv.

190 **"a rich evocation of underground America":** Lomax, *Mister Jelly Roll*, xv.

190 **"did not draw a color line":** Ramsey and Smith, *Jazzmen*, 5.

191 **"Alan Lomax. Author, *Mister Jelly Roll*":** Quoted in Ed Kahn, "1934–1950: The Early Collecting Years," in Ronald D. Cohen, ed., *Alan Lomax: Selected Writings, 1934–1997* (New York: Routledge, 2003), 7.

191 **Only William Russell continued to devote himself to the gospel of Dixieland jazz:** Russell moved to New Orleans in 1956; in 1958 he was appointed curator of the Archive of New Orleans Jazz at Tulane University. See Raeburn, "The Musical Worlds of William Russell," 13–18.

191 **Charles Edward Smith retreated from jazz research altogether:** See Russell, "Charles Edward Smith," 474–475.

192 **a new generation of folk music enthusiasts:** Robert Cantwell, *When We Were Good: The Folk Revival* (Cambridge, MA: Harvard University Press, 1996); Neil V. Rosenberg, ed., *Transforming Tradition: Folk Music Revivals Examined* (Urbana: University of Illinois Press, 1993); Benjamin Filene, *Romancing the Folk: Public Memory and American Roots Music* (Chapel Hill: University of North Carolina Press, 2000), 183–232.

192 **"For those of us whose revival began around 1958":** Cantwell, *When We Were Good*, 22.

the growth of a virulent critique of black social "pathology": See Daryl Michael Scott, *Contempt and Pity: Social Policy and the Image of the Damaged Black Psyche, 1880–1996* (Chapel Hill: University of North Carolina Press, 1997).

192 **"corrupted by city ways":** Blesh, *Shining Trumpets,* 112–113.

193 **"lascivious song":** Blesh, *Shining Trumpets,* 100.

194 **he wandered into the Village Vanguard:** Frederic Ramsey, Jr., "Leadbelly's Last Sessions," *High Fidelity* (November– December 1953), reprinted as liner notes to *Leadbelly's Last Sessions,* Smithsonian Folkways Recordings SF CD 40068/7.

194 **"was rough and grainy, and some of its raw tones came up":** Frederic Ramsey, Jr., "Leadbelly's Legacy," *Saturday Review* (February 1950).

194 **"record collector who, with a large library to choose from":** Ramsey, "Leadbelly's Last Sessions."

195 **"Rambling was strong in Leadbelly's blood":** Ramsey, "Leadbelly's Legacy."

195 **"Life in the country extremely old":** Frederic Ramsey to Moses Asch, March 30, 1954, FRP. My account of Ramsey's journey comes from his letters (to his family and to Moses Asch) and from early drafts of *Been Here and Gone,* all held in FRP.

196 **At first he kept his cameras and tape recorders in his bag:** Frederic Ramsey, Jr., *Been Here and Gone* (New Brunswick, NJ: Rutgers University Press, 1960), xi.

197 **"here, hands are still striving":** Ramsey, *Been Here and Gone,* 19.

197 **"men who carried the devil on their backs":** Ramsey, *Been Here and Gone,* 95.

197 **"I got the blues so bad":** Ramsey, *Been Here and Gone,* 108.

198 **"a personal expression":** Ramsey, *Been Here and Gone,* 31.

198 **"tractors will replace mules":** Ramsey, *Been Here and Gone,* xii.

199 **Looking back on his time with Leadbelly:** Frederic Ramsey, "Leadbelly: A Great Long Time," *Sing Out!* (March 1965). Interviewed in 1991, four years before his death, and asked about Leadbelly's links to "the liberal, progressive crowd," Ramsey replied: "In that group there were left wingers who regarded Leadbelly as their tool and they tried to make him a spokesman

for their political ends. I thought this was crap. He was an artist, he wasn't a PR vehicle. They totally misunderstood the guy. . . . Leadbelly was not a political person and I think they abused him." Sean Killeen, "Fred Ramsey (1915–1995)," *Lead Belly Letter* 5 (Winter–Spring 1995), 11.

199 **"I had looked vainly":** Ramsey, *Been Here and Gone,* xi.

199 **"The kids down South":** *New Yorker* (August 6, 1955), 14–15.

199 **"It is beginning to be evident":** Frederic Ramsey to Moses Asch, June 6, 1954, FRP.

Six: The Real Negro Blues

201 **If you had been walking past the building:** In this opening section I have tried to imagine a pivotal event from three sentences James McKune wrote in 1961: "I first heard Charley Patton on a beat [battered] record early in 1944. At first he seemed too primitive to me. But by the end of that year I told a few friends that he was the greatest blues singer I have ever heard" (James McKune, "The Great Country Blues Singers (1)," *VJM Palaver* [April 1961], 3). In 1944 McKune had not yet attracted his circle of acolytes, and so far as I know he never told anyone about how he came to collect race records. Yet even though much of this section is by necessity imagined, throughout I have tried to build upon facts, playing around with chronology where necessary. In devising this chapter's introduction, as in the opening to Chapter 3, I am much indebted to Rachel Cohen, *A Chance Meeting: Intertwined Lives of American Writers and Artists* (New York: Random House, 2004).

McKune speaks of his taste for Spanish and South American folk music in a 1951 letter to his friend Henry Renard, reprinted in Renard's article, "Letters from McKune," *78 Quarterly* 1, no. 3 (1988). His years of "reading up" on Old World folk dances are my invention, though here I'm alluding to what I've observed about collectors in general—their ability to careen abruptly between minutely focused and wildly disparate interests. (I was particularly struck by this when I interviewed Pete Whelan, whose other obsessions have included vintage cars, nineteenth-century physical anthropology, early Anglo-Saxon languages, crocodiles, and dwarf palm trees.) Stephen W. Smith's article, "Hot Collecting," in Frederic Ramsey and Charles Edward Smith's 1939 *Jazzmen*, filled me in on the growth of a collector's subculture. The account of McKune's experience clerking in a store selling race records draws on remarks he made to his friend Henry Renard. That he disliked what he heard is my inference, based on how wildly his blues aesthetic would diverge from early 1930s black popular tastes. In a 1969 interview (reprinted in Rani Singh's 1999 edited collection of interviews with Harry Smith, *Think of the Self Speaking*), Harry Smith spoke of receiving a letter from McKune in 1942 in which he enclosed the list of untouched Paramounts found at the Central General Store. (Many of those disks turned up ten years later on Smith's *Anthology of American Folk Music*.) That McKune was chagrined by having sent it is my inference. One year later, McKune began collecting blues recordings himself, and at that point I cannot imagine that he would have let those disks pass him by.

From McKune's early 1960s columns in *VJM Palaver*, a record trader's journal, I knew that he began listening to blues in 1943 and to Patton in 1944, and from Renard's "Letters from McKune," I learned that he compiled two major "want lists," one in January 1943 that stretched to sixteen typewritten pages and an expanded edition one year later that encompassed thirteen hundred titles. (No one that I've spoken to ever laid eyes on either the 1943 or the 1944 list. McKune sent them out to record dealers and kept no copies of either; later, he tried to retrieve them by placing an ad in the *Record Changer*, but without success.) For the possibility that he drew on Alan Lomax's "List of American Folk Songs on Commercial Records," I drew on the reminiscences of Harry Smith, who told several interviewers that by the mid-1940s Lomax's list had become a kind of collector's Bible. For McKune's reaction to specific recordings and the development of his blues collecting strategies, I have drawn on McKune's *VJM* columns, Renard's "Letters from McKune," and my interview with Pete Whelan.

210 **only the barest facts emerge from their stories:** Henry Renard, "Letters from McKune," *78 Quarterly* 1, no. 3 (1988), 54–62; Bernard Klatzko, "Postscript to the McKune Story," *78*

Quarterly 1, no. 4 (1988), 93; Stephen Calt, *I'd Rather Be the Devil: Skip James and the Blues* (New York: Da Capo Press, 1994), 216–217; Joel Slotnikoff, "Pete Whelan Interview," http://www.bluesworld.com/PeteWhelanInterview.html.

210 **"I don't know if this should be mentioned":** Slotnikoff, "Pete Whelan Interview," 3.

211 **"'sockless,' and seemingly brain-damaged from alcohol":** Calt, *I'd Rather Be the Devil*, 217.

212 **"There was a guy called Jim McKune":** Quoted in Jim O'Neal, "I Once Was Lost, but Now I'm Found: The Blues Revival of the 1960s," in Lawrence Cohn, ed., *Nothing but the Blues: The Music and the Musicians* (New York: Abbeville Press, 1993), 376.

212 **"He lived in one room in the YMCA":** Slotnikoff, "Pete Whelan Interview," 3.

213 **the Jazz Record Center, or "Indian Joe's":** Henry Renard, "The Life and Times of Big Joe Clauberg and His Jazz Record Center," *78 Quarterly* 1 (1989), 62–66.

214 **"We paced about the store":** Pete Kaufman, "A Recollection of Big Joe's. . . ," *78 Quarterly* 1, no. 2 (1968).

215 **"bananas are the ideal collector's food":** Frederic Ramsey, "Discollecting: How to Care for Records, Where to Find Them, Which Are Rare," in George S. Rosenthal and Frank Zachery, eds., *Jazzways* (New York: Greenberg, 1947), 91.

215 **"Only last night I gave a lady $2.00":** Letter from Emerson Parker to Frederic Ramsey, April 17, 1945, FRP.

216 **"There are collectors, and then there are Collectors":** *Record Changer* (May 1950), 13.

217 **the Popular Front's jazz-inflected imagination:** See Michael Denning, *The Cultural Front: The Laboring of American Culture in the Twentieth Century* (London: Verso, 1997).

217 **"a transcribed history":** Charles Edward Smith et al., *The Jazz Record Book* (New York: Smith and Durrell, 1942), vii.

218 **a major auction of choice jazz rarities:** Pete Whelan, "Jacob S. Schneider: 63 Years and 450,000 Records Later," *78 Quarterly* 1 (1967), 31.

218 **"the jerks who pay ten bucks":** Bill Grauer, "In Defense of Label Collecting," *Record Changer* (May 1950), 7.

219   **"a propaganda machine":** Slotnikoff, "Pete Whelan Interview," 7.

219   **"McKune had this way of talking":** Interview with Pete Whelan, July 6, 2003.

219   **the peculiarity of his wants had drawn him a circle of acolytes:** Kaufman, "A Recollection of Big Joe's. . . "

220   **He introduced them to the sites of collector's mythology:** Slotnikoff, "Pete Whelan Interview," 11–12.

221   **"I have read with enthusiasm":** James McKune to Frederic Ramsey, January 12, 1944, file "*Jazzmen* Correspondence—Misc and Fan Mail," Frederic Ramsey Papers.

222   **"On principle":** Interview with Pete Whelan, July 6, 2003.

222   **"all of them choice":** Interview with Pete Whelan, July 6, 2003.

222   **"treacle fanciers":** Undated letter from James McKune to Henry Renard, published in Renard, "Letters from McKune," 58.

222   **"considered worthless by everyone but [McKune] himself":** Calt, *I'd Rather Be the Devil*, 216.

223   **"He tells a story only in part":** James McKune, "The Great Country Blues Singers (2)," *VJM Palaver* (June 1961), 3.

223   **"conditions not conducive to good listening":** Letter from James McKune to Henry Renard, August 27, 1952, published in Renard, "Letters from McKune," 61.

224   **I said, "Are you sure? That's a long ways":** Interview with Dick Spottswood, July 2003, broadcast October 12, 2003, as part of "The Room Where the Blues Was Born," BBC Radio 3, written and presented by Marybeth Hamilton, produced by Tim Dee.

224   **Samuel Barclay Charters IV:** For information on Charters, see Goldsmith, *Making People's Music*, 255–256, 267–268.

225   **"In simple terms I was trying":** Samuel Charters, *The Country Blues* (New York: Da Capo Press, 1975; originally published 1959), ix.

226   **"became the emotional outlet for Negro singers":** Charters, *Country Blues*, 19.

226   **"keep the focus where the black audience put it":** Charters, *Country Blues*, xviii.

227 **"Collectors of the Negro country blues singers should read this":** McKune, "The Great Country Blues Singers (1)," 3–4.

229 **"hours in the hot sun":** Charters, *Country Blues,* 266.

230 **"It was real":** Slotnikoff, "Pete Whelan Interview," 2.

230 **"The voice is dark and heavy":** Pete Welding, "Stringin' the Blues," *Down Beat,* July 1, 1965, 22.

230 **"After you've listened to the real Negro blues for a long time":** James McKune, "The Great Country Blues Singers (3)," *VJM Palaver* (September 1961), 7.

230 **"an intensity devoid of dramatic effects":** McKune, "Great Country Blues Singers (3)," 7.

231 **Stephen Calt later estimated:** Calt, *I'd Rather Be the Devil,* 249. In 1967 Pete Whelan sold the OJL label to his partner Bill Givens, who moved the company to Berkeley. More information on its releases can be found at http://www.originjazz.com/ and http://www.wirz.de/music/ojlfrm.htm.

231 **"the definitive country blues anthologies":** Palmer, *Deep Blues,* 281.

231 **a view held as well by Jeff Todd Titon:** Jeff Todd Titon, "Reconstructing the Blues: Reflections on the 1960s Blues Revival," in Neil V. Rosenberg, *Transforming Tradition: Folk Musical Revivals Examined* (Urbana: University of Illinois Press, 1993), 224.

232 **a young historian named Lawrence Levine:** See Lawrence Levine, *Black Culture and Black Consciousness: Afro-American Folk Thought from Slavery to Freedom* (New York: Oxford University Press, 1977), 478, fn 16, and 483, fns 85, 87, where Levine draws on the OJL reissues.

232 **"The kind of blues on the present recording":** Marshall Stearns, liner notes to *Negro Blues and Hollers;* originally published 1962, reissued in 1997 on Rounder Records (CD 1501).

233 **even Samuel Charters agreed:** Samuel Charters, *The Bluesmen* (New York: Oak Publications, 1967), 27–32.

234 **"Don't know what the Delta along the way will hold":** Frederic Ramsey to Moses Asch, June 28, 1954, Frederic Ramsey Papers.

234 **The residents they interviewed uniformly attested that the region felt modern:** See the report of fieldworker Samuel Adams, "Changing Negro Life in the Delta," included

in Robert Gordon and Bruce Nemerov, eds., *Lost Delta Found: Rediscovering the Fisk University–Library of Congress Coahoma County Study, 1941–1942* (Nashville: Vanderbilt University Press, 2005), 225–290. For more on the study and its portrait of the Delta, see Marybeth Hamilton, "The Blues, the Folk, and African-American History," *Transactions of the Royal Historical Society* 11 (2001), 17–36.

234 **Lewis Jones found no recordings by local musicians:** "List of records on machines in Clarksdale amusement places," Folder 7 (Lists), Fisk University Mississippi Delta Collection, Archive of Folk Culture, Library of Congress, Washington, DC.

234 **he stumbled across a juke joint on the edge of a cotton field:** Alan Lomax field notes, July 1942, Coahoma County Survey materials, Alan Lomax Archives, Hunter College.

234 **"rural proletariat":** Lewis Jones's reflections on the study's findings appear in Charles S. Johnson and associates, *To Stem This Tide: A Survey of Racial Tension Areas in the U.S.* (Boston: Pilgrim Press, 1943), 28.

235 **"If the blues simply mirrored the protest of the moment":** Samuel Charters, *The Poetry of the Blues* (New York: Oak Publications, 1963), 17, 173.

235 **"All those guys on that Harry Smith Anthology were dead":** Greil Marcus, *Invisible Republic: Bob Dylan's Basement Tapes* (London: Picador, 1997), 94.

236 **the Delta blues acquired living, breathing embodiments:** For a scathing account of the revival by a McKune protégé, see Calt, *I'd Rather Be the Devil.*

236 **"of almost archaeological purity":** *Atlantic Monthly* (1961), quoted in Calt, *I'd Rather Be the Devil,* 218.

236 **Skip James, an immensely troubled man:** Calt, *I'd Rather Be the Devil,* 239–346.

237 **"cherished the physical symbols":** Grauer, "In Defense of Label Collecting," 7.

238 **"the rarest labels in the record collecting fraternity":** Whelan, "Jacob S. Schneider," 29.

238 **"record collecting was not like collecting stamps":** Interview with Pete Whelan, July 6, 2003.

239 **"scratches, pops, clicks and hiss":** Robert Santelli, *The Best of the Blues: The 101 Essential Albums* (London: Penguin, 1997), 57.

239   **"There is an honest and laudable interest"**: Charles Keil, *Urban Blues* (Chicago: University of Chicago Press, 1966), 38.

239   **"Are you another one of those guys"**: Keil, *Urban Blues,* 35.

240   **"a rich evocation of underground America"**: Lomax, *Mister Jelly Roll,* xv.

240   **"the blues of the professional jazzmen are never quite the real thing"**: Lomax, *Land Where the Blues Began,* 440.

240   **"anomie and alienation, orphaning and rootlessness"**: Lomax, *Land Where the Blues Began,* ix.

241   **"self-made outcasts"**: Ramsey, *Been Here and Gone,* 97–98, 122.

241   **"flight from commitment"**: Barbara Ehrenreich, *The Hearts of Men: American Dreams and the Flight from Commitment* (New York: Anchor Books, 1983).

241   **"beggar, outcast, near criminal"**: Frederic Ramsey, "'The Country Blues' in Word and Song," *Saturday Review* 43 (January 16, 1960), 78–79.

241   **"a frontiersman in the Wild West"**: Norman Mailer, "The White Negro," in Mailer, *Advertisements for Myself* (New York: G. P. Putnam's Sons, 1959), 339.

242   **"Knowing in the cells of his existence"**: Mailer, "The White Negro," 341.

242   **"His voice, guttural and hoarse"**: Lomax, *Land Where the Blues Began,* 18.

243   **to dissolve boundaries, renounce autonomy:** For a suggestive analysis of gender and primitivism, see Marianna Torgovnick, *Primitive Passions: Men, Women, and the Quest for Ecstasy* (Chicago: University of Chicago Press, 1996).

243   **a faintly colonialist romance with black suffering:** For a lucid reflection on blues history writing, see Luc Sante, "The Genius of Blues," *New York Review of Books,* August 11, 1994, 52.

245   **the lower floors retained a kind of lowlife glamour:** Thanks to Luc Sante for information about the history of the Broadway Central. The building burned down in 1973; the site now houses a New York University dormitory.

245   **When police found his body in September 1971:** Klatzko, "Postscript to the McKune Story," 9.

⸙ INDEX ⸙